AFRICA AND LAW

DEVELOPING

LEGAL SYSTEMS

IN AFRICAN

COMMONWEALTH

NATIONS

AFRICA AND LAW

DEVELOPING

LEGAL SYSTEMS

IN AFRICAN

COMMONWEALTH

NATIONS

Edited by Thomas W. Hutchison
in association with James N. Roethe
Harold P. Southerland, Nancy C. Dreher
Michael St. Peter, and other members
of the staff of
the *Wisconsin Law Review*

With an
Introduction by
A. ARTHUR
SCHILLER

THE UNIVERSITY
OF WISCONSIN
PRESS 1968
MADISON
MILWAUKEE
AND LONDON

Published by the
University of Wisconsin Press
Madison, Milwaukee, and London
U.S.A.: Box 1379, Madison, Wisconsin 53701
U.K.: 26-28 Hallam Street, London W.1

Printed in the United States of America
Library of Congress Catalog Card Number 67-26627

This book reproduces substantially
the Fall, 1966, issue of
the *Wisconsin Law Review*
with substitutions and additions
including a new Introduction
by A. Arthur Schiller

CONTENTS

INTRODUCTION

Two themes run through the studies which make up the contents of this volume. In the first place, it is apparent that the new nations of Africa are facing a host of difficult problems in fashioning national legal systems. Secondly, these questions are sufficiently akin to one another to be subsumed under the heading of "African law." The challenge is frequently raised, what is there in common to the legal experience or the legal problems of the former colonial possessions of diverse European powers on the continent to warrant the use of the generic term "African law"? Clearly we must now be prepared to recognize the existence of Ghanaian law, of Kenyan law, of Basuto law, of the law of the individual states of French-speaking Africa. But is there more reason to speak of African law than of North American law or of Asiatic law? I submit that there is some basis for considering the law of the continent as a whole.

Almost every country on the African continent has a plurality of legal systems within the bounds of the individual state. Two or more distinct legal systems existing side by side are clearly to be discerned in the new states of tropical or sub-Saharan Africa. Further reflection discloses that there is also a plurality of legal systems in the countries of North Africa and in the Republic of South Africa. The wave of Islamic law across northern Africa was later subjected to an incursion of Western (European) law, and both were superimposed upon an indigenous Beduin law. Some institutions of the latter still emerge in various localities. The Republic of South Africa has an internal plurality of legal systems even though allegedly driving to the settling of its population into separate states, each with its own distinct law. Africa is certainly not the only continent where there presently are states possessing a plurality of legal systems, but it is clearly the one where this fascinating type of legal structure prevails.

A second factor tends to justify the term "African law." Most of the states of Africa underwent common experiences in the first stages of the evolution of their law. At the moment of contact with the Western world, and during the subsequent period of rule by European powers, African peoples lived according to their own indigenous law. Some social anthropologists have described groups of peoples in Africa—one hesitates to speak of societies—with no semblance of government, "tribes without rulers," and concomitantly, lacking a legal system. Hence the repeated statement, "the Nuer have no law." Whether or not this is true—and a good deal depends on one's definition of "law"—the great mass of Africans were subject to rules of conduct whose infraction was met by some sort of legal sanction. European powers introduced their own law primarily to guide and control the colonial staff and the foreign entrepreneurs, and at the same time they retained the local indigenous legal system or systems for the regulation of most of the affairs of the native population. But the imported law did not continue to be solely the law for the colonial administration or the European immigrant. Increasingly, the Western law, modified to accommodate local conditions, permeated the life and actions of the African. The techniques utilized for the development of the law, whether imported or indigenous law, and the outlook basic to its administration were those peculiar to the mother country ruling the colony. Thus, when independence came, the colonial heritage largely shaped the form of the national legal system being fashioned. It is possible, for instance, to identify "code" states with a civilian approach to the development of the law and to single out "common law" states relying more or less on case law and precedent. To summarize briefly, at the close of colonial rule African law was characterized by the over-all presence of a plurality of legal systems, coupled with the inheritance of techniques and points of view peculiar to that mother country governing the colony.

Legal systems being fashioned in the new nations of the continent still merit the generic designation of "African law." The problems being faced by the several nations described in this volume have significance beyond the borders of the individual countries concerned. The new states seek economic development on a vast scale, and it must be provided within the shortest possible span of time. In his article, Professor Seidman points out that neither the customary (indigenous) law nor the Western imported (English) law fully meets the needs of the new governments. The postulate of state intervention—or "plan"—must be evolved to satisfy the demands of the public sector in economic development. The study of land law in Kenya by Mrs. Munro calls attention to one of the most pressing problems faced by all the states of Africa. The scheme adopted by Kenya well illustrates the role that government policy must play in the evolution of legal institutions. In the article by Mr. Asante we are given an overview of the interaction of law and society in a single-party state to compare and contrast with Professor Harvey's study of the legal structure of that same state following a coup. Mr. Thompson describes available sources for the development of the law in Sudan, calling attention to the uncertainties, the strains, and the pressures which must be taken into account if a viable legal system is to be founded. With modifications to suit local exigencies, the portrayal of the problems faced in the administration of justice in these several instances will serve for almost any of the emerging states in Africa.

The five studies in the volume are significant contributions to understanding the legal problems of the emergent states of Africa. Each is complete and noteworthy in itself. Little is to be gained by pointing out the crucial elements in the individual studies or by attempting to correlate one study with another. Any intelligent reader does this himself. I believe, however, that it is proper and might be fruitful to call attention to one area of African law that deserves more space than is given in the studies in this volume. I refer to customary law, or more properly, indigenous law, generally dismissed as of minor importance by the lawyer immersed in the legal problems of economic development, characterized as antiquarian by the policy-maker, and surrendered to the anthropologist, who normally attempts to reconstitute the pristine, primitive law untainted by contact with Western ways and modern life. I wish to turn again to that hackneyed topic, "the future of customary law," which at the moment seems to require a choice between Scylla and Charybdis. This is an area of African law deserving of attention and, to my mind, crucial to the successful development of these legal systems of the future. I extend my apologies to the reader, and more particularly to the competent contributors to this volume, for the nature of the remainder of the introduction. The contributors can justifiably accuse me of following a favorite line of my own. I admit my guilt.

Professor Seidman asserts that customary law cannot conceivably reflect the common consciousness of the people and, at any rate, does not relate to any of the important issues raised by development (pp. 28–29 *infra*). Again, customary law is keyed to precapitalist economy; transactions related to development must be controlled by the received common law or by statute (p. 46). Indeed, in the field of land law, customary law inhibits development in the agricultural sphere (pp. 48 ff.). Mrs. Munro's article emphasizes that any drive toward individual landholding under indigenous law—on the assumption that this would be progress—was hampered by colonial policy. Independent Kenya has turned to "plan" to write its land policy and institutions for the future. Mr. Thompson points out that in the Sudan customary law is the "nearly forgotten" source (pp. 148 ff.). Little is known of it and nothing is being done to foment change (pp. 158 ff.).

In spite of the sparse notices, all the contributors would concede that in colonial times the indigenous law was a primary source of a good portion of the legal system, and if there should be no direct abrogation this would continue to be the case, in sub-Saharan Africa at any rate. There exists the extremely negative view that customary law ceased to exist with the disappearance of the isolated, homogeneous community throughout Africa; indigenous law cannot survive within an official jurisdictional setup.[1] But even exponents of a modernist point of view, such as that of Professor Alliot of the Sorbonne, would concede that customary law cannot be eliminated for a good long time; he points particularly to the rules respecting parental relationship, marriage, dowry, and such matters as the taking of oaths.[2]

[1] NEKAM, EXPERIENCES IN AFRICAN CUSTOMARY LAW 6 ff. (1966).
[2] Alliot, *Les résistances traditionelles au droit moderne dans les états d'Afrique francophones et a Madagascar*, in ÉTUDES DE DROIT AFRICAIN ET DE DROIT MALGACHE 235, 247–48 (1965).

The new states have adopted policies with respect to the customary law which are quite diverse and often somewhat ambiguous. These policies are described as unification, harmonization, integration, codification of the law. Before undertaking to define these terms, it may be well to look into the various devices and techniques for discovering the nature and content of the customary law, which is the subject matter of the policy directives of the individual governments.

The first step recommended by a majority of persons interested in the future of the customary law is the recording or restatement of that portion of the law. There are arguments in favor of as well as against this preliminary effort. Restatement, it is said, affords legal security, assures a measure of primacy to the customary law enabling it to withstand outside influences, and makes the substance of the law available to the lay public. On the other hand, restatement tends to prevent the evolution of custom and paves the way for unification and the fashioning of a legal system more developed than customary law, two results which are frowned upon by many.[3] And it is argued that restatement tends to preserve a customary law that may of itself be in the process of withering away.[4] No uniformity of methods and ends is seen where recording or restatement has been undertaken, and indeed it may be true that a scholarly exposition of the traditional law cannot be reached by measures employed in recording customary law for the benefit of a legislative committee implementing government policy.[5]

There are further techniques for ascertaining the substance of customary law on which to base its future development, if that be the objective of government action. Many colonial legislative enactments provided for the declaration of the indigenous law by local authorities. If such a declaration was accurate, provided the possibility of modification, and at the same time was not repugnant to doctrines of equity and natural justice, it was recognized as the law in force; Northern Nigeria is an example.[6] In Tanzania, the declaration of the indigenous law is utilized at the present time to establish the binding principles of a good portion of the private law. Senegal has posed the question whether the principles of family law drawn up by the notables of Cap Vert should be accepted as authentic statements of the law of that region by the central government.[7]

---

[3] Gilissen, *La rédaction des coutumes dans le passé et dans le présent, Essai de synthèse,* in LA RÉDACTION DES COUTUMES DANS LE PASSÉ ET DANS LE PRÉSENT 15, 30, ff. (1962).

[4] Cotran, *The Place and Future of Customary Law in East Africa,* in EAST AFRICAN LAW TODAY, 5 COMMONWEALTH LAW SERIES 72, 84 (1965).

[5] W. TWINING, THE PLACE OF CUSTOMARY LAW IN THE NATIONAL LEGAL SYSTEMS OF EAST AFRICA 45 ff. (1963).

[6] Northern Region Native Authority Law, No. 4 of 1954, § 48.

[7] Cited by Forster, *La place de la coutume indigène dans le droit moderne de la République du Sénégal,* 66 ZEITSCHRIFT FÜR VERGLIECHENDE RECHTSWISSENSCHAFT 1, 9–13 (1964).

The studies in this volume call attention to the use of judicial decisions, case law, as a means of affording knowledge of the customary law as well as providing a technique for its development. Less than a decade ago, it was recommended that changes in the customary law ought to stem from the people themselves and that the courts could serve well as the device for making the principles of the law conform to the changing social conditions.[8] At the 1963 Dar es Salaam conference, however, the experts turned to the central government as the directing force in the evolution of the customary law.[9] As a result, case law would cease to be a primary factor in its development, for no one has yet suggested that the decisions of primary courts—where customary law would be most exhaustively fashioned by judicial action—should be reported. Without reports, it is not likely that case law could play a role in the evolution of the law. Strikingly, it is the expert in the indigenous law of the French-speaking countries who today would rely upon case law for the evolution of customary law. It has been stressed that the courts are largely responsible for the survival of Burundi customary law.[10] Herbots notes that experience shows that the legislator has not been at all effective in the development of customary law in the Congo; therefore, recourse should be had to the superior courts, where modification can be left to the judges' initiative.[11]

Formerly, legislation at the local level was one means employed to bring about radical change in the customary law. Today many states propose to continue the legislative process, particularly where it is thought that institutions of the customary law should be maintained. A recent Malagasy ordinance provides an instance where legislated customary law doctrines have filled the gap normally occupied by Western-enacted law.[12] The indigenous institution known as *fokon'olona*, providing for collective participation and responsibility by members of various traditional groups in the native society, has been made an institution of Malagasy statute law. The institution provides, *inter alia*, for mutual assistance and collective solidarity, for rural development and urban planning, for police corps and general security, for rural agents and agricultural inspection, for hygiene and public health, for education, and indeed for practically any undertaking involving group action and responsibility.

The knowledge of the customary law is at hand to permit its further development in the African states, to incorporate whatever

---

8 THE FUTURE OF LAW IN AFRICA 30 ff. (Allott ed. 1960).

9 McClain, *Recent Changes in African Local Courts and Customary Law*, 10 How. L. J. 187, 218 (1964).

10 Helvetius, *Les transformations du droit coutumier au Burundi*, 5 REVUE JURIDIQUE DU RWANDA ET DU BURUNDI 145, 148–49 (1965).

11 Herbots, *Les techniques des recours en droit congolais*, 20 REVUE JURIDIQUE ET POLITIQUE, INDÉPENDANCE ET COOPÉRATION 203, 221 (1966).

12 Ordonnance 62–004 of 24.7.1962, Jour. Off. Répub. Malg. of 11.8.1962, pp. 1559 ff. *Cf.* Raharijaona, *Le droit malgache et les conventions de fokonolona*, in ÉTUDES DE DROIT AFRICAIN ET DE DROIT MALGACHE 49–71 (1965).

part desired into the national legal system, or to abrogate the greater
portion or the whole of the traditional law. It is up to the governments to lay down the policies to be followed. The means to serve
the particular objectives are various. But unfortunately the terminology employed to describe distinct methods by which the aims
will be achieved has been both misleading and ambiguous. To take
a typical instance, "unification" of the law is used to describe the
drive towards consistency at all levels.[13] It may designate unification within the customary law, within the general law or Western
component, or a synthesis of the personal law or the criminal law.
At a higher level, it connotes the fashioning of a single legal system
in the state. Again, it may signify regional unification or even
uniform legislation throughout Africa. Another term, "integration,"
is sometimes employed to describe the unifying of diverse customs,
though normally this term is limited to the attempted combination
of Western and indigenous law. There is frequent reference to
"codification" of customary law. To my mind, it might be clearer
if in the future relatively fixed value is given to each of the terms
describing methods used to implement legal policy in the state:
unification, harmonization, integration, assimilation, and codification.

Unification is the attempt to eliminate diversity between individual rules of different systems of customary law. It serves a
practical purpose. Diversity of rules makes the administration of
the law difficult, confuses lawyers and members of nontraditional
courts, and prevents successful application of the customary law in
urban areas. Though no expressed policy towards unification came
during the colonial period, judicial decisions did sometimes bring
to pass a certain measure of this. With the coming of independence
the drive towards unification was specifically undertaken in several
states. At the London conference at the turn of the year 1959/60,
sharp differences of opinion existed over whether there was substantial lack of uniformity in given states, and if this was so, whether
it was a weakness which might be desirable or practicable to overcome.[14] Nonetheless, Kenya and Tanzania each instituted projects
to bring about uniformity of customary law within their respective
states.

In Kenya, this aim commenced with a restatement of the customary criminal law. When this was completed, it was proposed that
customary offenses capable of being defined should be incorporated
within the Penal Code. As of the moment, no concerted effort
towards the unification of the customary civil law exists, though
there is projected reform in many fields of the private law.[15] The

[13] Allott, *Towards the Unification of Laws in Africa,* 14 INT'L & COMP.
L. Q. 366, 375 ff. (1965).
[14] THE FUTURE OF LAW IN AFRICA 9 ff. (Allott ed. 1960).
[15] Cotran, *op. cit. supra,* note 4, at 81. Mr. Cotran has recently been
named by the Kenya government to direct the integration of the customary
law and the general law in various areas of the law of persons and of family
and of succession.

restatement of the customary law in Tanzania was from the start a first step towards the unification of the law. Nyerere called for a unified code as a vital element in the building of a nation state. Government officials met with tribal representatives chosen by district councils in order to ascertain the rules applicable in the fields of family law and succession throughout the Bantu patrilineal tribes of the country. They prepared uniform statements of the law and submitted these draft pronouncements to local authorities. Although in many instances the rules proposed varied considerably from the local practice, these declarations were accepted by the district councils and were promulgated as rules of law binding upon the courts. Hence, unification of the customary law of most of the Bantu peoples of Tanzania has been accomplished, at least in the printed notices issued as supplements to the official gazette.[16]

Many doubt the feasibility of a new customary law—insofar as it is not a continuation of the existing system—and question whether it can be imposed on fragmented and diverse societies characteristic of Africa today.[17] Tanner recently challenged the basic tenets of unification as they have been propounded in the Tanzanian scheme.[18] Were the representatives really expert in the customary law? Customary law is considered by many of those involved as nothing more than a colonialist theme, urban legislators are far removed from customary practice, unification and codification of the law are symbols of modernism. Which customary rules were chosen and why? Many rules are clearly outmoded, there exists no tie between the principles promulgated and the rules utilized in actual disputes before local courts. Can the rules in the declarations be enforced? Decisions by local magistrates running counter to accepted practice may well give rise to severe tension. All in all, Tanner believes that a great portion of the law is newly made and therefore foreign to many of the ethnic groups, resulting in a hotchpot satisfying no one—with inaccurate statements, outmoded principles, and poor organization of the individual rules within the drafted declarations.

A second design for further development of the national legal system depends upon the harmonization of the principles of customary law to accord with the rules and institutions of the general law of the country. Both systems of law (the traditional law and the mass of rules stemming from French-influenced legislation) exist side by side in Senegal. The integration of the courts into a single hierarchical scheme with unified jurisdiction renders it possible to apply the rules of indigenous law whenever these be pertinent to the case at hand.[19] In Rwanda a procedure has been established

---

[16] Cotran, *Integration of Courts and Application of Customary Law in Tanganyika*, 1 EAST AFRICAN L. J. 108, 119–20 (1965).

[17] Allott, *supra* note 13, at 386; McClain, *supra* note 9, at 225.

[18] Tanner, *The Codification of Customary Law in Tanzania*, 2 EAST AFRICAN L. J. 105–16 (1966).

[19] Lamy, *Le problème de l'intégration du droit congolais: son origine, son évolution, son avenir*, 41 REVUE JURIDIQUE DU CONGO 135, 171 ff. (1965).

whereby "custom-laws" are legislated and brought into harmony with the guiding principles of the new constitution of the independent state.[20] Many of the African states have made conscious effort to adjust the principles of customary law to the demands of the modern state.

A further step beyond harmonization is the integration of the customary law and the Western-adapted law into a single legal system capable of serving the needs of the present day. The creation of a general territorial law reconciling the principles of the received English or French law insofar as these are acceptable to African conditions, together with the principles of African customary law which have won acceptance throughout the territory, appears to be the desired and most appropriate aim of a majority of the new states. A typical instance of the integrated national legal system of the future is afforded by the development in Nigeria.[21] Case law and statutes will constitute the sources of the law. The former will be Nigerian common law and equity in place of the inherited principles of English common law and rules of equity. Customary law will cease to be a source of the law in its own right, but many of its institutions will have become a part of Nigerian law by reason of judicial decision or statutory enactment.

In the English-speaking countries of Africa we will find a common law of the country consisting of an amalgam of English common law and equity doctrines into African form together with such indigenous institutions as have been adjusted to the contemporary scene. According to Allott, the new governments will have to modernize their legal systems to meet economic and social needs, will have to replace the plurality of legal systems with a single national law, and at the same time will have to make them more genuinely African.[22] The situation is the same in French-speaking Africa. For the immediate future at least, most of the states have set their sights upon an integration of the civil law base with a measure of the customary law. A program looking towards the integration of the law in the Congo-Kinshasa envisages, with reference to the indigenous elements, a compilation of the customary criminal law in order to integrate it into the penal legislation, an extension of the portion of the Congo Civil Code devoted to obligations to all Congolese, a critical examination of the law of persons with a view to discovering those elements capable of being unified, and a codification of the customary land law in order to fashion a truly African law of property.[23] The drive towards integration of the plural legal systems is

[20] Ruhashyankiko, *La codification du droit au Rwanda*, 20 REVUE JURIDIQUE ET POLITIQUE, INDÉPENDANCE ET COOPÉRATION 114, 120 (1966).
[21] Park, THE SOURCES OF NIGERIAN LAW 142–43 (1963).
[22] Allott, *The Future of African Law*, in AFRICAN LAW: ADAPTATION AND DEVELOPMENT 216, 223 ff. (H. Kuper & L. Kuper ed. 1965).
[23] Lamy, *supra* note 19, at 198.

clearly uppermost in the policy aims of most of the countries of Africa today.

A particular technique affording full integration of the customary law into the general territorial law has been made available by a law of Ghana. "The common law, as comprised in the laws of Ghana, consists . . . of rules of customary law included in the common law under any enactment providing for the assimilation of such rules of customary law as are suitable for general application."[24] A traditional council or the House of Chiefs may undertake to draft a declaration of what in its opinion is the customary law relating to any subject. If the draft is accepted by the Minister of Local Government, it may be embodied in a legislative instrument for enactment, provided he is satisfied that the recommended customary law is not repugnant to the laws of Ghana as contrary to natural justice, equity, and good conscience.[25] In case of conflict with another rule of law, an assimilated rule shall prevail over any other rule. This procedure of providing precedence for certain customary rules has, to the best of my knowledge, not yet been utilized by the government of Ghana.

At least three of the African states have planned the complete absorption of the customary law into the general civil law. Ethiopia has already enacted its Civil Code and the same is envisaged for Senegal and Rwanda. Undoubtedly other states may travel the same road, but a brief reference to these must suffice.

Professor David of the Sorbonne, author of the Civil Code of Ethiopia, came to the conclusion that customary law played no significant role in that country. Moreover, his Ethiopian advisors were inclined to discard the traditional law as an antiquarian heritage and ill-suited to modern times. Although Professor David urged the cautious adoption of the new code spreading over a period of years, the Ethiopian government was unwilling to postpone the immediate enactment of the entire project.[26] As a result, in a few institutions only do the remnants of customary law persist until modern legal devices replace the older ways. The Code, its author admits, is not a statement of customary principles, though these principles have been taken into account. In the interests of certainty, the diversity of the customary rules rendered them inadequate as true principles of law. Nevertheless, in his promulgation of the Civil Code, the Emperor asserted that the new law was the ultimate

---

24 Interpretation Act, C.A. No. 4 of 1960, § 17 (1).

25 Chieftaincy Act, No. 81 of 19611, §§ 58 ff.

26 See generally, David, *"La refonte du Code civil dans les états africains,* 72 PENANT 352–64 (1962); David, *Les sources du Code civil Éthiopien,* 14 REVUE INTERNATIONALE DE DROIT COMPARÉ 497–506 (1962); David, *A Civil Code for Ethiopia: Considerations on the Codification of the Civil Law in African Countries,* 37 TUL. L. REV. 187 (1963). See also Krzeczunowicz, *New Legislative Approach to Customary Law,* 1 J. ETHIOPIAN STUDIES 57–67 (1963).

expression of the sense of justice of the Ethiopian people.[27] One commentator views the alterations from the model—the French Civil Code—as in part reflections of Ethiopian customary law and religious practices and in part modernization of the French Code.[28] Sohier seems to have struck more truly at the character of the Ethiopian project.[29] It appears to him that the legislators tried to innovate, and deliberately discarded, the customary law; the Code departs from its French model not under the impulse of customary law, but rather in attempted conformity to the development that has taken place in the evolution of Western World law. Professor David has looked upon this Code as a model for other African countries, hoping it may bring uniformity throughout the continent and at the same time preserve the legal institutions of the population. In truth, the Code is a far cry from a *Volksrecht* expressing the popular consciousness—to use Savigny's terms—either in its origin or in its reflection of the people's ways.[30]

The disappearance of the indigenous law in the criminal field, in commercial law, or in civil and criminal procedure, may well support the economic development of the new states. But the trend is also apparent in the sphere of private law. In Senegal, says the Code Commissioner, "the fashioning of a Civil Code will be necessary because an unwritten juridical system and heterogeneous customs are incompatible with the accession of international life and the obligations required for economic development."[31] Where a relatively homogeneous society exists, as in Rwanda, a project for a code of the law of persons, of the family, of succession, of property, and of obligations is already in the course of preparation.[32]

The policies that have been outlined run the gamut from unification to codification. In what way will customary law fit into the final picture? The predictions range from one end of the scale to the other.

> The force of traditional law is that it is African or Malgache. Its success proves the attachment of the people to their country, the impossibility of deliberately ignoring, the difficulty of combatting, and the wisdom of the legislators, convinced of the necessity of modernizing their law, of starting on a way of progress, of pressing for a written law, in that they would forge a modern law, but a modern law

---

[27] Civil Code Proclamation of 1960, Proclamation No. 165, *Negarit Gazeta*, Extraordinary Issue No. 2 of 1960, p. V.

[28] Allott, *La place des coutumes juridiques africaines dans les systèmes juridiques africains modernes*, in ÉTUDES DE DROIT AFRICAIN ET DE DROIT MALGACHE 256, 265–66 (1965).

[29] Sohier, *Propos sur le Code civil de l'Empire d'Éthiopie*, 41 REVUE JURIDIQUE DU CONGO 271, 272 (1965).

[30] Sand, Book Review, 30 RABELS ZEITSCHRIFT 539, 541 (1966).

[31] Quoted by Forster, *supra* note 7, at 6. The translation is mine.

[32] Ruhashyankiko, *supra* note 20, at 121.

authentically African or Malgache. The modern law of
Africa and of Madagascar ought at least to be a foreign law
laid down in the embodiment of their traditional law.[33]

Or again,

> The history of attempts at law reform show that the pre-
> dominant trend of thought among British legal officers and
> senior civil servants was in favour of the wholesale adoption
> of English law and the wholesale elimination of the African
> customary law. The likelihood is, however, that African
> governments, though perfectly prepared to make radical
> alterations in their local customary laws, will at the same
> time wish to build their legal systems on as African a foun-
> dation as possible.[34]

At the other extreme,

> Customary law remains outside the main flow of legal
> development, an oddity, a reservation, which cannot freely
> grow according to its own pattern and which, therefore, is
> doomed eventually to disappear.... From the point of
> view of the new states customary law is divisive, it is a
> centrifugal force. The new states will have to level it down,
> will have to transform it, make it innocuous.[35]

Or the legislator in Guinea, "The same law applies to all similar
litigants without distinction of personal, religious or regional
customs."[36]

Customary law will certainly not disappear overnight. Many
governments agree with a substantial number of the experts in
believing that there should be no replacement of customary law by
English or foreign law in the spheres of the law of persons, of
marriage and divorce, and of succession. Only those principles
incompatible with modern life should be altered by legislative
enactment. But there are signs that this viewpoint is weakening.
A recent Malawi Wills and Inheritance Ordinance, though couched
in language designed to conceal its radical break with tradition,
actually provides uniform mandatory rules for testate and intestate
succession.[37] The ordinance sets forth the procedure according to
which Africans can dispose by will of personal property and land
held in freehold or leasehold title, if adequate provision be made for
surviving spouse and dependent children. But more than that, on
intestacy, four-fifths of the deceased's property is to be divided
among surviving wives and children in accordance with principles

---

[33] Alliot, *op. cit. supra* note 2, at 256. The translation is mine.
[34] Allott, *The Changing Law in a Changing Africa,* 11 SOCIOLOGUS 115,
126 (1961).
[35] NEKAM, *op. cit. supra* note 1, at 12.
[36] Ordonnance No. 47, 29 Dec. 1960, art. 5.
[37] Ordinance No. 36 of 1964; *cf. Roberts, A Revolution in the Law of
Succession of Malawi,* 1966 J. AFRICAN L. 21–32.

set forth in the act, only the remaining one-fifth devolving according to customary law. This complete departure from any known system of indigenous law is still prospective, for the ordinance does not come into operation until promulgated in the *Malawi Gazette*, and to my knowledge this has not as yet occurred.

If African customary law should to a considerable degree disappear, will there be adverse repercussions in the social life of the people? Actually, we know very little about the reasons why disputants take their cases to the courts rather than settle them extrajudicially according to established indigenous norms.[38] There is some evidence that a court decision in one's favor merely adds another point of vantage in gaining a better settlement of the dispute. This may be one reason why so many judgments handed down were never brought to execution by the successful party. If future judgments are rendered by magistrates who are strangers to the community, and if they are based upon principles dictated by the central government and at odds with well-established and recognized rules of the local customary law, there is good reason to expect less resorting to the state judiciary. For these decisions would have little or no weight in enhancing one's position in the give and take leading towards settlement. A diminution in the use of the courts means an increase in the number of traditional arbitral hearings. The nullification of the judicial process on the part of a substantial element of the rural population is a serious danger. It is a giant step back on the road to tribalism! The new states will do well to consider very thoughtfully any policy to be followed with respect to the indigenous law of their citizens. Restatement of the law, certainly. Unification of the customary law, query. Integration of the indigenous and the general law, by all means. Codification of the law, not for the present!

A. Arthur Schiller
Professor of Law
Columbia University
School of Law

New York City
May 15, 1967

---

[38] A fine example of a thorough discussion of this problem among the agricultural Masai of Northern Tanganyika is Gulliver, Social Control in an African Society; a Study of the Arusha (1963).

AFRICA AND LAW

DEVELOPING

LEGAL SYSTEMS

IN AFRICAN

COMMONWEALTH

NATIONS

LAW AND ECONOMIC DEVELOPMENT IN INDEPENDENT, ENGLISH-SPEAKING, SUB-SAHARAN AFRICA

ROBERT B. SEIDMAN*

I. INTRODUCTION

The Declaration of Delhi of the International Congress of Jurists, held in New Delhi in 1959, states in flaming words that:

> [T]he Rule of Law is a dynamic concept . . . which should be employed not only to safeguard and advance the civil and political rights of the individual in a free society, but also to establish social, economic, educational and cultural conditions under which his legitimate aspirations and dignity may be realized . . . .[1]

To what extent do the several legal orders of the independent, sub-Saharan, English-speaking African states realize the substantive requirements of the "Rule of Law" as thus dynamically conceived? Put in less lofty terms, how relevant to development is the law of English-speaking, independent Africa?

Professor Harvey has defined law as "a specific technique of social ordering, deriving its essential character from its reliance upon the prestige, authority, and ultimately the reserved monopoly of force of politically organized society."[2] It is a value-neutral tool. In this view, law has no moral authority merely because it is law; rather, it embraces every aspect of state power. Indeed, as Hans Kelsen has pointed out, there is no difference between the state and law; they are merely different sides of the same coin.[3] Every state institution is a manifestation of state power and can be viewed either institutionally or legally.

Because law is itself value-neutral, an important task for those who wield state power is to determine the criteria pursuant to which it is to be used. Value-acceptances are essentially subjective.[4] Following the philosophies of William James[5] and Roscoe

---

* Professor of Law, University of Wisconsin. B.A., 1941, Harvard University; LL.B., 1948, Columbia University.

[1] INTERNATIONAL COMM'N OF JURISTS, THE RULE OF LAW IN A FREE SOCIETY: A REPORT OF THE INTERNATIONAL CONGRESS OF JURISTS 3 (1959).

[2] Harvey, *The Challenge of the Rule of Law*, 59 MICH. L. REV. 603, 605 (1961). See also Harvey, *A Value Analysis of Ghanaian Law since Independence*, 1 U. GHANA L.J. 4, 5 (1964). This position derives essentially from KELSEN, GENERAL THEORY OF LAW AND STATE 18-19 (1949).

[3] KELSEN, *Law, State and Justice in the Pure Theory of Law*, in WHAT IS JUSTICE? 288 (1960). The statement in the text is accurate only for a relatively centralized legal order (*i.e.*, not most customary societies).

[4] "Justice is an irrational ideal." KELSEN, *op. cit. supra* note 2, at 13. Pound himself at one point stigmatized this as a "give-it-up philosophy." POUND, JUSTICE ACCORDING TO LAW 23 (1951). In the same essay, however, he urges lawyers not to wait for philosophers to develop a theory of

Pound,[6] a democratic system of law must proceed to investigate what are, as a matter of fact, the empirically determined value-acceptances of a given society.[7]   These value-acceptances, re-phrased as "jural postulates" in terms relevant to law, should, so far as possible, determine the legal ordering of society.   They ought to be society's standard of justice.[8]

In order to determine the sufficiency of the law of the indepen-

---

values.   "Experience developed by reason and reason tested by experi-ence have taught us how to go far toward achieving a practical task of enabling men to live together in politically organized communities in civilized society with the guidance of a working idea even if that working idea is not metaphysically or logically or ethically convincingly ideal." *Id.* at 29.   But why should lawyers adopt as the basis for law *their* notion of a solution which is not convincing metaphysically, logically, or ethically?

[5] "Since everything which is demanded is by that fact a good, must not the guiding principle for ethical philosophy (since all demands conjointly cannot be satisfied in this poor world) be simply to satisfy at all times *as many demands as we can?*"   JAMES, THE WILL TO BELIEVE 205 (1897).

[6] Justice is "such an adjustment of relations and ordering of conduct as will make the goods of existence . . . go round as far as possible with the least function and waste."   POUND, SOCIAL CONTROL THROUGH LAW 65 (1942).

[7] According to Stone, Pound suggested that reference be made either to the jural postulates of the society or to the "scheme of interests" that he proposed at other times.   STONE, HUMAN LAW AND HUMAN JUSTICE 266 (1965).   If the referent for justice is the existing scheme of interests, it is difficult to see how Pound's system differs from Aristotle's "distributive justice," which saw the end of justice as giving each man that to which his rank in society entitled him.

[8] Stone says:
> In a given society at a given time, individuals are asserting inter-ests as worthy of protection by the law of that society. . . . In order to understand what law in that society should do, the first step, therefore, must be to observe and record the social phenomena with which the law is concerned, namely, the interests which human be-ings are actually pressing for recognition by law.   From this com-prehensive picture the jurist can also draw out, by as impersonal a synthesis as possible, the fundamental principles concerning human conduct (or the "jural postulates") which substantially all of the phenomena presuppose.

Id. at 267.   The problem lies in formulating "by as impersonal synthesis as possible" the jural postulates for the society.   Absent any scientific meth-odology for determining value-acceptances, the jural postulates that one infers from the claims made are very apt to be intuitive rather than im-personal.   In that case, a natural law theory is being imposed in the guise of an empirical theory.   Laski made essentially that criticism of Pound when he asserted of Pound's jural postulates for the United States that "after his long journeys through the immense literature of legal theory he arrives at a framework of principles which are the obvious outcome of his affection for the country town of Lincoln, Nebraska . . . they are framed, that is to say, for a community of small owners such as the Middle West knew in the epoch first following the Civil War."   LASKI, AMERICAN DEMOC-RACY 443 (1949).

In Africa, there are, so far as one can ascertain, no studies of value-acceptances except with respect to tribal societies.   Therefore, the author has attempted his own synthesis, realizing the danger implicit in the ab-sence of any scientific methodology that subjective and intuitive value judgments will mask themselves in the choice of supporting data.

dent, sub-Saharan, English-speaking African states to accomplish
the material requirements of the "Rule of Law" as described in the
Declaration of Delhi, one must first examine the society and the
law as it stood during the colonial era. One must then discover,
so far as one may, the claims, demands, and interests that clamor
for satisfaction from the legal order—*i.e.*, from the state—and
the jural postulates that they presuppose. The sufficiency of the
legal orders of these independent, sub-Saharan, English-speaking
African states to realize the *de facto* demands made upon them can
then be weighed in light of the empirically determined value-
acceptances of the society.

II. THE ECONOMIC, SOCIAL, AND POLITICAL MATRIX

When the colonial powers began their extensive exploitation of
Africa in the latter part of the nineteenth century, a sparse subsistence economy held the continent in its implacable grip. It
largely retains its hold today.[9] The technological basis of its
economy is farming of a very simple sort. Wherever one goes in
Africa, whether in a sun-lit clearing in the rain forests of the
West Coast, the limitless reaches of the Sudannese savannah, or the
sunny plains of East and Central Africa, the farmer and his wives
people the rural scene, their feet straddled wide, leaning from the
waist to hack the refractory soil with a heavy, short-handled hoe
and a matchet, almost the sole agricultural tools. Fertilizers are
rarely used, and productivity is extremely low. In Ghana, one
farmer supports but one and one-half workers.[10] In the United
States, one farmer produces sufficient food for himself and about
twelve working people.[11]

The culture of the subsistence economy, while rich and varied,
remains basically prescientific. Africans in the subsistence economy learn the manifold skills required to survive in a harsh environment, but these skills bear little relevance to modern technology. Today, Nigeria, the most heavily populated country in
Africa, is said to be seventy-five percent illiterate in Lagos and
parts of the eastern region[12]—its most progressive areas—and up
to ninety-eight percent illiterate in the northern regions.[13] There
is a lamentable paucity of high-level manpower. Zambia is said

---

9 The catchall phrase "subsistence economy" covers a wide variety of
activities. Included in the phrase are all agrarian and pastoral economies
whose main emphasis is on subsistence production. See Kamarck, *Economics and Economic Development*, in THE AFRICAN WORLD: A SURVEY OF SOCIAL
RESEARCH 221, 230-31 (Lystad ed. 1965). Barber prefers to denote it as "the
indigenous economy." BARBER, THE ECONOMY OF BRITISH CENTRAL AFRICA
5 (1961).

10 OFFICE OF THE PLANNING COMMISSION (Accra), SEVEN YEAR PLAN 10
(1964).

11 *Ibid.*

12 WEST AFRICAN DIRECTORY, 1965-66, at 291 (1965).

13 AFRICA—A HANDBOOK TO THE CONTINENT 240 (Legum ed. 1961).

to have had about 960 Africans of school certificate (secondary school) standard at independence—for a country of about 3,500,000 people.[14]

As a result of this low level of economic productivity and technological training, the standard of living remains pathetically depressed. In Nigeria, every other baby dies before maturity.[15] *Kwashiokor*—malignant malnutrition—is the most widespread disease in Africa. The average life expectancy of Africans is between thirty and forty years.[16]

The social structure of the subsistence economy is responsive to its problems but is hardly apt to meet the demands of modern industrialization. For example, polygamy, which is practically universal in the culture of the subsistence economy, embodies a sensible answer to the demands for sufficient labor for subsistence farming. It soon becomes dysfunctional when husband and wife work for a daily wage in an office or factory and live in a two-room flat with all the modern conveniences. The extended family provides a useful buffer for the storms that sweep the subsistence economy. A widow and orphan, for example, can readily be fitted into a farming household, in whose endless work they can participate. But the cash nexus erodes the extended family's *raison d'etre*. The family obligation changes from support in an agrarian household into cash payments to indigent members. The ceaseless leakage of cash in fulfillment of family obligations drains the accumulations of the family's more fortunate members and makes it difficult for them to enjoy the fruits of ambition and diligence. The extended family thus tends to negate the incentives on which the cash economy largely depends.

The colonial powers imposed upon the Africa of the subsistence economy an enclave of relatively modern technology, based in the main upon extractive industry—mining, forestry, and plantation crops.[17] Together with the extractive industries came the great trading firms—Unilever, which through the United Africa Company still dominates the trade of English-speaking West Africa, G. B. Oliphant, John Holt Batholomew, and a few others. They not only controlled the import of European manufactures, but

---

[14] Education Minister John Mwanakatwe, quoted in HALL, ZAMBIA 173 (1965).

[15] There are no accurate statistics; this estimate has been made by a responsible official of the Nigerian Ministry of Health. In East Africa, it is conservatively estimated that two-fifths of all those born die before reaching 14 years. HAILEY, AN AFRICAN SURVEY REVISED 1070 (1957).

[16] U.N. DEMOGRAPHIC YEARBOOK 1963, at 612-24 (U.N. Pub. Sales No. 64.XIII.I). The caloric intake in Ghana in 1957 was about 1,800 calories per day per person; that of the U.S. about 3,280 calories per day per person. U.N. STATISTICAL YEARBOOK 1964, at 372-75.

[17] See Okigbo, *Independence and the Problem of Economic Growth*, in ECONOMIC TRANSITION IN AFRICA 323, 326-27 (Herskovits & Harwitz ed. 1964).

they also came to control the export of the peasant-produced crops of the Gold Coast (now Ghana) and Nigeria.

The extractive industries and the trading firms required the construction of some modern infrastructure—roads, railways, ports. All were designed primarily to meet the demands of the colonial interest, not to service the subsistence economy. The railroad systems of the United States or of Europe, for example, form a network joining the various regions. But the railways of Africa are short lines leading from a center of extractive industry to the sea.[18] There is to this day no railway joining East Africa to West. To go by plane from Lagos to Nairobi requires that one go by way of Ethiopia—and even that is quite recent; formerly one had to fly to Europe for transfer.

Shaped by the imperatives of the profit motive, these colonialist enclaves primarily became funnels through which the rich raw materials of Africa were directed to the metropolis,[19] where they fed the smelters of Birmingham, the chocolate factories of Cadbury & Fry, and the soap factories of Unilever. Practically no secondary industries to process raw materials were erected in tropical Africa. Until this year, if a Ghanaian wanted cocoa in a usable form, such as drinking chocolate or a chocolate bar, he had to buy an imported product—and Ghana produced thirty-three percent of the world's cocoa! In all of Africa there was not one factory producing copper products—although the copperbelt in Zambia produces much of the world's copper. The paradigm is the oil wells of Nigeria that today pump oil automatically into tankers waiting offshore. Very few Nigerians learn any skill, or even receive any cash wages, as a result of the enterprise.[20]

Colonialist culture was, in the same way, mainly an enclave. In East Africa, the best areas of land were exclusively reserved for white settlers by statute.[21] In Rhodesia, Africans were forbidden to live in the colonialist metropolitan centers such as Salisbury.[22] In West Africa, the Europeans huddled in tight little com-

---

[18] 1 KIMBLE, TROPICAL AFRICA 337-38 (abr. ed. 1962); and see frontispiece.

[19] The economies of Africa are "pre-eminently export-oriented. The dependence of Africa's income on exports is greater than that of Latin America or Asia." Kamarck, op. cit. supra note 9, at 222.

[20] Barber urges that, rather than the model of subsistence economy and colonialist enclave, the economies of the countries of Central Africa at least are best conceived as dual economies, with a money sector and a subsistence sector. BARBER, op. cit. supra note 9, at xi.

[21] In Kenya in 1961, the average settler's farm had 3,460 acres, while the average African farm had 23.6 acres. FORRESTER, KENYA TODAY: SOCIAL PREREQUISITES FOR ECONOMIC DEVELOPMENT 73 (1962).

[22] In Southern Rhodesia, 42% of the land is reserved for use by 2,282,800 Africans (1957 population figures), but in fact the bulk of the population is limited to "native reserves" that comprise about 22% of the total land area. The white population of 178,000 persons (1956 figures) is exclusively

munities. Ikoyi, the most elegant residential district in Lagos, was reserved for Europeans until recently. Even today, one can see in Accra compounds in which are grouped all the bungalows of the expatriate personnel of a single trading firm. In colonial days, they had their own clubs, their own bars, their own bathing beaches, their own society.

The result was that the economy, the culture, the society, and, as we shall see, the law of tropical Africa at independence—and to a great extent, even to this day—were pluralistic. But the two enclaves were hardly equal. The subsistence sector, in which lived the vast majority of Africans, had a desperately low standard of living. The colonialist enclave had a high standard of living based upon the exploitation of African resources and African labor. In Africa today probably seven to ten percent of the population receives fifty percent of the income.[23] The average African per capita income in Tanganyika is about forty-five dollars per year; the average European per capita income is about 839 dollars per year.[24]

Much of the vast income that was earned in the colonialist enclave was in the form of profits to the great expatriate firms. These profits were sent home to the mother country and were reinvested there. To this day, it is estimated that about twenty-five percent of Africa's gross foreign earnings is shipped out of Africa.[25] As a result, there was precious little reinvestment of disposable surplus in Africa. The subsistence economy droned on, not significantly improving from year to year and leaving its inhabitants drowned in perpetual penury, disease, and—in terms of modern technology—ignorance. The colonialist enclave lived with rela-

---

entitled to use 50% of the land. BARBER, op. cit. supra note 9, at 22, 54, 160 n.1.

[23] While statistics are not, so far as can be determined, available for every country, a few are suggestive. In the Federation of the Rhodesias and Nyasaland, for example, the European population, comprising about 7.3% of the total population in 1956, received 64% of the total money income from wages, salaries, and unincorporated enterprise. If corporate profits were included, the amount would be even higher. Id. at 161 table II, 160 n.1.

[24] See Ghai, Some Aspects of Income Distribution in East Africa, 1964 (unpublished paper in Makerere University Library). In Kenya, the per capita money income in Nairobi (the center of European activity) is $708; the per capita money income in the Northern Provinces is $8. GOVERNMENT OF KENYA, DEVELOPMENT PLAN 1964-70, at 129 (1964).

[25] See U.N. Doc. No. E/CN. 14 (IV)/SR 7, at 27. The figure given is merely an estimate; it is impossible to give a precise figure for the profits, interest, and dividends which have been shipped out of Africa annually by the foreign firms, banks, and insurance companies which conduct the major share of the business in the colonialist enclave. In Northern Rhodesia (Zambia), the copper companies in 1951 exported overseas 58% of the total value of domestic exports in the form of interest, dividends, and undistributed profits; in 1952 and 1953, 39% and 35% respectively. BARBER, op. cit. supra note 9, at 110.

tively high incomes as a tight little island in the surrounding sea of poverty. It shipped out of Africa for the benefit of the home country the extraordinarily large disposable surplus earned by African resources and African labor.

III. THE PLURAL LEGAL PATTERNS AT INDEPENDENCE

A pluralistic legal system provided the norms for this plural society. To understand its functional relationships to the social and economic matrix, one must examine the customary law, the reception of English law, and the rules of internal conflicts of law.

A. Customary Law

Perhaps the only valid generalization that can be made about customary law in Africa is that, in all its diversity, it has been reasonably apt to answer the problems thrown up by the subsistence economy and the existing level of technology. The allocation of property rights in land offers a good illustration.

Professor Gluckman has said that "the incidence of rights over land varies with the technology of the tribe concerned . . . ."[26] The most widespread form of farming technology in Africa is shifting agriculture. A plot of land is burned over, cleared, and then tilled for a few years until the soil is exhausted, at which time a new plot of fallow land is similarly brought to cultivation. Meanwhile the old plot is permitted to lie fallow until it has regained its productive capacity.

The land law of the tribes, in all their infinite varieties, accommodates itself to the twin facts of a relative abundance of vacant land and plots brought to fruition by the efforts of individual families. In the more centralized states, allodial ownership is in the larger community—the stool in West Africa, the chief or other ruler in East Africa. In less centralized societies, allodial ownership is frequently in some smaller group—a village, lineage, or family.[27] However, the nominal "owner" must allocate portions of unoccupied land either directly to individual members of the relevant group[28] or to subgroups, who in turn must allocate on demand to their individual members, as for example, among the Lozi[29] or the Ashanti.[30] In most systems, the right to exclusive

---

26 GLUCKMAN, POLITICS, LAW AND RITUAL IN TRIBAL SOCIETY 36 (1965).

27 Bentsi-Entchill, *Do African Systems of Land Tenure Require a Special Terminology?*, 1965 J. AFRICAN L. 114, 124-26; Mugerwa, *Land Tenure in East Africa—Some Contrasts*, in EAST AFRICAN LAW TODAY, 5 COMMONWEALTH LAW SERIES 101, 101-02 (1965).

28 *E.g.*, the Tallensi of Northern Ghana. FORTES, *The Political System of the Tallensi of the Northern Territories of the Gold Coast*, in AFRICAN POLITICAL SYSTEMS 239, 250 (Fortes & Evans-Pritchard eds. 1940).

29 GLUCKMAN, *op. cit. supra* note 26, at 37-40.

30 OLLENNU, PRINCIPLES OF CUSTOMARY LAND LAW IN GHANA 31 (1962).

possession of the plot in the individual or family to whom it has been allotted cannot be tampered with by the allotting authority (save in very exceptional circumstances) so long as it is being used.[31] Upon its being abandoned to the bush, however, the former occupier has no further rights in the land, and it reverts to the control of the allotting authority.

Sir Henry Maine said long ago that "the movement of progressive societies has hitherto been a movement *from Status to Contract*."[32] In the tribal societies of Africa, as in early Europe,

> most of the transactions in which men and women are involved are not specific, single transactions involving the exchange of goods and services between relative strangers. Instead, men and women hold land and other property, and exchange goods and services, as members of a hierarchy of political groups and as kinsfolk or affines. People are linked in transactions with one another because of pre-existing relationships of status between them.[33]

Thus with respect to land, property right is a function of status, just as status is a function of property right.

B. *The Reception of English Law*

Upon this pattern of customary law the English grafted their own law. The reception of English law in tropical Africa came in a wide variety of forms. Sometimes a specific area of English law was adopted by reference; sometimes a specific English statute was made operative in a territory; and sometimes a whole area of common law was codified and enacted by a colonial legislature.[34]

The most common form of reception, however, was the general reception statute, that existed in almost every English-speaking African state.[35] That statute, of which Ghana's (the earliest) may be taken as an archetype, usually appeared either as local legislation or in the Order-in-Council establishing the colony or protectorate. The Gold Coast Supreme Court Ordinance of 1876 contained the following clause establishing the basic law: "The common law, the doctrines of equity, and the statutes of general application which were in force in England on the date when the Colony obtained a local legislature, that is to say, 24th July, 1874, shall be in force within the jurisdiction of this Court."[36] The exceptions to this broad reception statute, however, were far broad-

---

31 Bentsi-Entchill, *supra* note 27, at 127-28.
32 MAINE, ANCIENT LAW 174 (10th ed. 1920).
33 GLUCKMAN, *op. cit. supra* note 26, at 48-49.
34 ALLOTT, ESSAYS IN AFRICAN LAW 5-6 (1960).
35 The statutes can be found in JUDICIAL AND LEGAL SYSTEMS IN AFRICA (Allott ed. 1962).
36 Courts Ordinance, 1876, § 14 (Gold Coast).

er than the statute itself. The same statute provided that:

> Nothing in this Ordinance shall deprive the Supreme Court
> of the right to observe and enforce the observance, or shall
> deprive any person of the benefit, of any law or custom ex-
> isting in the said Colony and Territories subject to its juris-
> diction, such law or custom not being repugnant to nat-
> ural justice, equity or good conscience, nor incompatible ei-
> ther directly or by necessary implication with any enact-
> ment of the Colonial Legislature ... .[37]

Since numerically the persons who could claim the benefit of customary law—the entire African population—far exceeded the European population, in every English-speaking African state the
strange anomoly obtained that the "basic" law—English law—applied to a miniscule proportion of the population, but the "exceptional" law—customary law—applied to the vast majority.[38]

The English law received was basically the common law as it
stood in the late nineteenth and early twentieth centuries and the
"statutes of general application" (primarily statutes dealing with
commercial matters and decedents' estates).[39] Nineteenth-century
England had rapidly developed the modern tendency to separate
ownership of property and the sphere of work of the individual[40]—
a sharp contrast to the position in customary law, where the right
to use property was, in the main, intimately connected to the
actual fact of using it.[41] The concomitant was that the right to

---

[37] Courts Ordinance, 1876, § 19 (Gold Coast).

[38] The Sudan was a special case of reception that deserves mention.
There the British ruled in a unique condominium with Egypt. Because of
the vast difference between the English law and the pastiche of Islamic,
Ottoman, and French law obtaining in Egypt, as well as the dominant
Muslim character of northern Sudan, it was felt inadvisable to introduce
any specific sort of law at all. The courts were simply directed to decide
cases on the basis of "justice, equity and good conscience." Civil Justice
Ordinance, 1929, § 9, 10 LAWS OF THE SUDAN 13 (1955). However, the judges
were all Englishmen trained in English law; and with magnificent insularity
it developed that "justice, equity and good conscience" meant not merely
English common law but English statutory law as well. The author has
been told by an English barrister who tried a case in the Sudan some years
ago that he was amazed to discover that "justice, equity and good conscience" meant in his case the English Sale of Goods Act, 1862. See Gutt-
mann, *The Reception of the Common Law of the Sudan*, 6 INT'L & COMP.
L.Q. 401 (1957).

[39] In Nigeria only about thirty to forty such statutes have been held
applicable. PARK, THE SOURCES OF NIGERIAN LAW 35 (1963). Why such a
vague term as "statutes of general application" was used is difficult to
determine. It has led to continual confusion about the scope of the reception. See ALLOTT, *op. cit. supra* note 34, at 9.

[40] FRIEDMANN, LAW IN A CHANGING SOCIETY 72 (1959). This observation
is drawn from Renner's analysis. See Kahn-Freund, *Introduction* to REN-
NER, THE INSTITUTIONS OF PRIVATE LAW AND THEIR SOCIAL FUNCTIONS *passim*
(Kahn-Freund transl. 1949).

[41] There are exceptions—for example, the *milo* estates in Buganda and
the great Dahomey plantations of old described by Professor Herskovits.

property in English law depended not on status, as it had in feudal days, but on contract. Real property, like other sorts of property, was treated as merely one of the necessary factors of production and tended to be assimilated to the demands of the market.[42] Contract, not status, was the principal source of property right in the received law.

The received law thus accommodated well to the demands of the British in Africa. The economic activities of the new rulers were organized around the central notion of the exploitation of African labor in European-owned mines and on European-owned plantations.[43] In West Africa, a special variant developed in which the African peasant worked his own land but sold to the great English factors the products of his labor—rubber, groundnuts, cocoa, and oil-palm products. In each case, the control of the products of labor was separated from their production. The legal institution that provided the rules for this separation was contract.

But the English law that was received in Africa was not the English law of the home country. As early as the late nineteenth and early twentieth centuries, massive inroads were being made upon the freedom to use property under the imperatives of the welfare state. The apparatus of restriction—in connection with labor contracts, the use and ownership of land, the use of certain specific sorts of property, the imposition of standards on the producers of consumer goods, and the use of taxation as a method of controlling the use of property—was introduced in England by statute or delegated legislation. These statutes were never included in the phrase "statutes of general application." Therefore, the received English law embodied norms that found their principal source of legal right in contract and that were appropriate for the development of a sector of the economy largely dependent upon the private initiative and enterprise of the colonialists for its shape and direction.

C. Internal Conflicts

The body of law—customary or English—to be applied in a given case was determined by the rules of internal conflicts of law. These rules were originally framed to meet a single policy consideration: It was "fair" or "just" that the norm used to control a given transaction was the norm that the actors concerned anticipated would be applied. Thus the rules of internal conflicts were

---

HERSKOVITS, DAHOMEY—AN ANCIENT WEST AFRICAN KINGDOM 55-56 (1938). Some of the farms cultivated by the *gletanu*, or great cultivators, are described as comprising areas fifteen to twenty-five or thirty kilometers long and "several" kilometers wide. They were worked by the descendants of slaves who worked for half of each day on the *gletanu's* estate.

[42] Bohannan, *Land Use, Land Tenure and Land Reform*, in ECONOMIC TRANSITION IN AFRICA 133, 134 (Herskovits & Harwitz ed. 1964).

[43] WODDIS, AFRICA—THE ROOTS OF REVOLT *passim* (1960).

originally framed in ethnic terms. In cases between Africans, customary law was to be applied; in cases between non-Africans, English law was to be applied.[44]

The internal conflicts rules, however, served a purpose different from that originally planned—for transactions directly relating to the economy. Since at the time these rules were adopted every African lived and mainly worked within the subsistence sector and every European within the colonialist enclave, the rules allocated transactions arising in the subsistence sector to the customary law and transactions arising within the colonialist enclave to the English law. Thus each sector of the economy was controlled by norms of law appropriate to it.

It was at once apparent, however, that the ethnic touchstone was not entirely satisfactory for there might well be circumstances in which Africans might opt to transact business in the light of English law rather than customary law. Therefore the internal conflicts rules included two important exceptions to the ethnic test. If the parties intended English law to apply to the transaction, or if the transaction was unknown to customary law, English law was to be applied.[45]

In practice, the courts stretched these exceptions considerably, at least when dealing with commercial transactions, so that if the transaction was one typical of the colonialist enclave, English law would usually be applied, even if the transaction was between Africans. The use of a typical English form of lease or contract, for example, raised a presumption that English law was to control, either because the transaction was unknown to customary law[46] or because the use of English forms implied an intention to invoke English law.[47] Moreover, by declaring that a corporation or as-

---

[44] See, e.g., The High Court of Lagos Act § 27 (Nigeria): "Any such law or custom [i.e., customary law] shall be deemed applicable in causes and matters where the parties thereto are natives . . . ." Since English law was the "general" law, it applied unless (as in the quoted clause) it was excluded. For a typical example, see Labinjoh v. Abake, 5 Nigerian Law Reports 33 (1924) [Nigerian Law Reports will hereinafter be cited N.L.R.]. The statutes are collected and discussed in ALLOTT, op. cit. supra note 34, at 153-202.

[45] See, e.g., the High Court of Lagos Act § 27 (Nigeria):
No party shall be entitled to claim the benefit of any native law or custom, if it shall appear either from express contract or from the nature of the transactions out of which any suit or question may have arisen, that such party agreed that his obligations in connection with such transaction should be exclusively regulated otherwise than by native law and custom or that such transactions are transactions unknown to native law and custom.

[46] See, e.g., Griffen v. Talabi, 12 West African Court of Appeals 371 (1948) [West African Court of Appeals will hereinafter be cited as W.A.C.A.].

[47] See, e.g., Green v. Owo, 13 N.L.R. 43 (1936); Griffin v. Talabi, supra note 46. At one time it seems to have been the rule in West Africa that the use of writing automatically meant that the transaction was not one

sociation, even if composed entirely of Africans, was not "African"
for the purposes of the internal conflicts rules,[48] the courts withdrew from the operation of the rules a whole category of entities
that typically centered their activities in the money economy.
Perhaps the most extreme case is *Okolie v. Ibo*.[49] A member of
the Ibo tribe owned a gasoline station and another owned a lorry.
In a dispute between them over the sale of gasoline, the court
held that, in view of "their respective occupations and the nature
of the transaction between them,"[49a] neither their personal law
nor Islamic law (which was the law of the forum) could be applied.
Therefore English law governed.

Thus, the basic rules of internal conflicts more or less function-
ally allocated transactions arising out of the precapitalist sector to
customary law and allocated transactions arising out of the
colonialist enclave to the English law. But there were two
important exceptions: criminal law, and transactions between Africans and expatriates.

1. CRIMINAL LAW

English criminal law was in most territories the first body of
English law introduced.[50] It covered all serious crimes, although
in most colonies African courts continued to apply customary crim-

---

recognized by customary law, but that is no longer the position. PARK, *op. cit. supra* note 39, at 109; ALLOTT, *op. cit. supra* note 34, at 242-74.

[48] Mengo Builders and Contractors Ltd. v. Kasibante, 1958 East African Court of Appeals 591 (Uganda). *But see* Interpretation and General Clauses Ordinance, 1951, § 3(8) (Uganda). See also PARK, *op. cit. supra* note 39, at 103.

[49] 1958 Law Reports of the Northern Region of the Federation of Nigeria 89 [Law Reports of the Northern Region of the Federation of Nigeria will hereinafter be cited N.R.N.L.R.].

[49a] *Id.* at 90.

[50] English criminal law was introduced into the Gold Coast in 1853. Supreme Court Ordinance (1853). The Indian Penal Code was introduced in East Africa early in the century. The Queensland Criminal Code was introduced into Northern Nigeria in 1904 and into Southern Nigeria in 1916. The Sudanese Criminal Code (1907), modeled in large part upon the Indian and the Pakistan codes, was introduced into Northern Nigeria in 1959. During the 1930's, the colonial office drafted a new criminal code based in large part upon the Queensland code. It was introduced into Kenya, Uganda, Tanganyika (Tanzania), Zanzibar, Nyasaland (Malawi) and Northern Rhodesia (Zambia). It is an intriguing fact that the Queensland code, upon which most of the African codes are now modeled, in turn drew, *inter alia*, upon the Penal Code of New York for inspiration. See Read, *Criminal Law in Africa of Today and Tomorrow*, 1963 J. AFRICAN L. 5-17. Any resemblance between the mores immanent in the codes and those of the people subject to them would seem largely accidental, like the broken clock that is right twice a day. See Seidman, *Witch Murder and Mens Rea: A Problem of Society Under Racial Social Change*, 28 MODERN L. REV. 46 (1965); Seidman, *Mens Rea and the Reasonable African*, 15 INT'L & COMP. L.Q. (1966); Seidman, *The Inarticulate Premiss*, 4 J. MODERN AFRICAN STUDIES 567 (1966).

inal law to minor offenses.[51] English criminal law preempted the
field because it met most aptly the requirements of the Dual Mandate.[52] In the first place, the English required a monopoly of force
if there was to be a settled society in which trade might flourish.[53]
The existence of competing power centers threatened imperial rule.
A case that arose in the Gold Coast in 1895 aptly demonstrates
that English criminal law was introduced to meet the requirement
of a monopoly of force in society. Pursuant to well-defined custom, the elders of the Anlo tribe (a portion of the Ewe nation)
condemned and executed some criminals—the so-called "Fifth
Landing Stage" executions. By so doing, they acted as the responsible agents of their society in ridding the community of intol-
erable criminal elements. For their temerity, the elders—who had
acted reasonably and pursuant to the imperatives of their own
society for law and order—were themselves tried for murder and
hung by the British before some ten thousand of the Anlo people
gathered for the occasion.[54] The real offense of the elders was
that by purporting to try and execute criminals they threatened
the imperial monopoly of state power.

But the Dual Mandate also imposed a "civilizing mission" upon
the British rulers. Its requirement in the early years was primarily that "barbarous native customs," chiefly slavery and human sacrifice, should be eradicated.[55] The requirements of public
order and the "civilizing mission" met happily—to British minds—

---

[51] Read, *supra* note 50, at 15-16.
[52] The "Dual Mandate" was Lord Lugard's name for the twin imperatives of British imperialism: to benefit England's economy, and to uplift
the "savage races." See LUGARD, THE DUAL MANDATE IN BRITISH TROPICAL
AFRICA (5th ed. 1965).
[53] The history of the introduction of criminal law in the Gold Coast is
instructive. The Fante Bond of 1844 provided in part that "Murders, Rob-
beries and other Crimes and offenses" were to be tried by the Queen's
judicial officers and the chiefs, "moulding the customs of the Country to
the general Principles of British Law." Quoted in NEWBURY, BRITISH POLICY
TOWARDS WEST AFRICA: SELECT DOCUMENTS 1786-1874, at 298 (1965). At
this time the British control over the Gold Coast was very tenuous, both
legally and factually, and it was impossible to impose British rule directly.
See Dispatch from Governor Winniett to Earl Grey, Secretary of State, 31
January 1849, in ADM 1/450 (National Archives, Accra). By 1853 the
British felt secure enough to create a Supreme Court that was to apply
the common law of crimes. Supreme Court Ordinance (1853) (Gold
Coast). The colony was formally created in 1874. The Supreme Court
Ordinance, 1876, gave the Supreme Court exclusive jurisdiction over serious crimes. The chief's courts retained only a very narrow jurisdiction
over minor crimes, and their power to punish was limited to fines of thirty-
two "ackies" of gold, imprisonment for not more than three months, "or
. . . some other native punishment of not greater severity not repugnant
with natural justice or with the principles of the law of England." Native
Jurisdiction Ordinance, Schedule, §§ 3-4 (1883).
[54] GOLD COAST PRISONS DEPARTMENT, ANNUAL REPORT (1895).
[55] See, *e.g.*, the Fante Bond of 1844 (Gold Coast), described in note 53
supra.

in the common law of crimes. It at once provided a minimum guarantee of a peaceful society, and, by embodying English notions of morality, it fulfilled the minimum requirements of the "civilizing mission."[56]

In Northern Nigeria and Buganda, however, a different pattern arose. There the British found strongly entrenched, hierarchical societies with well-developed systems of public order: the Buganda customary courts and law in the one case, the Alkalis (or judges) and the Malaki school of Islamic law in the other. It was in these two countries that the doctrine of indirect rule flourished. Hence, until very recent times, the indigenous law of public order also flourished, but subject to supervisory control by the Resident or Judicial Advisor.[57] But the principle involved was the same: The monopoly of power was still firmly in British hands through the control exercised by the Resident, and the civilizing function was exercised (if on occasion only rather gently) by the supervisory function.[58]

2. TRANSACTIONS BETWEEN AFRICANS AND NON-AFRICANS

A second major exception to the general rule held that transactions between Africans and non-Africans were to be governed by English law unless it was proven that the parties intended some other law to apply.[59] The most frequent form of such transactions was contract: contracts of employment in the great mines and plantations of South, Central, and East Africa, and contracts for the sale of produce and manufactured goods in West Africa.

British exploitation of its African empire required exploiting African labor, either through employment or through the purchase of peasant-produced crops. Similar exploitation in French West

---

[56] Judge Ollennu asserts that English criminal law was introduced into the Gold Coast because "having seen the application of the English criminal law as it was administered within the settlements, and compared it with their own customary systems, the aborigines themselves were left with no doubt that the English system was more satisfactory and more effective in dealing with crime than their own . . . ." Ollennu, *The Influence of English Law in West Africa*, 1961 J. AFRICAN L. 21, 25. *But cf.* King Aggrey's complaint that the president (and effective ruler) of the trading forts imposed criminal law by the strong right arm of his soldiery. KIMBLE, A POLITICAL HISTORY OF GHANA: THE RISE OF GOLD COAST NATIONALISM 1850-1928, at 204 (1963).

Allott agrees that British law was not accepted voluntarily by the people, with the possible exception of the Gold Coast. Allott, *The Changing Law in a Changing Africa*, 11 SOCIOLOGUS 115 (1961). However, as King Aggrey's complaint suggests, it is far from clear that the Fante Chiefs understood the implications of the Bond of 1844.

[57] The history of the gradual replacement of Islamic criminal law in the Alkali courts of Northern Nigeria by "English" criminal law is described in OKONKWO & NAISH, CRIMINAL LAW IN NIGERIA 4-12 (1964).

[58] See BOHANNAN, AFRICA AND AFRICANS 17-20 (1964).

[59] See generally ALLOTT, *op. cit. supra* note 34, at 189-201.

Africa and in Portuguese Africa was frequently accomplished by the use of forced labor.[60] In British Africa, however, forced labor was inconsistent with the Dual Mandate, although it was occasionally invoked.[61] Hence exploitation in British Africa was usually marked by a contractual relationship.

These contracts were measured by English law under the internal conflicts of law rule. In legal fiction, they were based upon the individual's freedom to contract. But the economic imperatives were such that relative equality of bargaining power, which alone makes freedom to contract meaningful, was notably absent. There can be no "freedom to contract" between an African laborer and the great foreign mining firms or plantations. In West Africa, produce export was firmly in the hands of a very few English trading firms. During the 1930's these firms formed a trust in order to fix a low price for cocoa and other primary products.[62] To enforce contracts made under such conditions of inequality of bargaining power was to paper over the exploitative relationship with a thin veneer of "voluntary agreement."

Patent inequalities in bargaining power in England and the United States have led to a host of laws that limit freedom of contract in the interests of the weaker party—labor laws, hire-purchase (conditional sale) laws, insurance law, and many others.[63] In South, Central, and East Africa— the great settler colonies—and to a lesser degree in West Africa, the thrust was largely in the opposite direction. In the first place, contract law offered precious little protection to the European employer because an African laborer could hardly respond in damages for breach of contract. To remedy this situation, master and servant laws were enacted in every colony making it a criminal offense to breach a contract of employment without adequate cause.[64] In the second place, not enough Africans were willing to leave the subsistence economy to enter upon employment with European entrepreneurs. Various compulsions were devised to force them to do so. Hut taxes and poll taxes were originally imposed not to raise funds for the government but to create compulsions upon Africans to work in European-owned enterprises.[65] A variety of pass laws and other

---

[60] HAILEY, op. cit. supra note 15, at 1367; WODDIS, op. cit. supra note 43, at 70-75; KLOOSTERBOER, INVOLUNTARY LABOUR SINCE THE ABOLITION OF SLAVERY 140 (1960).

[61] WODDIS, op. cit. supra note 43, at 64-70.

[62] REPORT OF THE COMMISSION ON THE MARKETING OF WEST AFRICAN COCOA, Cmnd. 5845 (1938).

[63] FRIEDMANN, op. cit. supra note 40, at 106-09.

[64] The standard Blue Book forms (statistical and other returns completed annually by every British Colony) included a separate statistical return for convictions under the master and servant laws. See HAILEY, op. cit. supra note 15, at 1413-18.

[65] AARONOVITCH, CRISIS IN KENYA 99 (1946); 1 BUELL, THE NATIVE PROBLEM IN AFRICA 331 (1928); SCHAPERA, MIGRANT LABOUR AND TRIBAL LIFE 7, 108, 151 (1947).

measures were enacted to achieve the same purpose.[66]

But in West Africa there never was a large settler population. In the main, peasant farmers produced cash crops for export instead of working on European plantations, and as early as 1911 the Gold Coast economy had acquired the outline that it now has.[67] Peasant-produced crops were purchased by the great European trading firms. Marketing boards were created for a variety of reasons, but at first in the interests of the buying firms themselves. The first chairman of the Cocoa Marketing Board, for example, was a representative of Cadbury's.[68] In Nigeria, the English firms were the principal buying agents for the boards at the outset and continue as such to this day. However, in time the board's function changed. It became essentially a device to stabilize prices to the peasant producer.[69] The price to the producer for cocoa in Ghana remained stable from 1945 to 1966. Legally, the function of the boards was to provide a buffer between the producers and the buyers. They reflected the plain fact that there was no meaningful freedom of contract between the small peasant producers and the buying corporations.

D. Conclusion

This broadly sketched picture of the law of the African colonies just prior to independence suggests the consequences of British rule. Africans in the indigenous economy were to remain there, controlled by their own customary law. Persons and transactions in the colonialist enclave were to be controlled by English law, thereby creating a legal environment favorable to private enterprise. But under the guise of "freedom" to contract, the labor market in East, Central, and South Africa was highly structured by the use of a variety of compulsions to persuade Africans to work for European enterprise. In West Africa, where the main British economic interest was in the form of the purchase of peasant-produced crops, the oligopolistic market, controlled by the great British trading firms, was the device by which the British bent the African economy to the uses of British commerce. Overall, law and order were maintained by the monopoly of violence embodied

---

[66] HAILEY, op. cit. supra note 15, at 1418-24.

[67] SZERESZEWSKI, STRUCTURAL CHANGES IN THE ECONOMY OF GHANA 1891-1911, at 2 (1965).

[68] The history of the board is summarized in Green, Multi-purpose Economic Institutions in Africa, 1 J. MODERN AFRICAN STUDIES 163, 166 (1963). The board was first suggested in the Newell Commission Report. REPORT OF THE COMMISSION ON THE MARKETING OF WEST AFRICAN COCOA, Cmnd. 5875 (1938). This commission was appointed in response to a "hold-up" by producers against the "Cocoa Ring." However, it was not implemented until World War II, when demands for a board were voiced by the companies themselves. Green comments that at first the Board "reinstated the 1937 Pool with government sanction although with limited profits." Green, supra at 167.

[69] Id. at 168-69.

in the English criminal law, with control over petty offenses within the subsistence sector delegated to customary courts and customary law.[70]

To continue these laws and these institutions at independence meant to continue economies structured as they were during colonialism. The mark of difference between South Africa and the independent states is that the former proposes to institutionalize the dichotomous economic structure by apartheid and the *Bantusans* policy.[71] The independent states, on the other hand, are faced with new imperatives blown up by the winds of change. Before one can examine the problems posed for the law by these new imperatives, one must examine the *de facto* claims, demands, and interests that clamor for legal protection.

IV. THE IMPERATIVES OF INDEPENDENCE

Independence changed the color of some of the faces in the colonialist enclave, but it did not of itself change either the structure of the economy or the basic character of the legal system. It came about simultaneously with a new pattern of *de facto* claims made upon the state and the legal order. From an examination of these claims one can determine the imperatives to which the independent African states must respond. They may be subsumed under two headings: development and social engineering on the one hand, and legality on the other.

A. Development and Social Engineering

The criticial issue for a theory of justice based upon a jurisprudence of interests is to determine the serial order in which the *de facto* claims are to be recognized.[72] Pound assumed that in a "civilized" society "most" *de facto* claims, demands, and interests would be animated by a commonly accepted set of jural postulates. As early as 1942, however, Pound himself expressed a vague uneasiness that this assumption was doubtful when applied to the United States. He said that his system was

> less useful . . . . indeed, [is] embarrassed in [its] operation, because of transition from a social order . . . the jural postulates of which were clearly understood, to one which

---

[70] But *cf.* Allott, *supra* note 56 at 119 ("The British imposed their own laws for ease of administration, and also from a conscious policy of ameliorating the conditions under which the subject populations lived"); Roberts-Wray, *The Adaptation of Imported Law in Africa*, 1960 J. AFRICAN L. 66 ("British administration in overseas countries has conferred no greater benefit than English law and justice . . . . It has been said so often by so many people—as many laymen as lawyers and perhaps more Africans than Englishmen—that it must be assumed to be true ").

[71] Schiller, *Law,* in THE AFRICAN WORLD: A SURVEY OF SOCIAL RESEARCH 166, 176 (Lystad ed. 1965).

[72] DE JOUVENAL, SOVEREIGNTY 154 (1957).

has not sufficiently found itself to admit of formulating an ideal which all accept (as all the schools accepted that of the last century) or formulating jural postulates the validity of which may be assumed.[73]

What was vaguely characteristic of the United States of 1942 is the outstanding quality of the Africa of 1966.[74] Three sets of claims, demands, and interests appear to struggle for recognition. One set is predicated upon customary law; one set looks for satisfaction under the received English law; and a third set makes claims upon the national government in the name of national development. Each presupposes its own set of jural postulates. These jural postulates differ from each other in a host of particulars. However, legal philosphers from the extreme right to the extreme left agree, says Professor Friedmann, "that property and its distribution occupies a central—and in the view of many, a decisive—position in modern industrial society . . . ."[75] For the purposes of economic development, the same is plainly true in Africa.

Ownership of property confers on the proprietor a dual power, to enjoy and command.[76] The differences between the three sets of jural postulates that clamor for recognition in Africa can best be understood by their posture towards the central concept of property.

Ownership and labor are usually closely connected in subsistence economies.[77] Thus, ownership has only a very limited command function—command function being the power to exercise a quasi-public authority over people and social relationships. In customary law, the enjoyment of property and the limited command function are tightly tied to ownership. Ownership, in turn, hinges upon one's place in the social order—as a member of family, village, lineage or tribe; i.e., it depends upon status. The principal postulate of the customary legal order and of the claims made upon it reflects this central theme.

The claims, demands, and interests that seek satisfaction under the received "English" law, on the other hand, reflect a different set of jural postulates about property. In English law, the right to

---

[73] POUND, SOCIAL CONTROL THROUGH LAW 122 (1942). See STONE, HUMAN LAW AND HUMAN JUSTICE 277-79 (1965).

[74] Cf. id. at 279.

[75] FRIEDMANN, op. cit. supra note 40, at 65.

[76] Id. at 71-72.

[77] It is an intriguing fact that where the indigenous economy has moved from the subsistence to the market economy (as in the cocoa-belt in Ghana and the coffee and cotton-growing areas of Uganda) ownership and labor have tended to become discrete functions. In Ghana in the 1950's, for example, more than 200,000 migrant workers came annually to work in the cocoa farms. ROPER, LABOUR PROBLEMS IN WEST AFRICA 14 (1958). The number is said to be half again as large today. In addition, many farms are worked by abuoso (sharecropping) tenants.

enjoy property and the right to command tend to be joined in the owner, reflecting the tendency for ownership to be dissociated from labor in a modern economy.[78] The Austrian writer Renner, in a classical study made early in this century, demonstrated how the owner of industrial assets became a "commander" merely by virtue of his ownership of the tools of production.[79] He achieved this control largely through the device of contract—contracts of employment, of lease, of loan, of conditional sale, of purchase and sale. Contract thus became the theme of the law of modern capitalism. In modern economies dominated by corporate mega-liths, contract has also been the principal device by which the right of ownership has become separated from the right of con-trol.[80] But the central perception of Renner remains true: Con-tract is the main legal institution by which owners or the new class of corporate managers exercise their functions.

Contract is also the principal theme of the jural postulates un-derlying the claims about property that look to the received law for their realization. In the imperial era these claims were almost entirely generated within the colonialist enclave; they embodied par excellence the interests of the colonialist. But every year the private sector includes more and more African businessmen who work sometimes in cooperation with, and sometimes in competition against, the expatriate firms. Today, the same enclave forms the core of the nonagricultural private sector of the economy of every African state and of the agricultural private sector of some.

The *de facto* claims made by these entrepreneurs upon the law assume the basic jural postulates of the modern common-law juris-dictions. The principal function of the state is to remain the im-partial, aloof arbiter between conflicting private interests. It may insist upon limitations on the use of private property or on oppor-tunity only where necessary to avoid injury to others, but it may not require an affirmative use of property or opportunity in directed functions. It assumes that the private entrepreneur is the principal engine of progress, not the state. It requires a stable, clearly articulated set of rules by which the game is to be played.

The legal expression of private enterprise is the bargain struck between private individuals. Thus, property rights conditioned upon contract and state power invoked primarily to enforce bar-gains are the underlying postulates of the received English law and the claims made upon it by the entrepreneurs within the private sector. In Africa, contract did not develop from status, as Sir Henry Maine's model would require. Instead, the received

---

[78] FRIEDMANN, *op. cit. supra* note 40, at 71-72.
[79] RENNER, THE INSTITUTIONS OF PRIVATE LAW AND THEIR SOCIAL FUNC-TIONS (Kahn-Freund transl. 1949).
[80] BERLE & MEANS, THE MODERN CORPORATION AND PRIVATE PROPERTY (1932).

English law, which embodied preeminently the concept of contract, was imposed upon a legal order in which status was the dominant theme.

The third set of demands are novel to our epoch. They are the claims made by the population at large, and articulated by practically every African political leader, for "all the good things which western civilization has produced in the two millennia of its history."[81] Africans demand better education, better health standards, better roads, water, and electricity, better houses, more and better food and clothing, automobiles and bicycles, radios and television. And they demand them *now*. In short, Africans demand development.

But economic development on any scale whatsoever is inseparably social and political transformation.[82] Many, perhaps most, Africans and their leaders are unwilling to wait until such transformation occurs through the unhurried dialectic of the market. They would agree with Professor Harvey that "an affirmative response of government to pressing human needs seems to provide the only hope of bringing together sufficient capital resources to remove, through economic development, the grinding heel of poverty from the majority of the world's people."[83]

To meet this demand for development, "socialism" of one definition or another has been the common currency of African politics.[84] The label of "socialism" contains no more common specific content than an acceptance of the idea that the values clustered around the concept of contract are subordinate to the demands of

---

[81] SPIRO, POLITICS IN AFRICA: PROSPECTS SOUTH OF THE SAHARA 6 (1963). But *compare* BAUER & YAMEY, THE ECONOMICS OF UNDERDEVELOPED COUNTRIES 149-50 (1957) ("We believe that the widening of the range of effective choice is the most valuable single objective of economic development as well as the best single criterion of its attainment") *with* BARBER, THE ECONOMY OF BRITISH CENTRAL AFRICA 8 (1961) ("It is proposed to treat the development condition as satisfied when two conditions have been met: (1) the money economy expands in real terms; (2) the *per capita* real income of the indigenous population also improves through time ").

[82] FRANKEL, THE ECONOMIC IMPACT ON UNDERDEVELOPED SOCIETIES 74 (1953).

[83] Harvey, *The Challenge of the Rule of Law*, 59 MICH. L. REV. 603, 612 (1961).

[84] BROOKWAY, AFRICAN SOCIALISM *passim* (1963); HUNTER, THE NEW SOCIETIES OF TROPICAL AFRICA: A SELECTIVE STUDY 288-89 (1962) ("The serious content [of socialism in Africa] includes above all the devotion to central planning of the use of resources, both human and material, for the common good . . . . Planning, in African circumstances, does in fact mean not only State control but a great deal of State enterprise, particularly in the field of industry, finance and marketing "); Roberts, *A Socialist Looks at African Socialism*, in AFRICAN SOCIALISM 89 (Friedland & Rosberg ed. 1964) ("In the words of a Tanganyika student, 'socialism in Europe is to take the wealth and spread it out, but African Socialism is the common effort to create wealth' ").

planning.[85]   African notions of socialism cover a broad spectrum from the "pragmatic" to the Marxist varieties.[86]

State intervention in the economy necessarily implies planning of one sort or the other.   "The major economic mobilization and reorganization of resources that these transactions imply cannot be realized without planning, direction, control and co-operation," declares the Kenya Sessional Paper on African Socialism.[87]   Dr. Fatouros summarizes the position:

> Thus, the conditions today prevailing in the underdeveloped countries make it necessary for their governments to undertake a wide range of functions. They have to provide the basic facilities which are lacking, to substitute for reluctant or missing entrepreneurs in founding new industries, and to protect the weaker classes from exploitation. In the developed countries, some of the corresponding functions belong to the private sector, while others are exercised by the government through indirect measures, which cannot be very effective in less developed countries.
>
> The ultimate synthesis of all state measure of inference in a given country is the national plan, which provides a classification of particular measures and specific objectives.[88]

The jural postulates about property presupposed by state planning are very different from either status or contract. Planning assumes that the command function of property inheres in the state, even though the state may delegate certain aspects of command to private individuals in specific circumstances. It assumes that the right to enjoy the fruits of ownership of the means of production properly inheres in the population at large, for whose benefit the plan is formulated and enforced. Professor Berman, speaking of the Soviet experience, has summarized the relation-

---

[85]   I look on Government participation [in economic development] as absolutely essential, not so much because it is ideologically desirable, but because it is inevitable if there is to be the swiftest possible development and if the meagre financial and technical resources are to be exploited in full. Government can participate either by owning certain parts of industry; or by creating the infrastructure which would guide the country into certain areas of development; or simply by working out an economic plan into which any development must be fitted.
MBOYA, FREEDOM AND AFTER 169 (1963); Morse, *The Economics of African Socialism* in AFRICAN SOCIALISM 35 (Friedland & Rosberg ed. 1964).

[86]   *Id.* at 36-37.

[87]   Sessional Paper No. 10 of 1963/65, *African Socialism and Its Application to Planning in Kenya,* ¶ 3 (1965) (Gov't. Printer, Nairobi).

[88]   FATOUROS, GOVERNMENT GUARANTEES TO PRIVATE INVESTORS 35 (1962). See also ADU, THE CIVIL SERVICE IN THE NEW AFRICAN STATES 227 (1965). Compare Chief Awolowo's statement of the program of the Action Group in 1951 in Awo, THE AUTOBIOGRAPHY OF CHIEF OBAFEMI AWOLOWO 224 (1960). See further *id.* at 269-79, 283-84; ROPER, *op. cit. supra* note 77, at 8-9; Okigbo, *Independence and the Problem of Economic Growth*, in ECONOMIC TRANSITION IN AFRICA 323, 324 (Herskovits & Harwitz ed. 1964).

ship between planning and law:

> Plan is that aspect of the social process which is concerned
> with the maximum utilization of institutions and resources
> from the point of view of economic development; law is that
> aspect of the social process which is concerned with the
> structuring and enforcing of social policy (plan) in terms
> of the rights and duties arising therefrom.[89]

The jural postulates that underpin the claims and demands made
in the name of development, therefore, assume that the state has
the duty of structuring and enforcing a plan that will rapidly
achieve the desired objectives. They imply that the state may consciously direct productive forces into desired paths rather than
wait for the self-generating processes of the market to bring about
the required transformations. They embody the theme of administration—the conscious articulation and enforcement of state directives concerning the use of property.

This theme is largely novel to the common law, for the great
progenitor jurisdictions of the common law were antipathetical to
planning concepts during the formative years of the common law.[90]
This is not to say that the colonial governments did not purport
to plan or that those who see in contract the central jural postulate
of a just legal order do not pay at least lip service to planning.[91]
Rather, it is to say that the claims made about development in
Africa do not assume that the principal jural postulates of the
new legal order ought to center the command function in private
ownership. Instead, the claims suggest that the central jural
postulate ought to lodge the command function with the state. In
the exercise of a wise administration, certain command functions
may wisely be delegated to private entrepreneurs—in the African
circumstance, usually very wide powers. But the implicit assumption—the jural postulate—of most economic plans in Africa is that,
if it were desirable, the state could and should place any limitations
it chooses upon both the command and enjoyment functions of private property. As Fatouros puts it, "that the underdeveloped
countries must plan can hardly be disputed, but the precise content of particular plans as well as the degree and manner of state

---

[89] BERMAN, JUSTICE IN THE U.S.S.R. 101 (rev. ed. 1963).

[90] See, *e.g.*, GRIFFITH & STREET, PRINCIPLES OF ADMINISTRATIVE LAW 1-2
(1952); HEWART, THE NEW DESPOTISM *passim* (1929).

[91] Colonial "plans" tended to be quite limited. Speaking of Uganda,
Professor Elkan says:

> One has to be quite clear about the nature of these plans. None of
> them is an overall plan, setting out targets or allocations for the
> economy as a whole, as in the case with, for instance, the Russian or
> the Indian Development plans. They are all plans for action in the
> public sector only . . . . [I]n the words of the East African Royal
> Commission, "the most important economic expansion of East Africa
> occurred independently of these plans and owes nothing to them."

ELKAN, THE ECONOMIC DEVELOPMENT OF UGANDA 46-47 (1961). Some "plans"
in independent Africa have been but little more.

interference are highly controversial issues."[92]

Thus the claims made by Africans upon their pluralistic legal system seem to suggest three fundamentally antithetical sets of jural postulates: status, contract, and state intervention (or plan). The interaction among these postulates will necessarily produce the direction of change in African law, the scope and shape of the transformation of economic and social institutions. The role of the social scientist, the politician, and the lawyer must be directed to the social engineering function which the resolution of their frictions requires.

B. Stability and Legality

The social engineering function of law does not exhaust the demands made upon the law of this epoch. Overriding every claim made upon the several legal orders of Africa are claims of stability. These claims are of two sorts. In the first place, there is the problem of political stability.[93] Development cannot proceed without governments that can carry out long-term projects. Neither private capital nor public international agencies will invest in an unstable situation.[94] A complete discussion of the legal problems of development would require attention to the constitutional arrangements of the several African states, a topic beyond the scope of this article.

A second aspect of the notion of stability is one peculiarly of interest to the law and lawyers. One of the principal functions of the legal order is to ensure that state power will be applied to individuals only in relatively predictable ways.[95] Both private enterprise and public planning require a society that is stable in this sense.

In a society in which the state has had thrust upon it the imperative of effectuating massive transformations of the economy and the social structure, the demands for stability of this sort are the more urgent. Social transformation will be *orderly* only if there is stability. However, the political and social matrix of English-speaking Africa, unhappily, imposes few restraints upon the governing elite.

---

92 FATOUROS, *op. cit. supra* note 88, at 35.

93 See pp. 66-72 *infra*.

94 BAUER & YAMEY, *op. cit. supra* note 81, at 164; BUCHANAN & ELLIS, APPROACHES TO ECONOMIC DEVELOPMENT 289 (1955). Professor Hanson interposes a mild dissent. Successful development requires "not a stable government with a consistent policy, but the right kind of stable government with the right kind of consistent policy. To obtain such a government with the right kind of consistent policy, an underdeveloped country may have to go through an extended Time of Troubles characterised by political instability of the most extreme kind." HANSON, PUBLIC ENTERPRISE AND ECONOMIC DEVELOPMENT 51 (1959).

95 Pound, *My Philosophy of Law*, in THE GREAT LEGAL PHILOSOPHERS 532, 533 (Morris ed. 1959).

The prevailing political pattern in Africa at independence was a variety of the Westminster model. In England, the relationship of executive and legislature at least theoretically makes the executive the servant of the legislature. In Africa, for a variety of reasons, the legislature has tended to be a rubber stamp for the executive. In pre-coup Nigeria, the average time that bills were before the Federal Parliament for consideration is said to have been two hours. So far as one knows, no government bill has ever failed of passage in independent, English-speaking Africa.[96]

Moreover, there are few societal restraints upon the executive. Societies for the Prevention of This and That, which exercise so salutary an influence in many of the more developed countries, are not often found in Africa. Trade unions are rudimentary; the size of the industrial proletariat is small numerically and proportionally. The press is either government-owned, as in Ghana, or so dominated by factional interest as to be largely irrelevant, as in Nigeria.

Finally, the countries of Africa emerged from the independence struggle with one party effectively dominating the political machinery. Even pre-coup Nigeria, on its surface a multiparty democracy, was in fact a loose federation of three (later four) one-party states. The party was given exclusive hegemony by constitutional amendment in pre-coup Ghana and in Tanzania. In fact, the party has hegemony almost everywhere else in Africa. The last African testing ground for multiparty democracy in the traditional Western sense may have been the Western Nigerian elections of October 1965. The result of the exercise was riot, arson, and deaths numbering in the thousands; these, in turn, were the preconditions for the coup of January 1966.

The judiciary has not always been a significant bastion against the arbitrary exercise of state power. In Ghana, the judiciary acquiesced in the broadest construction of the Preventive Detention Act[97] despite a number of avenues by which it at least might have been furnished with a procedural basis to somewhat alleviate its arbitrary character. In Nigeria, despite a Privy Council holding that the central government's imposition of Chief Akintola upon the Western Region was unconstitutional,[98] the central government

---

[96] *Cf.* BRETTON, POWER AND STABILITY IN NIGERIA 24 (1962) ("The status quo forces [in Nigeria] have recognised in the British [Westminster] model a device for the protection of their interests, for the relative absence of a separation of powers in it more readily permits the welding of basic and superficial power positions for the mutual protection and preservation of the status quo"); Mackintosh, *The Nigerian Federal Parliament*, 1963 PUB. L. 333, 352, 359-61.

[97] Re Akoto, Civil Appeal No. 42/61 (Ghana 1961). Compare the arguments to the contrary in RUBIN & MURRAY, THE CONSTITUTION AND GOVERNMENT OF GHANA 223-26 (1st ed. 1961).

[98] Adegbenro v. Akintola, [1963] A.C. 614 (Nigeria).

retroactively approved legislation validating the action.[99] Whether the judiciary in the East African states can stand against the executive remains to be seen.

The most significant restraint upon the leadership of English-speaking Africa has been its nominal adherence to the tradition of submission to the rule of law. The leadership groups have all been educated in England or the United States. Their articulated ideals have been those compatible with "a government of laws, not of men." Even after then-President Nkrumah of Ghana summarily dismissed several judges without explanation, the government newspaper editorialized that no one could doubt Dr. Nkrumah's devotion to the ideal of an independent judiciary.[100]

Africa is full of leaders-in-a-hurry. They may be hurried because they are fired with zeal to improve the harsh lot of their country-men. Or they may be hurried because they are fired with zeal to line their own pockets. But everywhere the sense of overwhelm-ing urgency pervades the political atmosphere. Leaders-in-a-hurry, restrained mainly by their own respect for the forms of law, can usually achieve their objectives within the form of law but out-side its real content. To a depressingly great extent, Africa has become a continent of legalisms rather than legality.

The most obvious aspect of the common disregard for legality is the widespread corruption that permeates the fabric of most African states. Corruption is the negation of legality, for it implies that the state structure is being used for purposes irrele-vant to its intended function. Corruption has become the central enemy of development, at least in West Africa.

This, then, was the matrix for the law of English-speaking Africa at independence: a dichotomous society, sharply split between the subsistence economy with its associated culture and law and the commercial-industrial, private, Westernized sector; a pluralistic legal order; demands upon the legal orders that implied funda-mentally irreconcilable jural postulates—status, contract, and plan; and a governing elite for whom law was more frequently a restriction to be avoided than a tool for the rational application

---

99 NWABUEZE, CONSTITUTIONAL LAW OF THE NIGERIAN REPUBLIC 230 (1964). "Under our law, a decision of a court of law given against the Government cannot be enforced by the levy of execution upon property belonging to it, and though the Government is required to give effect thereto it may be too much to expect it to do so in matters of profound constitutional im-portance involving political interests." *Ibid.*

100 In the debate on the Criminal Code (Amendment) Bill, 1961 Ghana, to establish a special criminal division of the high court to try state offenses, from which there would be no appeal, the then Minister of the Interior Kwaku Boateng asked who could believe "that Kwame Nkrumah who is so constitutional in all his deeds, so wise and kind as he has always been . . . could create a system of Court offensive to our motto: Freedom and Jus-tice?" AUSTIN, POLITICS IN GHANA 1946-60, at 406 (1964).

of state power. This matrix imposed two central imperatives upon the legal order: first, the social engineering function of providir.g institutions to accommodate the several sets of demands, or, where necessary, to choose between them; and second, the further function of guaranteeing a regime of legality. Social engineering and legality are the specifically African forms of Dean Pound's famous paradox that the law must at once provide for change and for stability. How well did the received law respond to these imperatives?

V.   The Sufficiency of the Customary and the Received Law

The model that has been described can serve as a tool for the analysis of the sufficiency of the law presented to the African states at independence. First, we shall examine the sufficiency of the existing law to meet the several sets of demands. Secondly, we shall examine the frictions arising between the different sets of demands. Finally, we shall examine the sufficiency of the law to guarantee the regime of legality.

A.   Customary Law

Excepting problems of land tenure, most of the claims made upon customary law are not claims of development. The sufficiency of customary law to meet these demands would not require attention here were it not that a certain segment of academic lawyers sees a sort of legal salvation in customary law. As Professor Allott has said,

> If [a] uniform legal system [for a whole territory] is to evolve in a satisfactory manner, one which expresses the characteristic ethos and ways of life of the people, it is essential that immediate attention should be paid to the present customary law, which reflects, par excellence, the people's own choice of legal system. So far as possible, one wants to avoid revolution in the legal sphere, and abrupt discontinuity with the past and present. What one seeks is a smooth evolution of legal institutions, so that the new law is based on and is in harmony with the old.[101]

This modern invocation of the *Volksgeist* may encapsulate a useful idea for the law of marriage, the family, and descent and inheritance. But, there is small reason to construct a pastiche of the many varieties of customary law and received law in the name of "the people's own choice of law" for the sake of development. Two reasons suggest themselves. The customary law enforced by the

---

[101] Allott, *The Study of African Law*, 1958 Sudan L.J. Rep. 258. The author is indebted to his former colleague at the University of Ghana, Dr. Chiojioke Ogwurike, for many of the concepts in this section of the article. See generally Ogwurike, *The Source and Authority of African Customary Law*, 3 U. Ghana L.J. 11 (1966).

courts cannot conceivably reflect the common consciousness of the people, and, at any rate, it does not address itself to any of the important issues raised by development.

1. CUSTOMARY LAW AND THE *Volksgeist*

There are several factors that explain why the customary law cannot reflect the common consciousness of the people. Before a court applies a rule of customary law in a specific case, it must pass through several filters. The judge must find as a matter of fact that the law is the present custom of the people.[102]   It has frequently been reiterated that the essence of customary law is that it changes and adapts to changing circumstances.[103]   But communities, even closely knit tribal ones, do not change their ideas in concert as a monolithic organic unit. In practice, the judge is presented with evidence by both sides to the litigation, each asserting contrary rules of customary law. The judge cannot avoid making a normative choice. A choice of what the law ought to be masks itself in the guise of a factual inquiry, just as in the endless search for the hypothetical "reasonable man." In *Golightly and Tettey Gbeke II v. Ashrifi*,[104] for example, there was at issue the right of individuals to sell land in an area that was formerly bush used for slash-and-burn farming but that was then in demand for housing estates in a rapidly growing area of Accra. The trial court found as a matter of fact, based upon evidence of chiefs and linguists, that the customary law of the family owning the land forbade any effective alienation of stool[105] land unless a stool debt was in existence. The appellate court reversed on this point, relying on the following for its factual determination of what the customs were: very old works of Redwar and Casely Hayford that had no specific reference to the stool in question, a 1909 Lagos case that concerned land in Lagos, and another Nigerian case of 1930. "In our opinion the existence of a stool debt was not at the times material to this inquiry a necessary preliminary condition to the sale of stool land."[106]   The court's inquiry, presumably a factual one concerning the existence of a custom among the people involved, was really normative in character.

The rule must pass through other filters as well. Customary law in most states must not be repugnant to "equity, justice and good conscience".[107] Even in those jurisdictions that no longer re-

102 Eleko v. Officer Administering the Gov't of Nigeria, [1931] A.C. 662, 673 (Nigeria); ALLOTT, ESSAYS IN AFRICAN LAW 72-98 (1960).

103 Eleko v. Officer Administering the Gov't of Nigeria, *supra* note 102, at 673; Allott, *supra* note 56, at 115.

104 14 W.A.C.A. 676 (Gold Coast 1955).

105 The stool is the symbol of sovereignty in the Akan tribes of Ghana.

106 Golightly and Tettey Gbeke II v. Ashrifi, 14 W.A.C.A. 676, 681 (Gold Coast 1955).

107 For examples of the operation of the rule, see, *e.g.*, Edet v. Essien,

30 Robert B. Seidman

quire this test, public policy presumably serves the same purpose. Customary law also must not contradict any written statute.[108] Judges take judicial notice of customs approved in earlier cases, just as they did in the *Golightly* case, even where the custom noticed was not that of the community concerned.[109] As a result, the law announced by the courts may reflect the ethos of the judges; it reflects only accidentally, if at all, the common consciousness of the tribes.[110]

Besides the filtering issue, the diversity of African ethnic groups and customary laws presents a problem. Forging a "common" customary law based upon the lowest common denominator actually creates a new "customary" law that, more likely than not, reflects nobody's *Volksgeist*, except perhaps the compiler's.[111]

---

11 N.L.R. 47 (1932) (customary rule that child born before marriage price is returned on divorce "belongs" to husband instead of natural father held repugnant); Re Offiong Ata, 10 N.L.R. 65 (1930); Mariyana v. Dadikro Ejo [1961] N.R.N.L.R. 81 (customary rule that a child born within ten months of divorce "belongs" to former husband instead of natural father held repugnant); Guri v. Kadejia N.A., 4 Fed. Sup. Ct. 44 (Nigeria 1959) (written Malaki [Islamic] rule that persons accused of highway robbery had no right to defend themselves in court held repugnant). It is impossible to discover any consistent standard in these cases. In some, the judges use the common law as a test. Amachree v. Kallio, 2 N.L.R. 108 (1914) (customary property rights in navigable streams held repugnant). In others, the test seems to be the morality of Englishmen. Gwao bin Kilimo v. Kisunda bin Ifuti, 1 Tanganyika Law Reports (Revised) 403, 405 (1938) ("I have no doubt whatever that the only standard of justice and morality which a British Court in Africa can apply is its own British standard"). In most cases, however, the standard seems to be an ill-defined appeal to intuitively apprehended natural law.

[108] See, *e.g.*, Tanganyika Order in Council, 1920, Article 24 ("[E]very Court . . . shall be guided by native law so far as it is not . . . inconsistent with any Order in Council or Ordinance or any Regulation or Rule made under any Order in Council or Ordinance . . . ").

[109] See, *e.g.*, Biei v. Akomea, 1 West African Law Reports 174, 176 (Gold Coast 1956) ("This court cannot allow local customs to override general principles and practice in these days of changing conditions ").

[110] Judge Ollennu has described the process in Ghana in some detail, but he reaches a contrary conclusion from that stated in the text:

> "All this time there has been a steady marrying of the two systems of law . . . . It is correct to say that in the process of marrying the two systems, the principles of English law, the English rules of practice and procedure and rules of evidence have been effectively employed by lawyers trained in the tradition of English law to excavate and crystallize the principles of customary law."

Ollennu, *The Influence of English Law in West Africa*, 1963 J. African L. 24, 25.

[111] See Professor Twining's criticisms and Mr. Cotran's reply in Twining, The Place of Customary Law in the National Legal Systems of East Africa 25-54 (1964) and Cotran, *The Place and Future of Customary Law in East Africa*, in East African Law Today, 5 Commonwealth Law Series 72, 84-89 (1965). See also Cotran, *The Unification of Laws in East Africa*, 1 J. Modern African Studies 209 (1963); Twining, *The Restatement of African Customary Law: A Comment*, 1 J. Modern African Studies 221 (1963).

Finally, the folkways of Africa are rapidly being transformed by the erosions of the cash nexus and by changes induced by the operation of the received English law itself. In Ghana, the use of English forms of conveyancing have contributed to radical changes in the customary law.[112] Similarly, Professor Bohannan has shown how the customary land law of the Tiv, the Yoruba, and the Giguyu have changed under the impact of English law.[113] To say that the customary law today still embodies the *Volksgeist*—if it ever did—is to rest on a mystical faith, not fact.[114]

If the customary law does not reflect the "ethos and way of life of the people," there would seem small reason to invoke it in meeting the legal imperatives of independence. But there is a final reason for seeking elsewhere the institutions and laws required for transformation: Customary law simply contains insufficient responses to the demands of development.

2. THE DEMANDS OF DEVELOPMENT

As Professor Schiller has said, "It is generally recognized that the indigenous systems of law in Africa are deficient in the areas of commerce, finance, labor and social welfare. Further, the indigenous law is considered inadequate in the field of obligations and property . . . ."[115] To take a single example, Islamic law is treated as a form of customary law in those areas in which it is prevalent, most strikingly in Northern Nigeria, the most populous single region in English-speaking Africa.[116] Yet the Shari'a does not admit of executory contracts, since they are regarded as a form of gambling, a sin expressly forbidden by the Koran.[117] In East Africa, "actions for debt are often dealt with under customary law and there are well-developed principles in relation to certain types of agreement, but customary concepts do not seem to be adequate to deal with many of the types of commercial transactions that will become more and more common as the economy develops."[118]

If customary law is deficient in the area of commercial and business law, it is completely empty in the area of modern public law.

---

[112] Asante, *Interests in Land in the Customary Law of Ghana—A New Appraisal*, 74 YALE L.J. 848, 862-63 (1965).

[113] Bohannan, *Land Use, Land Tenure and Land Reform*, in ECONOMIC TRANSITION IN AFRICA 133, *passim* (Herskovits & Harwitz ed. 1964).

[114] Professor Schiller states that "the indigenous law of primitive peoples seems to have had little in common with the external expression of popular consciousness of the particular society—the German people—to which the term 'customary law' (Gewohnheitsrecht) was first applied." Schiller, *op. cit. supra* note 71, at 170.

[115] *Id.* at 178.

[116] See generally ANDERSON, ISLAMIC LAW IN AFRICA 171-225 (1954).

[117] FITZGERALD, MUHAMMADAN LAW: AN ABRIDGEMENT ACCORDING TO ITS VARIOUS SCHOOLS 181-84 (1931).

[118] TWINING, *op. cit. supra* note 111, at 18. See also Cotran, *The Unification of Laws in East Africa* 1 J. MODERN AFRICAN STUDIES 209, 217 (1963).

There simply is not even the germ of such institutions as planning, state enterprises, import control, central banking, exchange
controls, limitations on the repatriation of profits, income taxation,
trade unions and labor law, and a host of others. To search the
interstices of customary law for aid in formulating the response
to questions posed by the demand for institutions of this sort is
to search in vain.[119] Development requires economic transformation mainly of the institutions of the subsistence sector. One could
hardly expect to find a tool for their transformation in the very
law that describes them.

B. The Legal Environment of the Private Sector

The dominant property theme of the received common law is
that rights in property are primarily a function of contract. The
principal jural postulate of the demands made by the entrepreneurs
in the private sector likewise finds its central theme in contract.
Most of the claims upon the legal order emerging from the private
sector, therefore, can readily be answered in terms of the received English law.

The principal demand in the private sector is for an adequate
legal climate for private enterprise. In Africa, as elsewhere, the
private entrepreneur, whether foreign or domestic, requires a legal
framework that is sufficiently clear and firm to permit him to
make investments with some sense of security—i.e., with assurance
that his agreements will be enforced in a way reasonably anticipated. In addition, he requires a large variety of possible forms
for carrying out his business activities—permissible varieties of
business enterprise, legally enforceable credit mechanisms, and recognized devices for the sale, transportation, and delivery of
goods.[120] The development of a legal climate to meet these functional requirements in Africa calls for three sorts of legal reform:
modernization, codification, and adaptation.

Modernization of the law affecting business is the first requirement. At independence, the basic norms controlling economic
affairs in English-speaking Africa were too frequently those obtaining in England at the time of attaining a colonial legislature—1874 in Ghana, the other colonies mainly in the early years
of this century—or in some later but still out-of-date modification.
Nigeria's Company Law was based on the English Act of 1908 and
Ghana's on the English Act of 1862.[121] Ghana's mortgage law today

---

[119] This is not to say that the rules concerning these matters need not
be shaped to take customary law into account. See THE FUTURE OF LAW IN
AFRICA 41 (Allott ed. 1960).

[120] Mentschikoff, *Federalism and Economic Growth*, in FEDERALISM AND
THE NEW NATIONS OF AFRICA 194 (Currie ed. 1964); NWOGUGU, THE LEGAL
PROBLEMS OF FOREIGN INVESTMENT IN DEVELOPING COUNTRIES 17 (1965).

[121] COMM'N OF ENQUIRY INTO THE WORKING AND ADMINISTRATION OF THE
CO. LAW OF GHANA, FINAL REPORT 2 (1961) [Hereinafter referred to as

is that which was in force in England in 1874.[122] Bankruptcy law did not exist in many of the West African colonies. Ghana adopted a general insolvency law in 1962;[123] Nigeria and Sierra Leone still do not have one.[124] In particular, modern credit laws seem to be required; there is no law equivalent to a modern trust receipts act. Even chattel mortgages are of questionable validity in many countries.[125] Yet, as Professor Mentschikoff has pointed out:

> Commercial lending is the greatest yet relatively untapped source of capital [in Africa] and requires the existence of a money economy as well as certain legal reforms or additions to make simple the use of secured credit. Commercial credit is on two levels; the level of financing both of industrial equipment and of consumer goods. One important consideration is that, at least in the United States, equipment loans can be obtained not only from banks but also in very large volume from finance companies. The study of operations of these companies and the important way in which they have opened up new sources of credit to American business could prove fruitful to new nations. The importance of finance companies in the consumer-credit field is probably greater than that of the banks and their potential as financers of goods to be sent abroad has yet to be fully explored.[126]

The list of areas requiring modernization to create a suitable legal climate appropriate to modern systems of trade, industrialization, and finance could be multiplied almost endlessly.

Codification is a second requirement for an adequate legal environment for modern business. Discovering the law of agency, partnership, contract, banking, or insurance in a proliferation of common-law cases (the reports of which are frequently unavailable) is plainly unsatisfactory. Even in England this was found

---

the GOWER REPORT]. This report is frequently called the "Gower Report" because the Commission consisted solely of Professor Gower.

[122] Bentsi-Entchill, *Agricultural Credit in Ghana*, in I ATTI DELLA SECONDA ASSEMBLA, INSTITUTIO DI DIRETTO AGRARIO INTERNAZIONALE E COMPARATO 323 (1964).

[123] Pub. Act 153 (Ghana 1962).

[124] In East Africa, by contrast, bankruptcy laws have existed since about 1930. In general, the East African territories seem to have been better furnished with modern commercial laws than those of West Africa.

There are specific problems of adapting insolvency laws in Africa— *e.g.*, the nature of land tenures as affecting security devices in land, and the traditional liability of families and of family and stool property in some cases for debts of members. GOWER REPORT. See also Kahn-Freund, Comment, 25 MODERN L. REV. 78 (1962).

[125] In Ghana, for example, the common law of sales applied until 1962. See note 127 *infra*. At common law, a chattel mortgage was valid as between the parties but gave no priority on the insolvency of the debtor. 27 HALSBURY'S LAWS OF ENGLAND 163 (3d ed. 1959). Query whether the Sales of Goods Act, 1962, remedies this position?

[126] Mentschikoff, *op. cit. supra* note 120, at 194-95.

to be an unhappy solution. For example, England had codified
the common law of sales in the Sale of Goods Act, 1893, but Ghana
continued to operate under common law until 1962.[127]

The problem is especially complicated because one cannot predict
beforehand which jurisdiction's common law will be applied in any
particular instance. For example, the suspended Ghanaian constitution authorized the Supreme Court to select any formulation
of a common-law rule from any common-law jurisdiction.[128] Even
those countries whose courts are required to follow the English
common law retain the option of refusing to do so when the court
thinks that the English rule is inappropriate to local conditions.[129]
Since the course of litigation has not raised, yet alone solved, many
problems in the common law of Africa, the applicable law is extremely hypothetical. Codification provides one obvious step towards a solution.[130]

Codification has a particular attraction in terms of the unification
of the commercial law of the several African states. Inter-African
commercial contacts are growing and must continue to grow if
Africa is to develop and if African unity is to be more than a gleam
in the eyes of its proponents. The advantages to inter-African commerce if the basic norms of commercial life are the same in
each African country are obvious. Moreover, there is, more or less,
a commonly agreed set of norms controlling international trade.
FOB and CIF contracts have—or ought to have—the same core of
meaning everywhere. Commercial codes embodying the norms of
international trade are obvious demands of the entrepreneurs in
the private sector.[131]

The most difficult problem in developing a proper legal environment for the private sector is developing a law specifically
adapted to African problems. Modernization and codification of the
law can be accomplished merely by careful consideration of the

---

[127] Sale of Goods Act, 1962, Pub. Act 137 (Ghana). Before its enactment, however, the courts in fact tended to follow the English Act. See
DANIELS, THE COMMON LAW IN WEST AFRICA 232 n.20 (1964).

[128] Interpretation Act, 1960, C.A.4, § 17(4) (Ghana). See also BENNION,
THE CONSTITUTIONAL LAW OF GHANA 405-06 (1962).

[129] ALLOTT, op. cit. supra note 102, at 21-27.

[130] Tanganyika, Kenya, and Uganda repealed the Indian Contracts Act
in 1960 and 1961. Kenya and Uganda adopted in its place the common law
of contracts, uncodified; Tanganyika substituted the Law of Contract Ordinance, 1961 (No. 1 of 1961), reenacting the Indian Contract Act with some
substantial clarifying and modernizing amendments. COLE & DENNISON,
TANGANYIKA—THE DEVELOPMENT OF ITS LAWS AND CONSTITUTIONS 177 (1964).
Ghana has adopted the Contracts Act, 1961, Pub. Act 25, which makes certain modernizing amendments to the common law of contracts; it is not,
however, a complete codification of the subject.

[131] Mentschikoff, op. cit. supra note 120, at 198; THE FUTURE OF LAW IN
AFRICA 41 (Allott ed. 1960); Farnsworth, Law Reform in a Developing
Country: A New Code of Obligations for Senegal, 8 J. AFRICAN L. 6, 7-8
(1964).

law in the books, but adaptation requires empirical studies of the law in action. The greatest single hiatus in the study of African law is the lamentable absence of such empirical studies.[132] Without such studies, the scope and direction of adaptation can only come from intuition.

The difficulty in developing a proper legal environment for the private sector can be seen in the experience of the Commission of Enquiry into Trade Malpractices in Ghana. Following a rapid and—as subsequent events suggest—cataclysmic rise in prices, the Commission was appointed to investigate the pricing and distribution of goods. It found that kickbacks and favoritism by local store managers when dealing in scarce commodities was the major source of the price rise.[133] Whether there was such a causal relationship,[134] there was doubtless corruption of the sort described that was widespread and widely resented. However, the Attorney General promptly announced that these were "social evils" for whose correction there was no legal instrument.[135] The internal coherence of the private sector may well require that legal norms inhibit the ability of strategically placed individuals to structure the market artificially in their own interest during conditions of serious inflationary pressures and built-in shortages of many commodities.

The same Commission described the "passbook" system. This is a well-defined Ghanaian institution for wholesale dealings between the great importing companies and the richer market traders, almost all women, and many of them illiterate. It is a system whose legal relationships can be fitted into the received categories of contract law only with some effort. Absent norms of some sort, it is an institution that readily lends itself to abuse. An empirical study of the device must be made before legislation can be attempted, although the Commission has suggested enough to indicate the parameters of the problem.

The report on the Company Code in Ghana[136] is replete with the sorts of changes in English company law required to fit the African circumstance: minimum capital requirements for doing business, sensitivity to the demands of both foreign capital and local African business, the requirements of simplicity and clarity, and a host of

---

[132] A notable exception is Professor Gower's work on company law in Ghana. See the GOWER REPORT.

[133] COMM'N OF ENQUIRY INTO TRADE MALPRACTICES, REPORT (Gov't Print., Accra 1966).

[134] It has been strongly urged that corruption was a peripheral factor in the rise in prices. Lawson, *Inflation and the Consumer Market in Ghana: Report of the Commission of Enquiry into Trade Malpractices in Ghana,* 10 THE ECONOMIC BULL. OF GHANA 36 (1966).

[135] Whether the Attorney General was entirely correct may be questioned. See Criminal Code, 1960, Pub. Act 29 § 145 (Ghana).

[136] See GOWER REPORT.

others.[137] The report goes on to recommend a novel institution, the incorporated partnership, designed to preserve the goodwill of the African firm in the event of the death of a partner.[138] Its frequent use in Ghana suggests its utility. Similar work of adaptation is required in almost every field of commercial law.

The consonance between the themes of contract and private enterprise suggests that there are no great policy decisions to be made in the modernization, codification, and adaptation of English law to the African circumstance. More difficult problems beset public law in Africa primarily because there are but small legal beacons in the common-law world to light these stormy and rock-strewn waters.

C. The Legal Environment of the Plan

A third set of demands, those upon the public sector, make claims upon the state for a variety of services. These demands require an adequate legal environment and tend to be predicated upon the notion of a plan. While the received business and commercial law is relatively densely detailed and requires principally modernization, codification, and adaptation, very little in the English experience is relevant to planning or public enterprise.

1. THE PLAN AND PLANNING PROCESSES

It is self-evident that the rational allocation and utilization of public funds in development starts with a plan. An indication of the colonial governments' devotion to development is that colonial "planning" was frequently just a list of projects submitted annually by each ministry. This was true in Uganda, where a three year expenditure forecast was presented to the legislative council each year. This forecast estimated the amount of money likely to be available, set a ceiling upon aggregate expenditures, and made a provisional allocation of the total sum among the several ministries and departments. The allocations were the result of bargaining between the ministries. There was no central staff concerned with the analysis of alternative development proposals.

The mission of the International Bank for Reconstruction and Development summarized the essential requirements for adequate planning in Uganda as demanding:

    a. A continuous flow of ideas and schemes from the ministries and departments, and from sources outside the Government, on better uses of existing funds, on productive uses of new funds, and on ways and means of stimulating private economic activity.

    b. Machinery at the center capable of

---

137 See Kahn-Freund, *supra* note 124.
138 Incorporated Partnership Act, 1962, Pub. Act 152 (Ghana).

  i. assessing the availability of resources for development and developing new sources of funds;
  ii. recommending priorities for public investment;
  iii. reviewing and recommending public action relating
    to the private sector; and
  iv. following and evaluating the progress made.
 c. Adequate staff work in the fields of statistics and economics to service this machinery.
 d. A system of communication between the executive and
  legislature and between the Government and the public
  conducive to the open discussion of development issues
  and capable of marshalling the support of the nation
  behind the development program.[139]

There were very few norms of public law relevant to these functions anyplace in English-speaking Africa prior to independence.
Regrettably, there are precious few even today. The power of
planners to get information even about government projects is
mainly nonexistent. In his last budget speech in Ghana before the
coup, the Minister of Finance rather pathetically pleaded for legislation requiring managers of state enterprises to furnish required
information to the Ministry and the Planning Commission.[140] The
power of planners to get information about private enterprise is
even less. The Commission of Enquiry into Trade Malpractices in
Ghana reported that it was unable to obtain such information
about trade in the private sector because of the obduracy of private
enterprise. Planning based on no information or misinformation
can hardly be successful.

The requisite decisionmaking at the center cannot be made rationally unless the decisionmakers have directed their attention to
all the relevant interests, claims, facts, and values. If planning
is to be rationally accomplished, institutional devices guaranteeing
that their attention is so directed are necessary. But procedural
statutes detailing planning processes are largely absent from the
African lawbooks. There are few requirements for public hearings
or even for consultation of affected interests before proposals are
adopted. There are no requirements for feasibility reports on
proposals. There is not even any requirement that interested parties or ministries be advised that specific proposals are under consideration. In Ghana, this reached the ludicrous result that many

---

[139] INTERNATIONAL BANK FOR RECONSTRUCTION AND DEVELOPMENT MISSION,
THE ECONOMIC DEVELOPMENT OF UGANDA 53 (1962) [International Bank
for Reconstruction and Development will hereinafter be referred to as
I.B.R.D.]. See also I.B.R.D. MISSION, THE ECONOMIC DEVELOPMENT OF
TANGANYIKA 339-43; Bentsi-Entchill, *Agricultural Credit in Ghana*, in ATTI
DELLA SECONDA ASSEMBLA, INSTITUTIO DI DIRETTO AGRARIO INTERNAZIONALE
E COMPARATO 323; HANSON, PUBLIC ENTERPRISE AND ECONOMIC DEVELOPMENT
106-14 (1959). The I.B.R.D. report on Uganda insufficiently emphasizes
the implementation function if planning is to be successful.
[140] 1966 Budget Statement ¶ 53 (Ghana).

important projects were begun before the affected ministries even knew about them. There has been testimony in Ghana that the cocoa storage plant at Tema, a multi-million dollar project, went forward without *any* feasibility study.

Finally, there are few, if any, statutes in Africa authorizing the use of state power in the implementation of the plan. Instead, implementation tends to depend upon wheedling and persuasion. The Ghanaian Finance Minister in his budget speech complained of ministries charging ahead with projects never considered by the Planning Commission and not included in the plan.[141] They could do this because there was no statutory requirement that projects be approved by the Planning Commission before they go forward. As a result, the plans of Ghana, and of most African countries, remain mere paper projects to a distressing degree.[142]

2. THE PUBLIC SERVICES

Perhaps the central reason for the failure of planning implementation lies in the failure to assimilate planning concepts to the ministerial system of government and civil service.[143] The basic pattern of public services throughout English-speaking Africa remains in most aspects a reflection of the British model. Each function of government is allocated to a minister. He is supposed to formulate broad policy with the advice of a nonpolitical senior civil servant. The civil service formulates and carries out operational policies pursuant to basic ministerial directives.

This system of supplying public services differs markedly from the colonial pattern in two respects. In the first place, the colonial civil service, unlike the civil service in England, was not the silent, efficient, nonpolitical, loyal servant of government; it *was* government.[144] It not only implemented policy, it made policy. In the second place, the substantive scope of its activities was much more limited than it is today.

> [T]he old colonial administration and technical departments were concerned with such matters as maintenance of law and order, local administration, the provision of a moderate level of social services, elementary communications

141 *Id.* at ¶ 98.
142 Green, *Multi-Purpose Economic Institutions in Africa*, 1 J. MODERN AFRICAN STUDIES 163, 170-84 (1963). He quotes Adedeji, *Economic Planning in Theory and Practice*, Nigeria Journal of Economic and Social Studies, March 1962: "[T]here is little discernible relation between what is contained in a Plan and what in fact gets done." See also Bognar, *The Importance of Devising Effective Machinery for the Implementation of Development Plans*, 7 THE ECONOMIC BULL. OF GHANA 77 (1963).
143 Green, *supra* note 142, at 272-73 (British administrative and institutional structure "inherently unsatisfactory for development-centered government ").
144 ADU, THE CIVIL SERVICE IN THE NEW AFRICAN STATES 31 (1965).

networks, and the husbandry of natural resources. There were no five or ten year development plans, no infrastructural services, nor any full development of the economy, no balance of payment difficulties, no talk of deficit financing policies, no central banking nor the creation of money markets, and no external relations problems whether political, economic or commercial.[145]

The new functions of the civil service created sharp tensions. The new ministers were, at least at first, deeply suspicious of the civil service; and the civil service in turn gave the ministers grudging cooperation at best.[146] More important, however, was the lack of technical *expertise* among the civil servants who were inherited by the new African governments. Training and orientation programs rank very high among Mr. Adu's recommendations for the reform of the civil services.[147]

But it may be that the whole organization of the civil services requires reappraisal. To meet the demands of the new era, the immediate response everywhere has been a proliferation of administrative decisions. In Kenya, there are twelve statutory commodity boards, six for individual crops or industries and six set up under the Marketing of African Produce Act; a jute controller; and a wheat board that acts in an advisory capacity.[148] Similar lists of quasi-independent institutions with plainly overlapping areas of interest could, no doubt, be compiled for every African country.

The personnel policies of the civil service are based upon an older and more relaxed period of administration. As an example of its outlook, in 1920 a former assistant colonial secretary with military training, but with no penological background at all, undertook the basic reform of the Ghanaian prisons system. The appointment was considered an excellent one. This attitude manifests itself today in such ways as the moving of "permanent" secretaries from ministry to ministry like so much furniture. An implicit faith that "administration" is a separate skill divorced from content underlies such policies. This faith may be tenable when the technical scope of activity is relatively limited. But as the work of the ministries becomes more and more involved in the details of economic development, one may well question its utility.

---

[145] *Id.* at 226. Bognar, *supra* note 142, at 80, suggests that in view of the relative scarcity of experts in Africa, they ought to be concentrated in a ministry of economics.

[146] *Cf.* HANSON, *op. cit. supra* note 139, at 54.

[147] ADU, *op. cit. supra* note 144, at 232-35.

[148] McAuslan, *Administrative Law in Kenya—A General Survey*, in EAST AFRICAN LAW TODAY, 5 COMMONWEALTH LAW SERIES 23, 39 (1965). See also Green, *supra* note 142, at 273: "The ad hoc creation of state corporations which are not subject to any clear or effective control in their productive operations has further weakened co-ordination."

A more basic question relates to the whole role of the civil service in a public administration whose central thrust is dominated by planning concepts. As McAuslan sums up regarding Kenya:

> It may not be enough to tinker with the system and leave it at that. What are two of the most important constitutional and political facts about Kenya today? First, that it is moving towards becoming a one-party state, and, second, that the Government of that state is putting great effort into economic development via an agricultural and industrial revolution. We must be prepared to apply these facts to the system of administrative law in Kenya and, if necessary, strip that system to the ground and reconstruct it accordingly. We must attempt to supply answers to such questions as: What is the role of the party to be in the administrative system? Are the present legislative controls designed for a one-party parliament; if not, ought we to try and design some new controls? Should the civil service remain insulated from politics and should politics be forbidden to the civil service? Is the present administrative system and law helping, hindering or remaining neutral in the drive for economic development . . . ?[149]

The principal difference between a ministerial government in the British model and the sort of demands imposed by planning is in the degree of control from the center. Cabinet control in the British model is relatively relaxed and decentralized. Planning, if it is to succeed, calls for immense discipline in all the reaches of the public service.[150] Until the relationship between the plan and the ministries is sufficiently articulated, one may well doubt that the public services will be completely integrated into the drive towards development.

Specific institutions within the public services may also require empirical study to determine their utility to the tasks thrust upon them. Many, no doubt, are functional as received; but some may not be. One example of the latter sort (although somewhat to one side of the mainstream of development) is the prisons department in Ghana. The basic form of the Prisons Act and the regulations remain today what they were in 1876. In fact, whole sections of the regulations read exactly as they did ninety years ago. The paper rules governing the conduct of criminal prisoners require them to maintain a regime of silence by day and prescribe solitary confinement for them at night. The Act still distinguishes between hard labor of the first and of the second class,

---

[149] McAuslan, *op. cit. supra* note 148, at 69-70.
[150] 1966 Budget Statement ¶ 98 (Ghana). In Ghana, the lack of discipline within the ministries and in the cabinet itself was notable. For example, the seven year plan allotted £2,500,000 for a national conference hall to be spread over seven years; no part of its expenditure was scheduled for 1965. The government nevertheless spent £8,000,000 on the conference hall in 1965.

a distinction harking back to the days of "strictly penal labour"— the treadmill, shot drill, and the crank. None of these pillars of the penal system have been in force for decades; the separate system at night has never been enforced since it was enacted in 1876. The prison's staff has all been trained in England, and English notions of penology permeate the institution. But nobody has ever made an empirical study to determine whether the imposed British system is appropriate to the Ghanaian circumstance. Until such a study is made, it is impossible to determine its sufficiency.

3. THE BUSINESS RELATIONSHIPS IN THE PUBLIC SECTOR

Perhaps the most important of the specific institutions received at independence is the public corporation, the typical means by which African countries undertake enterprises in the public sector.

a. The Institutional Form

It has been stated that "the most critical control point [of public corporations and other public enterprises] is the law, decree or other basic authority providing for the creation of a public enterprise" and that "this is likely to determine in large measure all other organizational relationships."[151] While it has been suggested that this is exaggerated,[152] nevertheless it seems clear enough that the organic law of any public enterprise ought to respond to the functional demands made by the specific environmental circumstances.

In its original employment in England, the public corporation was viewed as providing a resolution to the competing considerations of the need for relative independence in business operations and the need for general policy direction from the appropriate minister or department.[153] The resolution of the competing considerations took place in the board of directors of the public corporation. This form has been employed throughout English-speaking Africa as the principal form of public enterprise.

On the whole, its success has not been spectacular. In both Nigeria and Ghana, and perhaps elsewhere, exactly the opposite of its presumed advantages seem to have occurred. There has been continual political interference in the operations of government corporations on the personnel level, with "jobs for the boys" play-

---

[151] U.N. TECHNICAL ASSISTANCE ADMINISTRATION, SOME PROBLEMS IN THE ORGANISATION AND ADMINISTRATION OF PUBLIC ENTERPRISES IN THE INDUSTRIAL FIELD 18 (1954).

[152] HANSON, op. cit. supra note 139, at 360.

[153] Friedmann, A Theory of Public Industrial Enterprise, in PUBLIC ENTERPRISE—A STUDY OF ITS ORGANISATION AND MANAGEMENT IN VARIOUS COUNTRIES 11 (1954); ROBSEN, NATIONALISED INDUSTRY AND PUBLIC OWNERSHIP 74 (1960).

ing a dominant role. But at the point where ministerial control should be most important—the point of financial accountability—it has been the most weak. Nigerian government auditors reported plaintively that it was impossible to obtain explanations of questioned expenditures from various government enterprises. The same complaint has too frequently been heard in Ghana. In Kenya, as a result of political appointments to the boards of corporations, the boards became subservient to ministerial suggestion.[154] This result was plainly true in Ghana as well.

The reason for the failure may lie in the grossly different environment in which the public corporation operates in Africa. In England, nationalization occurred in an economic and social system already highly developed and dominated by private enterprise.[155] It took place in a country with a well-developed tradition of rectitude in appointments to public bodies and of relative ministerial abstention from interference in the operation of semiautonomous public or quasi-public institutions. It developed in a country with enough managerial personnel, a country in which the civil service, albeit honest and efficient, was regarded as being unnecessarily bound by red tape and conservative, bureaucratic attitudes. In such circumstances, the central tension was plainly between efficient, businesslike management and the requirements of public control.

In Africa, the significant factors are different. The plan is of much greater importance to the economy than it is in England, for a far greater proportion of the economy is dominated by state action. Public bodies are too often viewed as opportunities for political placement, and there is a strong feeling of omnicompetence on the part of ministers. Most important, there is a desperate paucity of managerial personnel. The civil service, instead of being the most inefficient sector of the social structure, is frequently the principal source of high-level manpower.

As a result, the form of the public corporation in Africa addresses itself to the wrong issues. Placing policy direction in a board of directors that is largely politically appointed does not insulate the corporation from bureaucratic civil servants; instead, it insulates the corporation from the largest available pool of trained personnel. It does not free the corporation to compete with private enterprise in a basically private enterprise economy; rather, it tends to insure that they will have the maximum freedom from planning control in an economy where scarce resources must be carefully husbanded through central direction. It does not protect the corporation from political interference in personnel appointments; it insures such interference.

---

154 McAuslan, *op. cit. supra* note 148, at 38.
155 Friedmann, *op. cit. supra* note 153, at 16.

In the Soviet Union, public enterprises took a very different form than they took in England because of the very different pressures of that economic, political, and social structure.[156] Africa, too, may well require its own unique solution for the problem. However, absent basic empirical studies, one cannot determine whether public enterprises are needed and, if needed, the preferred form.

Turning to the typical form of state-private enterprise partnership, a form used with great frequency throughout Africa, a much more favorable picture emerges. In these situations the typical vehicle has been an ordinary private corporation, with the government (or perhaps an industrial development corporation) holding shares representing the public interests and with management usually in the hands of the private partner. In Ghana and in Nigeria, the results have been much better, at least on the level of the profit and loss statement.[157] It would be instructive to have a detailed study of the two forms to determine why the one has been so much more successful than the other.

b. Contractual Relationships

Relationships between privately owned firms in the free sector of the economy are controlled mainly by English contract law. The same law controls relationships between firms in the public sector, and, more significantly, between private firms and government enterprises.

There are important concepts of contract law that are irrelevant to agreements between government enterprises. Classically, contract law is built on four cornerstones: freedom of movement, insurance against calculated risk, freedom of will, and equality of bargaining position.[158] These cornerstones are cemented together by sets of rules governing offer and acceptance, consideration, and damages. The first theoretically ensures that parties will be held liable only for agreements freely entered into; the second underlines the requirement of a bargain or exchange as the essence of contract; and the third expresses the notion of insurance against calculated risk.

None of the cornerstones of contract law are relevant to contracts between government agencies, at least with the content given these concepts in the received English law. Freedom of movement of government enterprise in a planned economy is the antithesis of planning, as is the notion of freedom of will. Whether government agencies have equal bargaining strength is not a sig-

---

[156] *Ibid.* See also BERMAN, JUSTICE IN THE U.S.S.R. 110 (rev. ed. 1963).

[157] Joint state-private enterprises in Ghana returned a profit of 60% on the total investment in 1965; the government corporations returned a net loss. 1966 Budget Statement ¶ 50 (Ghana).

[158] FRIEDMANN, LAW IN A CHANGING SOCIETY 90 (1959).

nificant issue as between organizations that each have an assigned function in the plan. Insurance against calculated risk is almost equally irrelevant when government must bear the loss in any event.[159] With the undermining of the purposes of the received contract law, the conceptual cement of offer and acceptance, consideration, and damages dissolves. What emerges as a substitute is a system of administration in which relationships between public enterprises are controlled by altogether different norms.[160] That is the Senegalese solution.[161]

Contractual relationships between public and private enterprises pose a different and more complex problem. In developed countries these tend to be mere contracts of adhesion, with the government imposing the details of the relationship. This is apparently the case with construction contracts in Kenya.[162] On the other hand, there are cases, unknown in England or the United States, where the bargaining power of a foreign firm far outweighs that of the contracting government. The assets of Unilever, for example, are greater than those of most African governments. When Kaiser Engineers contracts with an African government, Kaiser's form contract is used, not the government's.[163] Empirical studies are necessary to determine whether the received norms of private contract law are relevant to the solution of the sorts of problems raised.

Finally, one must consider the scope of the criminal law as it bears upon the control of the public sector. The absence of the test of profitmaking as a simple standard against which to measure the performance of the manager of a state enterprise leads to difficult questions about the control of management. Demands arise that managers and others using public property be placed under the strictures of the criminal law with respect to their stewardship. In Ghana, for example, this has resulted in very broadly worded criminal legislation that declares a person guilty of an offense if, "by reason of a careless or dishonest attitude" towards the affairs of a state corporation, he "so mis-manages the affairs thereof as to cause the dissipation of or grave damage to public property."[164]

Whether the criminal law is an apt tool to solve problems of managerial efficiency may be questioned. Yet the test of profitability may not be available as a measure of managerial compe-

---

[159] In a developed centralized planned economy, the requirement for insurance against calculated risks seems to reemerge, as the Soviet experience suggests. See BERMAN, *op. cit. supra* note 156, at 114-44.

[160] FRIEDMANN, *op. cit. supra* note 158, at 371.

[161] Farnsworth, *supra* note 131, at 11-12.

[162] McAuslan, *op. cit. supra* note 148, at 68.

[163] The contract provides that it shall be controlled by California law!

[164] Public Property (Protection) and Corrupt Practices (Prevention) Act, 1964, Pub. Act 121 (Ghana).

tence because enterprises in the public sector may well be undertaken in order to achieve objectives other than immediate profit—
to exploit a potential pole of growth, for example, or to provide
off-season employment for farmers. Absent that test, either the
criminal law must be employed or some other device must be
found for policing managerial performance.

D. Summary

The first problem that arises in analyzing the sufficiency of the
various sorts of law in Africa to meet contemporary demands
made upon them is whether they sufficiently resolve the problems
posed to each. Customary law may be placed to one side with
respect to development, since customary law cannot be an important source of the institutional transformations required.

The received English law probably responds adequately to the
demands of the existing private sector. This is hardly a surprise
because before independence it served well the colonialist enclave
from which the present private sector has developed. The changes
that are desirable are no more far-reaching than those required in
most contemporary legal systems.

However, the received law fails to respond adequately to the demands of the public sector. This also is hardly a surprise.
The central jural postulate of the received law—contract—is antipathetical to the jural postulates that underlie the demands for
state intervention into the economy in the interests of development. So long as it is agreed that there is to be some degree of
planning, the formulation of adequate norms for the public sector
raises no great issues of policy. But when one considers potential
frictions between the several legal orders, important policy questions emerge.

VI. CONFLICTS BETWEEN THE SEVERAL LEGAL ORDERS

The determination of priorities between interests within a discrete sector of the economy can readily be made in light of the
agreed jural postulates appropriate to that sector. But what
principle of adjudication can be invoked to resolve conflicts that
arise between interests that claim under different sets of jural
postulates? Before reaching that question, however, it is necessary
to consider the most abrasive points of tension.

A. Internal Conflicts

Thus far we have assumed, rather loosely, that there are several
legal orders in the African states. This, of course, is something
of a misstatement. Actually there is but a single legal order de-
scending pyramidally from the constitution (Kelsen's *Grundnorm*).
But there are different sets of substantive norms to be applied in

different situations. The rules of internal conflicts of laws embody the central "rules of recognition."[165] These rules direct the judge to use one or the other of the different bodies of substantive norms in any particular case. Analytically, the entire system is unaesthetic. Everyone would concede a priori that it would be desirable to have a legal system whose hierarchies of power and substantive norms are unified. Two alternative but complementary policies have been invoked. One accepts the pluralism of the substantive law and seeks mainly to clarify the internal conflicts rules; the other looks to unification of the whole legal system.

1. CLARIFICATION OF INTERNAL CONFLICT RULES

If the institutions described by the law outrun too far the existing social institutions, the law will simply be inoperative.[166] All the power that the state can muster may be insufficient to compel obedience unless there is a high incidence of voluntary submission. Hence, a pluralistic legal system will necessarily be retained so long as the economy and social structure remains pluralistic. This view appears to be accepted by every independent state.[167] The immediate requirement, therefore, is for clarification of the rules of internal conflicts.

One function of the rules of internal conflicts is to allocate a transaction to the particular legal order appropriate to it. A two-part policy consideration is involved. On the one hand, an individual's legal relationships ought to be governed by the law by which he actually or presumably desired to have them governed. On the other hand, customary law is appropriate only to transactions arising in the sphere of the precapitalist economy; most of the transactions related to development must be controlled by received or statutory law.

Under the conditions obtaining when the internal conflicts rules were adopted, there was a coincidence between the two functions, for there were no Africans acting as entrepreneurs in the colonialist sector. Today, however, there are Africans who live entirely within the modern sector of society, and there are even more whose business relationships are within the money economy but whose personal relationships are still dominated by polygamy and the extended family. Thus, the single test of ethnic origin to deter-

---

165 "Rules of recognition" is H.L.A. Hart's suggested nomenclature. See HART, THE CONCEPT OF LAW 97 (1961).

166 Whatever the jurisprudential school, this much is commonly agreed today. Some writers go further. See, e.g., Rheinstein, *Problems of Law in the New Nations of Africa*, in OLD SOCIETIES AND NEW STATES: THE QUEST FOR MODERNITY IN ASIA AND AFRICA 220, 224 (Geertz ed. 1963): "Law is not a body of rules that can be unified or modified at will by governmental fiat."

167 Schiller, *Law*, in THE AFRICAN WORLD—A SURVEY OF SOCIAL RESEARCH 166, 177 (Lystad ed. 1965).

mine if customary law applies[168] is no longer a sharp enough scalpel to serve well, and the exceptions devised by the courts are not altogether satisfactory.

Kenya and Uganda made a first approximation at a resolution of this problem before independence. Typically, it was still phrased in racial terms. A person partly of non-African descent who did not own or occupy land in accordance with customary tenure, and who was not living in any African community in the customary way, could obtain a certificate exempting him from the jurisdiction of the native courts (and hence from the control of customary law).[169]

Tanzania has tried to solve the problem by abandoning the ethnic test and substituting the concept of "membership in a community." Membership in a community may be acquired either by adoption of the way of life of the community or by community acceptance of a person as one of its members. Membership in one community may be lost by acquiring membership in another community. The adoption of membership may be general or may operate for certain acts or transactions only. Moreover, the matter will be controlled by some law other than customary law if it is apparent from the nature of the act or transaction or from the manner of life or business of the parties that they intended the matter to be so regulated.[170]

Ghana has left the matter rather vague, presumably to permit the courts to work out detailed rules. A person is entitled to have applied in any case his "personal law," which is presumed to be the common law unless some system of customary law is to be applied.[171] It has been remarked that "if with the spread of industrialization and urbanization in Ghana, the courts tend to adopt the view that customary law ties are being severed by more and more Ghanaians, there is an opening here for accelerating the demise of customary law."[172] Probably the Ghanaian courts will not so construe the statute, although no reported cases on the subject can be found.[173]

---

[168] See text accompanying note 44 *supra*.

[169] Uganda: Interpretation and General Clauses Ordinance § 3(1)(b); Kenya: Interpretation and General Clauses Ordinance (No. 36 of 1956) § 5(c).

[170] See Cotran, *The Place and Future of Customary Law in East Africa*, in EAST AFRICAN LAW TODAY, 5 COMMONWEALTH LAW SERIES 72 (1965).

[171] Courts Act, 1960, § 66 (Ghana).

[172] BENNION, CONSTITUTIONAL LAW IN GHANA 452-53 (1962).

[173] Professor Rheinstein raises the question of inter-tribal conflicts of laws. Rheinstein, *op. cit. supra* note 166, at 227-28. The Nigerian statutes are clear: In the absence of a clear indication of choice of law by the parties, the law of the forum is to be used. Eastern Region: Customary Courts Law § 23(1)(a); Northern Region: Native Courts Law, 1956, §20 (a). See Regina v. Ilorin Native Court, 20 N.L.R. 144 (1953).

None of these attempted solutions appears to furnish a wholly satisfactory rule. Perhaps the lack of clarity results from an attempt to ride two policy horses at once. To make the basic rule of internal conflicts one of personal law emphasizes the policy of judging a case by the law that a party would choose to have it judged at the expense of the policy of using norms appropriate to the subject matter. Consequently, it is difficult to ensure that transactions relevant to development will be controlled by a suitable body of substantive norms. Yet, if it turns out that commercial transactions between Africans are to be controlled by norms of customary law, development may be adversely affected.

2. UNIFICATION

Only South Africa (and perhaps Rhodesia) proposes to continue the plurality of legal systems forever. Every other African state looks forward to a unified system composed partly of elements from the received law and partly of elements derived from customary law.[174] However, the overwhelming bulk of the corpus of the law respecting economic development cannot be customary law. For the purposes of this article, therefore, one need not enter upon the vigorous discussions that have been conducted by academic lawyers concerned with the manifold problems of collecting, restating, codifying, or declaring the customary law.[175]

So long as specific claims, demands, or interests can be satisfied within the legal order to which they look, there is a happy coincidence between the jural postulates of the law and the value-acceptance implied by the claim. However, where claims made under the several sets of laws impinge upon each other, courts are required to choose between the several jural postulates urged upon them. This is the major policy choice thrust upon the law and the state by the demands for development.

B. Customary Law

Undoubtedly, the hardest single rub in all African law lies between the norms of customary land tenure and the demands for development. This is inevitable. "The bond between man and

---

174 Schiller, op. cit. supra note 167, at 177.
175 See, e.g., THE FUTURE OF LAW IN AFRICA 9-13 (Allott ed. 1960). See also Cotran, op. cit. supra note 170. Among academic lawyers, there is a divurgence between writers who believe that the unification of laws can be imposed by government and those who believe that unification can only arise as African society loses its present pluralistic character. Compare, for example, THE FUTURE OF LAW IN AFRICA 23 (Allott ed. 1960) ("Should there be a single system of law, which embraces English law, and the other special types of law?") with Rheinstein, op. cit. supra note 166, at 225 ("In African countries, diversity of mores is marked and is bound to exist for a long time to come. As long as it exists, legal pluralism will have to continue.").

land that is described by the manner through which the land is distributed, maintained, and transferred, is a basic bond that conditions all human progress."[176]

Traditional African agriculture is, as has been frequently pointed out, extraordinarily well adapted for the level of technology and the geographical environment in which it occurs.[177] "Nevertheless, when all is said . . . traditional systems, unaltered simply will not sustain economic progress, and they are being and will be replaced by new crops and new methods."[178]

These new methods require, above all else, a stable investment in the land. They require a production unit of a single enclosed area that is large enough to accommodate the use of modern cultivating machinery. They require soils capable, when properly managed, of sustaining high yields over many years. They require an annual reinvestment of a substantial surplus in the land.[179]

Development of this sort is the very negation of the shifting agriculture that is the technological underpinning of most customary land law.[180] Such a transformation requires long-term capital investment in the farm. Patently, the norms of customary law are inappropriate in some ways to accomplish an end so different from that predicated on shifting agriculture. However, the changes required in the customary law are different if the development of modern agriculture is to be undertaken primarily by individual farmers impelled by ordinary market incentives, or if it is to be mainly directed by the state in response to the demands of a central plan.

The East Africa Royal Commission on African Land Tenure advocated the former solution, "a land policy which would have as its cardinal features the pregressive [sic] encouragement of individualisation of title in African lands . . . ."[181] The Swynnerton Plan adopted in Kenya in 1954 stated that

Holdings of an economic size [should be created] by consol-

[176] Translation by the author of "Le lien entre l'homme et la terre qui est représenté par la façon dont la terre est distribuée, conservée et transférée, est un lien fondamental qui affecte tout le progrès humain." Resolution of the Conference I.N.C.I.D.I. (La Haye 1953) as quoted in AFRICAN AGRARIAN SYSTEMS 1 (Biebuyck ed. 1963).
[177] ALLAN, THE AFRICAN HUSBANDMAN 3 (1965); HUNTER, THE NEW SOCIETIES OF TROPICAL AFRICA—A SELECTIVE STUDY 96-97 (1962).
[178] Id. at 98.
[179] ALLAN, op. cit. supra note 177, at 470.
[180] Clauson asserts that shifting agriculture and tenures dependent upon continued use inevitably result in "soil-mining" since the usufructury owner has only a limited interest in maintaining soil fertility. CLAUSON, COMMUNAL LAND TENURE—AN FAO LAND TENURE STUDY 38-39 (1953). See also LIVERSAGE, LAND TENURE IN THE COLONIES 116 (1945): "The tenant who has no security will sow only where he can reap."
[181] LA. ANYANE, GHANA AGRICULTURE—ECONOMIC DEVELOPMENT FROM EARLY TIMES TO THE MIDDLE OF THE TWENTIETH CENTURY 191 (1963).

idation ... or by enclosure of communal lands; the able African must not be debarred from acquiring units in excess of any minimum laid down for the area .... The commitment ... that he will be "sold up" if he defaults must be accepted by any farmer in applying for loans .... Once registered, farmers will be able to buy and sell land, amongst other Africans only, and to mortgage .... [A]ble, energetic or rich Africans will be able to acquire more land, and bad or poor farmers less, creating a landed and a landless class. This is a normal step in the evolution of a country.[182]

If the direction of agricultural development is to be as envisaged by the East Africa Commission or by the Swynnerton Plan, a sound legal environment would require permanency of tenure, clarity of title, freedom of alienability, and relative freedom from fragmentation.

1. INDIVIDUAL EFFORT

If private capitalist farming for the market is the objective, the first requirement would seem to be permanence of tenure. It is frequently stated that the weakness of customary law is that the farmer does not "own" the land; the family, the community, or the chief is the allodial holder. Yet in most systems of African customary law, the occupant does have the permanent right of occupation so long as he uses the land.[183] The difficulty with customary systems of land tenure from the point of view of the private sector lies in its imprecision, lack of freedom of alienability, and (in some areas) its susceptibility to fragmentation.

Stable, long-term investment in land requires clarity of title. That want of clarity of title inhibits commercial development[184] as well as capital-intensive farming seems self-evident. Yet land titles under customary law are frequently far from clear. The tragic (and sometime hilarious) rough-and-tumble Ghanaian land litigation is notorious.[185] Customary rules by their nature are unwritten and hence subject to misinterpretation and dispute. Moreover, boundaries are imprecise and frequently depend upon the memory of neighbors for their effectiveness.

The suggested solution everywhere has been the adoption of a

---

[182] A PLAN TO INTENSIFY THE DEVELOPMENT OF AFRICAN AGRICULTURE IN KENYA 8-10 (1954). See also I.B.R.D. MISSION, THE ECONOMIC DEVELOPMENT OF TANGANYIKA 95 (1961).

[183] Bentsi-Entchill, *Do African Systems of Land Tenure Require a Special Terminology?*, 1965 J. AFRICAN L. 114, 124-26. In some countries, security of title has been impaired by governmental action, as under the Southern Rhodesian Land Husbandry Act, 1951. *Id.* at 134.

[184] SIMPSON, A REPORT ON THE REGISTRATION OF TITLE TO LAND IN THE FEDERAL TERRITORY OF LAGOS ¶ 19 (1957).

[185] See, *e.g.*, MEMORANDUM ON THE CLEARING OF CLOUDED AND UNMARKETABLE TITLES IN THE GOLD COAST AND FOR THE INSTITUTION OF A SYSTEM OF LAND REGISTRATION 3 (Gov't Print., Accra 1954).

land registration scheme of some sort.[186] Registration at least makes a determination, by a sovereign act of state, of the extent of the then existing interests in land. At that point, title is clear.

Having made such a determination, what law is to control dealings in the land? English land law is dismayingly dysfunctional even to the problems of England; it has been said by a most experienced commissioner of lands in Africa that it, like the English weather, is "tolerable only in England."[187] Since it was devised mainly in response to the desires of aristocratic landowners to control their estates from the grave, it has almost no direct relevance to modern conditions. Indeed, the incredible complexities of English real property law are largely a catalogue of devices to avoid the true implications of English real property law. On the other hand, one may well question whether customary law resolves the problems adequately. Alienability of land is important if land use is to be maximized in the private sector.[188] Yet alienability under customary law is at best doubtful.

Land in every customary system is alienable by the allodial owner—the chief in most cephaloid societies, the family, lineage, or other subgroup elsewhere.[189] Such alienability may be sufficient to provide land for commercial and industrial development. But alienability by the user is also a necessity for the development of investment in land. The occupier frequently will not invest in land if he knows that he may be unable to realize his investment if he must move.

It is an intriguing fact that modern economic and social pressures tend to produce a restricted sort of alienability of land, even under customary systems of tenure.

> The general effect of modern changes particularly with permanent crops, and increasing population pressure and land shortage, is to eliminate or hasten the elimination of the holders of estates of administration in hierarchical systems, and the groups' estates of control in lineage systems. Often the Chief retains some claim, even though it may be no more than the right to a small gift to mark his ultimate

---

[186] See THE FUTURE OF LAW IN AFRICA 42 (Allott ed. 1960). Registration statutes are operative in most of English-speaking Africa. Except for Kenya, they have been invoked mainly for European-held property in the "white" enclaves of East and Central Africa and in some of the larger cities. In Lagos, for example, only 2,400 freehold and 500 leasehold parcels out of a total of 20,000 parcels on the rating list had been registered in 1956. The registration ordinance had been in effect for twenty-one years. Simpson, *op. cit. supra* note 184, at ¶ 19.

[187] *Id.* at ¶ 34.

[188] MEMORANDUM ON THE CLEARING OF CLOUDED AND UNMARKETABLE TITLES IN THE GOLD COAST AND FOR THE INSTITUTION OF A SYSTEM OF LAND REGISTRATION 16 (Gov't Print., Accra 1954).

[189] See GLUCKMAN, POLITICS, LAW AND RITUAL IN TRIBAL SOCIETY 41 (1965).

ownership: but in the end result no one intervenes between chief and individual landholder, and the latter may
sell to whom he wishes or mortgage as he pleases.[190]

This has been the development in Ghana, in large part because
cocoa trees remain in the same place and will bear for forty years.[191]
An analogous result seems to obtain among the coffee-producing
tribes of Uganda[192] and in some areas of Tanzania,[193] and in Ibo-
land (Eastern Nigeria).[194]

Despite these changes in specific areas, the individual farmer's
power to alienate land is still sharply limited under most customary
law. Even in Ghana his rights can be exercised only through legal
fictions. While customary law is sufficient for shifting agriculture,
the transition to intensive farming in the private sector will be
made easier if the norms determining alienability can be made less
restrictive. To do so requires that the decisionmakers choose between rights asserted under customary law and new claims arising
in the private sector.

Where population pressures have reduced the amount of land
available to farming so that shifting cultivation becomes less and
less feasible, holdings tend to become excessively subdivided and
fragmented.[195] This has been so pronounced in Kenya that the
principal thrust of efforts at land reform in that country during
the colonial period was towards the consolidation of holdings, usually by way of voluntary agreement negotiated by government
panels.[196] By October 1960, about 2,000,000 acres of Kikuyu land
had been consolidated and enclosed into separate holdings for
200,000 farmers. Over 137,000 individual titles were registered.
Between 1954 and 1959 alone, recorded sales of African produce
increased from £5,500,000 to £9,000,000.[197]

The principal source of such fragmentation usually lies in customary rules governing the evolution of property on death. The
Kara live on twenty-nine square miles of Ukara island in Lake
Victoria. The climate is favorable, and they use farming methods
that should result in high productivity. They have developed techniques of heavy manuring because they have come to regard their

---

190 Allan, op. cit. supra note 177, at 367.
191 Asante, Interests in Land in the Customary Law of Ghana—A New
Appraisal, 74 Yale L.J. 848, 878 (1965).
192 Allan, op. cit. supra note 177, at 367-68.
193 I.B.R.D. Mission, The Economic Development of Tanganyika 93
(1961).
194 Chubb, Ibo Land Tenure ¶ 30 (2d ed. 1961). See also Liversage, op.
cit supra note 180, at 66.
195 Clauson, op. cit. supra note 180, at 35; Hunter, op. cit. supra note
177, at 115.
196 Working Party on African Land Tenure, Report—1957-58, at 8-9
(1958).
197 Hunter, op. cit. supra note 177, at 115-16.

cattle instrumentally rather than as status symbols; they rigorously observe crop rotation and soil conservation measures; and they have a system of land tenure that amounts to virtual ownership of land by male heads of family. Yet, because of the fantastic fragmentation of the land, all they can manage is a bare subsistence. Holdings consist of a number of widely scattered tiny plots that rarely exceed a tenth of an acre and *average* a twentieth of an acre. Plots as small as twenty-five square yards are common. The division of land among inheritors primarily accounts for this fragmentation.[198]

Systems of inheritance are perhaps the most intractable rules of law to change in any society. Frequently carrying a heavy overlay of religious sanction, they are closely intertwined with society's system of care for widows and children and with the maintenance of group solidarity. Moreover, they cannot readily be changed unless alternative devices for social security exist. In particular, the rules that produce fragmentation cannot be changed unless there are employment opportunities elsewhere for the disinherited.

2. PLAN

Clarity of title, alienability, and relief from fragmentation seem to be the principal demands if land law is to accommodate to the imperatives of the private sector. However, if agricultural development is envisaged as coming about mainly by way of cooperatives and state farms, the direction of desirable change in customary land tenures may be different.

Cooperative efforts have frequently been observed occurring indigenously. For example, travelers in Northern Nigeria have noticed parcels of fifty acres or more of one crop. These large fields are usually either a "farm" being worked under the overall direction of the head of an extended family, or a number of contiguous plots worked by related individuals. Among the Gusii, as well, it is the custom to work contiguous plots together.[199]

Upon this basis, Clauson points out that what he has termed "tertiary communal land tenure" can emerge easily from customary forms. Normally, the group not only owns or controls the land but also more or less jointly farms it. It develops indigenously

---

[198] See ALLAN, *op. cit. supra* note 177, at 203-06. Professor Allott suggests that many criticisms of customary land tenures are too sweeping. Insecurity of tenures, he claims, are frequently a reflection of deficiency in land use, not in land law. Fragmentation is mainly a function of succession laws, not of land law. Moreover, he asserts that customary law can adapt successfully to new circumstances, presumably without legislative interference. Allott, *Legal Development and Economic Growth in Africa,* in CHANGING LAW IN DEVELOPING COUNTRIES 194, 200-01 (Anderson ed. 1963).

[199] Baldwin, *Land Tenure Problems in Relation to Agricultural Development in Northern Nigeria,* in AFRICAN AGRARIAN SYSTEMS 64, 78 (Biebuyck ed. 1963).

under the impact of bulk buying, which almost inevitably forces the producers to organize themselves as sellers to protect their own interests.[200]

This, coupled with the manifest advantages of mechanized tillage, induces farmers to cooperate. The existing forms of customary land tenure make the transition easy and do not require more than marginal changes in customary rules of land tenure. Most important, it does not require any changes that convert the system of land tenure from one depending upon status to one depending upon contract. Therefore, it can be made without doing violence to the value-acceptances of those within the customary land system.

Finally, if the direction of development is to be primarily towards large-scale resettlement or towards state farms, the thrust of change may well be different. In such case, the emphasis must inevitably be on assurances that government has adequate powers of eminent domain, not on changes in customary tenure per se.

Since independence, the several African governments have given some indication of the thrust of their policy. Kenya appears to be continuing the pre-independence policy of transforming customary tenures into relatively consolidated parcels held in what comes very close to a registered freehold title. Uganda likewise appears to have taken the position that individual land holding is the most appropriate path to agricultural development. The Public Lands Ordinance, 1962, leaves intact all existing private titles to land; however, it vests the freehold title to Crown lands in various public authorities. These authorities have power to make grants in freehold or leasehold regardless of customary tenures presently existing.[201] In Buganda, much private land is held in *milo* estates granted to notables in freehold by the 1900 Agreement.[202]

Tanzania seems to be moving towards another sort of solution. The Freehold Titles (Conversion and Government Leases) Act, 1963, vested all land in Tanzania in the President. Henceforth, no freehold exists in Tanzania, and the maximum private estate a person can have in the land is ninety-nine years.[203] Its purpose was to "convert freehold land into leasehold and to make rights of

---

[200] See CLAUSON, *op. cit. supra* note 180, at 41.

[201] See Mugerwa, *Land Tenure in East Africa—Some Contrasts*, in EAST AFRICAN LAW TODAY, 5 COMMONWEALTH LAW SERIES 72, 112-13 (1965).

[202] The 1900 Agreement was concluded by the English and the Kabaka (King) of Buganda. By its terms, the English got roughly half of Buganda's land, the other half going to the Kabaka, senior chiefs, and 1,000 chiefs and private landowners. The land that went to the notables was parceled out in square miles, and such estates became known as *milo* estates. See MORRIS & READ, UGANDA—THE DEVELOPMENT OF ITS LAWS AND CONSTITUTION 17 (1966).

[203] See Mugerwa, *op. cit. supra* note 201, at 112-13.

occupancy granted for agricultural purposes subject to up-to-date
Land Regulations" in order to procure "the development of land to
the greatest possible speed."[204]   In contrast to the Kenyan and
Ugandan developments, Tanzania relies upon plan as the theme of
agricultural development, not upon contract.   As it concludes in its
Proposals, the "Government considers that the urgent need for
raising the standard of living of the people of Tanganyika and the
vital importance of agriculture in the country's economy, compel
it to use its power to procure development of land."[205]

Ghana—at least prior to the recent coup—was embarked upon a
course in a similar direction.   Dr. Asante has summarized the
development:

> The increased proprietary capacity of the government [as
> the result of a whole spectrum of recent legislation] has
> had the following impact on the customary scheme of
> interests in land: The bold assertion of government con-
> trol of land makes any concept of absolutist ownership,
> which recent cases seem to project, quite illusory.   The
> subject's estate may be immune from restrictions by the
> stool, but is considerably curtailed by the Republic's pow-
> ers of expropriation and its wide powers of control of user.
> Furthermore, if the Administration of Lands Act applies
> to the subject's estate, then ownership will be severely
> curtailed by governmental supervision of dispositions. . . .
> Further, with regard to the effect of recent legislation on
> the institution of stool lands, it is no exaggeration to assert
> that the stool's ownership of unencumbered stool lands is
> now an empty concept devoid of all substance.[206]

Thus the rub between customary land law and the claims and
demands within the private sector, and between customary land
law and those claims generated within the public sector, lead
to different conclusions about the desirable direction of the change
of land tenures.   To do nothing is itself a policy decision to leave
much of African agriculture in its present deplorable state.   But the
direction of legal change cannot be determined without a basic
normative decision.

C.   *Conflicts between Contract and Plan*

An important policy issue in Africa is the extent to which the
state should intervene in the economy in order to bring about
economic development.[207]   In law, that issue underlies the conflict between those claims or demands that are predicated upon

---

[204] GOVERNMENT OF TANGANYIKA, PROPOSALS FOR LAND REFORM ¶¶ 1-2
(1962).

[205] *Id.* at ¶ 10.

[206] Asante, *supra* note 191, at 885.

[207] See Kamarck, *Economics and Economic Development*, in THE AFRICAN
WORLD: A SURVEY OF SOCIAL RESEARCH 221, 236 (Lystad ed. 1965).

contract and those that are predicated upon plan. These conflicts arise in two principal areas. To what extent should the state direct the activities of the private sector? To what extent should the state preempt whole sectors of the economy to the exclusion of private enterprise?

1. DIRECTION OF THE PRIVATE SECTOR

The state can structure the market artificially by rewarding desired action or by punishing undesired action. Both are sanctions. In either case, the individual chooses the course most desirable to himself, and the state imposes the sanction.[208]

In one sense, law is an order of norms directing state officials in specific circumstances to impose sanctions upon individuals.[209] There is a continuum in severity of sanctions available to the state to control the activities of private enterprise. The claims that bottom themselves on the jural postulates of plan would have the state administer the command and enjoyment functions of private property by the selective use of sanctions. The claims that look to contract for their realization would leave these functions of private property undisturbed in the private owners of the means of production. The conflict between the two raises serious policy questions in a broad range of laws.

a. Colonialist Restraints on a Free Market

The colonial legal structure included a variety of compulsions exerted on the market. Hut taxes, poll taxes, and pass laws controlled the labor market. Stringent restrictions on the alienation of land, especially in the "white" areas of Kenya and the Rhodesias, limited the real estate market. Africans were required to produce certain crops and forbidden to produce others. Marketing boards paid artifically fixed prices for commodities, sometimes differentiating between producers on ethnic grounds. Custom duties were manipulated to favor firms from the metropolitan country. The infrastructure was designed to encourage certain producers and products. It has been said of Kenya, for example, that the market forces there were "deliberately founded upon an elaborate

---

[208] *But cf.* Bauer & Yamey, The Economics of Underdeveloped Countries 160 (1957).

[209] Every legal norm can be rephrased in the form of a hypothetical judgment. Thus restated, the "commands" of the law are addressed primarily not to the subject but to officials. Kelsen, General Theory of Law and State 45 (1945). Every rule of law is therefore a rule for the application of the reserved monopoly of force in the state. H. L. A. Hart has criticized this view as failing to comprehend all the meanings of the word "law." Hart, The Concept of Law 35-41 (1961). Whatever may be the further reach of the concept of law, Hart does not deny that rules of law do embody commands addressed to officials concerning the application of state power.

base of legal and administrative compulsions."[210]

The direction of thrust of these compulsions was different from the direction that the independent states seek to follow.

> But whereas colonial governments tend to place their main emphasis on the expansion of agricultural, extractive and processing activities, those of independent states, while by no means neglecting these aspects of development, tend to find their *summum bonum* in the creation of manufacturing industries such as appear to have brought power and prosperity to the more developed lands. The reason for this difference in relative emphasis is well known. A colonial government normally aims at creating an economy which will be complementary to that of the metropolitan country; an independent government thinks in terms of an internally-balanced, diversified and comparatively self-sustaining economy.[211]

Many of the most obnoxious of the restraints under colonialism were removed during the imperial twilight; others hang on today. Whether they ought to remain raises issues for economists and lawyers.

b. *Marketing Boards*

The agricultural market was dominated almost everywhere in colonial Africa by the use of marketing boards. Acting as the sole authorized purchaser from the peasant, they then sold to foreign firms (cocoa in Ghana) or to local markets (maize in Kenya). There were various reasons, some incompletely formulated, for setting up these boards. They have been attacked as an unwarranted interference in the market economy: Increased prices to the peasant would have increased production, and the peasants would have made wiser investments with the surplus than did the government. And they have been defended: They stabilized prices to the peasants, provided a unified bargaining unit vis-à-vis the great exporting firms, and provided a surplus for investment pursuant to a plan.[212] Whether they ought to be retained in their received form, if at all, is a critical policy question in those countries where the marketing boards dominate the export trade.[213]

---

[210] Douglas, *Structure and Advice: The Case of Kenya*, 24 AMERICAN J. ECONOMICS & SOCIOLOGY 397, 403 (1965).

[211] HANSON, PUBLIC ENTERPRISE AND ECONOMIC DEVELOPMENT 3-4 (1959).

[212] The literature is voluminous. Citations are collected at *id.* at 281-82 n.1. See also *id.* at 281-87.

[213] In Zambia, two copper-mining firms produce a major proportion of Zambia's foreign exchange earnings and are her largest employers. Their pricing policies thus necessarily embody major decisions concerning the public welfare. Yet those decisions are, naturally, taken with a view towards maximization of profit.

c. Labor Law

A second area raising difficult policy questions is that of labor law. The African worker is peculiarly ill-equipped to bargain with his employer as an individual, but he is also peculiarly difficult to organize into trade unions. Many Africans are migratory laborers, some are seasonal workers. Both of these groups are notoriously the most difficult to organize.[214]

Literacy is not common, and it is difficult to organize workers without sufficient literacy at least to keep books.[215] The worker has little understanding of trade unions. Consequently, many African unions are poorly led and as poorly supported. Many workers are wholly ignorant of their rights.[216]

In addition, there are specific problems concerning the labor market. In West Africa, the marked predominance of government employment tends to make the government the leader in setting wages.[217] In the Rhodesias, there were special problems arising from the existence of unions organized on racial lines, with the white unions having as one of their chief goals the protection of "European" jobs and "European" rates against African penetration.[218]

It was upon this background that the colonial office imposed a set of labor laws basically modeled upon those obtaining in the United Kingdom. The provisions of the Colonial Development and Welfare Acts after 1940 required the Secretary of State for the Colonies to satisfy himself, before paying for the execution of any works, that the law of the territory concerned contained reasonable provisions for the establishment of trade unions.[219] In an important departure from the English model, which was otherwise followed, the laws imposed an additional requirement that all trade unions had to register before being permitted to perform their functions.[220]

Whatever the sufficiency of the received labor law to solve industrial tensions in pre-independence Africa, the demands of development raise yet another issue to bedevil the problem. However poorly organized by the standards of English or American

214 See INTERNATIONAL LABOUR ORGANISATION, SURVEY OF AFRICAN LABOUR 217-18 (1958) [International Labour Organisation will hereinafter be referred to as ILO]; Moore, The Adaptation of African Labour Systems to Social Change, in ECONOMIC TRANSITION IN AFRICA 277, 281-85 (Herskovits & Harwitz ed. 1964).
215 Cf. ROPER, LABOUR PROBLEMS IN WEST AFRICA 105 (1958).
216 YESUFU, AN INTRODUCTION TO INDUSTRIAL RELATIONS IN NIGERIA 158 (1962).
217 ROPER, op. cit. supra note 215, at 92-94.
218 See HAILEY, AN AFRICAN SURVEY REVISED 1439 (1957).
219 ILO, op. cit. supra note 214, at 223.
220 YESUFU, op. cit. supra note 216, at 223.

trade unions, the organized African worker is in a far stronger
position to protect his economic position than are the mass of poor
farmers or the unorganized workers. Since government is the
chief employer, higher wages for the organized workers will be
gained at the expense of the development program.[221] In Ghana
and Tanzania, this has led to the paradox of serious strife between
governments with expressly socialist orientations and the trade
union movement.[222]

d. Business "affected with a public interest"

While market forces were manipulated under the colonial regimes
in ways that may not now be acceptable, many colonies were
notably lacking in controls over businesses—especially those "affected with a public interest"—that are common in the United
States and England. They were imposed in England by statutes
that were either adopted after the reception of English law or
that were not comprehended within the term "statutes of general
application." As a result, there were fewer controls on many business institutions in the colonies than there were in England. Tanzania as late as 1959 had no banking statute; Ghana still does not
have one. Tanzania (again as of 1959) had no statute limiting the
activities of insurance companies. Ghana enacted a temporary
Insurance Act in 1962[223] but had to wait until 1965 for a statute
that reasonably approximated a modern one.[224] Zambia, in 1964,
had an insurance ordinance consisting of four paragraphs.[225] There
was no provision for an insurance commissioner, no provision for
regulation of premiums, no provision for standard clauses in policies, and no provision to assure the financial stability of insurance
companies. Reform of the law in these areas deserves examination in all the independent states.

e. Torts

A word must also be said of the problem of tort law. In nineteenth-century England, with an economy dominated by independent, "free" entrepreneurial units, the law of contract regulated
the consensual relationships between them. Not infrequently,
however, these "free" entrepreneurial units interfered with the
interests of each other or of the general public. The law of torts
responded to the disputes that arose.

The shape taken by the law of torts was the result of multifarious historical circumstances—the dead hand of antique forms

221 See Roberts, *A Socialist Looks at African Socialism*, in AFRICAN SO-
CIALISM 89, 90 (Friedland & Rosberg ed. 1964).
222 AUSTIN, POLITICS IN GHANA 1946-60, at 400-01 (1964).
223 Insurance (Temporary Provision) Act, 1962, Pub. Act 111 (Ghana).
224 Insurance Act, 1965, Pub. Act 288 (Ghana).
225 LAWS OF ZAMBIA, Cap. 201 (1964).

of action, the sorts of cases that the common-law judges were called upon to decide, or perhaps (if we follow the more extreme legal realists) what the judges ate for breakfast. Underneath, however, was a profound policy judgment, stated characteristically by Justice Holmes:

> A man need not, it is true, do this or that act—the term *act* implies a choice—but he must act somehow. Furthermore, the public generally profits by individual activity. As action cannot be avoided, and tends to the public good, there is obviously no policy in throwing the hazard of what is desirable and inevitable upon the actor.[226]

As a result of this policy decision, the law of torts in the main came to hold that the actor was not responsible for injury to another unless he acted negligently or intentionally.[227] As a result, many of the losses inevitably arising in the course of industrial development were cast, not on the entrepreneur, but upon the innocent victim.

The same rule of the common law controls the law in Africa today. If the central thrust of development is to be placed upon the state, rather than upon private economic activity, perhaps some alternate rule would be desirable. Absolute liability in the actor is a conceivable jural postulate to govern tort claims; universal insurance by the state is an alternative solution. Whether the law of torts in its received form is functional to development raises much the same policy choice that must be made in other areas of conflict between claims raised under the jural postulate of contract and those that imply plan as their major theme.

f. Capital Formation and Investment Decisions

The El Dorado of takeoff requires that disposable surplus be reinvested in the economy in areas most useful to generating productive investment. Those who assert claims and demands under the system of received English law would let market forces determine the amount and location of such investment. On the other hand, those who assert demands under a system of planning would have some or all of these decisions made centrally by government.[228] Again, a sharp policy issue is framed for the law to resolve.

---

[226] HOLMES, THE COMMON LAW 95 (1881). See also FRIEDMANN, LAW IN A CHANGING SOCIETY 127 (1959).

[227] There are many exceptions, of course. The entire law of workmen's compensation has developed in reaction to the principal rule; and, as Friedmann points out, many of these inroads upon the principle of fault have developed as a result of the "growing emphasis on the responsibility of the community for the accidents that befall the individual." *Ibid.*

[228] *Introduction* to AFRICAN SOCIALISM 5-6 (Friedland & Rosberg ed. 1964). Dr. Okigbo puts it with restraint: "Where the bulk of the population heavily discount the future in favour of the present, attempts by

A special set of devices to foster a proper reinvestment of surplus by foreign investors has been frequently employed. A stated minimum proportion of profits is sometimes required to be reinvested; sometimes a high surtax is imposed on exported profits beyond a stated minimum. Limitations upon the repatriation of capital have been urged. Exchange restrictions frequently achieve the same end, although they may be imposed to use limited foreign exchange for development or even to prevent the flight of domestic capital. Screening devices of various sorts have been employed in an effort to direct new foreign capital into areas of production acceptable to the planners.[229] The received law of African states did not contain provisions of these sorts. They have all been devised since independence by those states that have adopted them.

A second set of devices has been used in some states to capture surpluses of domestic private enterprise or to direct their investment. The principal examples are the marketing boards in West Africa, whose surpluses have been used extensively to finance development. The same result could be attained (assuming sufficiently competent personnel to make it effective) through a proper income taxation scheme. In underdeveloped states, private domestic risk capital traditionally tends to be invested in luxury real estate. If the interests asserted in the name of development and planning are to be given priority, devices must be employed to direct these surpluses into industrial or agricultural development rather than into speculation.

A third set of devices for the direction of investment is frequently found in the control of credit. Ghana, for example, made some effort to limit the extension of credit, even by private bankers, by requiring lenders to favor certain areas of investment over others.

Finally, a problem analogous to the question of the use of state power to compel capital formation in the private sector and to direct its deployment is that of Africanization. Many states require as a condition of entry that foreign enterprise employ stated percentages of indigenous citizens at various levels of employment.[230] This, too, is a *pro tanto* structuring of the labor market in the interests of planned development.

In all of these areas, the received colonial law was all but completely mute. To continue the law as received effectively makes a

public authorities to raise investment to the rate warranted by the target rate of growth of income are bound to interfere seriously with the autonomy of the individual." Okigbo, *Independence and the Problem of Economic Growth,* in ECONOMIC TRANSITION IN AFRICA 323 (Herskovits & Harwitz ed. 1964).

229 See generally NWOGUGU, THE LEGAL PROBLEMS OF FOREIGN INVESTMENT IN DEVELOPING COUNTRIES 9-33 (1965); PROEHL, FOREIGN ENTERPRISE IN NIGERIA *passim* (1965).

230 NWOGUGU, *op. cit. supra* note 229, at 12.

policy determination in each case favoring the sets of claims made
under the rubric of contract against those claiming under the
heading of plan.

g. Taxation

The tax structures of all the former British colonies are identical
in general outline. In each there is an income tax modeled
originally upon the Colonial Model Income Tax Ordinance, prepared in 1922 by an interdepartmental committee in the United
Kingdom for use in those "colonies not possessing responsible government."[231]   There is also a personal tax, usually a flat rate.
These taxes were originally hut taxes or poll taxes designed primarily to coerce Africans out of the subsistence economy into
European employment.[232]   Indirect taxes and export duties usually
play a much larger role in public finance than they do in most
developed countries. For example, in 1962 Ghana obtained only
fifteen percent of its tax revenue from direct taxes but eighty-five
percent from import duties and indirect taxes.[233]

Land taxation is a relatively underemployed system of taxation
throughout Africa. Its employment seems to be largely a function of clarity of title. In Ghana, for example, where urban land
titles are frequently obscure, only buildings are taxed. In East Africa, where the urban areas were mainly created by Europeans using
European methods of land registration to protect their titles, the
reverse is true: only the land is taxed.[234]

Each of these taxes in its received form is subject to specific
technical criticisms. Developing countries "have critical fiscal
problems in the old-fashioned sense; they need taxes which illiterate subjects can understand, administrative assessment and collection methods within the capacity of their administrations to manage, honesty and efficiency in handling of the revenues, full accountability for all persons concerned . . . ."[235]   In 1961, Ghana
abandoned the traditional British deductions against income in
favor of a single consolidated allowance in order to simplify administration. Such technical adjustments do not raise serious
policy issues. Amendments to the British model based upon empirical studies would not raise serious policy issues either. The
empirical studies would have to relate tax problems to African
conditions: For example, how can an income tax be administered

---

[231] Due, Taxation and Economic Development in Tropical Africa 32
(1963).
[232] See Douglas, supra note 210, at 399 n.10; Moore, op. cit. supra note
214, at 281.
[233] Due, op. cit. supra note 231, at 26.
[234] Id. at 103, 110.
[235] Sawer, Taxation in a Federation, in Federalism and the New Nations of Africa 261 (Currie ed. 1964).

when some of the individuals subject to it are illiterate, when many do not keep account books, and when only a few use checkbooks?[236]

Ghana's new Estate Duty Tax of 1965, is an instructive example of slavish devotion to English models since it was a rather hit-and-miss copy of the English estate duty. Aside from the question of the utility of copying a taxing act that only an odd English lawyer would defend even in England, the statute makes no provision for the taxability of family-owned property on the death of the occupier. Since much, if not most, of the property that passes at death in Ghana is property of this sort, the reach of the statute on its face seems very limited indeed.[237]

But taxing policy raises the familiar conflict between the jural postulates supporting the notion of private incentive as the main source of movement in the economy and those supporting plan. Professor Due has outlined four functions that the tax system of a developing country may be expected to accomplish:

1. Curtailing consumption and thus freeing resources for governmental services or capital formation.
2. Reallocating resources from investments regarded as having little beneficial effect upon development (e.g., office buildings) to those of greater benefit for growth.
3. Providing a flow of funds into government hands to facilitate the transfer of resources.
4. Providing incentive to economic behaviour in such a way as to facilitate economic growth, such as providing added incentive to save, to enter the market sector, to work longer periods, to undertake private-sector capital formation.[238]

There is a patent tension between the first three (which imply that government has a responsibility to direct the rate of capital formation and the area of investment) and the last (which leaves investment decisions about time-choice in capital formation and about specific areas of investment to market forces).

Real property tax offers the best source of new tax revenue in Africa.[239] Levies based upon its valuation offer the fewest disin-

---

[236] Ghana has made an attempt at solving this problem by the use of a standard assessment on certain categories of taxpayers. The taxpayer can then claim a rebate by proving his actual income to have warranted a lesser tax. Just before the February coup, the Minister of Finance proposed legislation to require all traders and retailers to pay for purchases in excess of £50 from wholesalers or importers with certified checks or bankers' drafts and to keep proper records. 1966 Budget Statement ¶ 137 (Ghana).

[237] Park, *Ghana, The Estate Duty Tax, 1965*, 9 J. AFRICAN L. 162 (1965).

[238] DUE, *op. cit. supra* note 231, at 146. See also Kaldor, *When Will Developing Countries Learn to Tax?*, 41 FOREIGN AFFAIRS 410 (1963).

[239] See Groves, Book Review, 1966 WIS. L. REV. 1269. See generally DUE, *op. cit. supra* note 231; Kaldor, *supra* note 238.

centives to enterprise, and, if the tax is related to land value, actually offer an incentive to improve the property. Yet insofar as these taxes cannot be levied for want of clarity of title, tax policy would seem to require much the same sort of clarification of titles under customary law as is demanded by agricultural policy itself.

h. Guarantees to Private Investors

Taxing policy clearly threatens the private sector with policies designed to match the jural postulates of plan. This threat is so important that various methods are required to guarantee private investors—especially foreign private investors—against too great an invasion of the market economy. The problems raised by such laws have been extensively examined elsewhere.[240] We need only note here that they were not included in the received law and that even today there are some African countries without investment guarantee acts.

2. THE EXCLUSION OF THE PRIVATE SECTOR

The use of all these techniques—and a host of others—requires policy decisions from the lawmakers. But, assuming that the law-makers propose to keep a private sector in existence in the areas affected, the decision is largely controlled by a pragmatic consideration: How far can private enterprise be controlled by fiscal and other policies before the incentives to private business are so far eviscerated that private capital will simply no longer be invested? In that sense, the advocates of increased public control over the private sector are engaged in a process of haggling with private business.

There are some sectors of the economy that the advocates of plan frequently assert must be entirely within the public sector. Whatever the areas selected, however, new institutions must be created by law to carry out the assigned functions. A number of states have instituted a central bank; Ghana has introduced a state commercial bank as well. Agricultural banks and similar institutions for the extension of agricultural credit are frequent. State marketing boards to monopolize internal wholesale distribution of certain commodities as well as to control the export trade in major foreign-exchange earners are relatively widespread. Railroads, communication networks and some public utilities were in the public sector everywhere, in colonial days. Heavy industry, to a great extent, is in the public sector today. Even light industry and plantation crops have been undertaken in the public sector.

Monopolization of any segment of the economy by public en-

---

240 See FATOUROS, GOVERNMENT GUARANTEES TO PRIVATE INVESTORS *passim* (1962); NWOGUGU, *op. cit. supra* note 229 *passim*.

terprise is a policy decision of overwhelming importance. While this article will not discuss it in detail, two observations can be made. In the first place, the policy determination of the extent to which public enterprise will engulf the economy is analytically distinct from the issue of creating an adequate legal climate for planning, whatever its scope and extent. The latter is a mediate decision[241] required to ensure a fine hone to the legal tools of planning, whatever the uses to which they may be put. The former requires a major policy determination. Too often, however, opponents of the planning process oppose the mediate decision, not on grounds truly relevant to that decision, but because they fear coming to grips with the larger issue of the ultimate reach of governmental control of the economy—the "creeping socialism" argument.[242] Yet, surely these are distinct issues. So long as there is to be any planning, a rational legal environment for it is desirable, whatever its scope.

Secondly, it is a truism to assert that to do nothing is itself to make a decision. The colonial governments did not structure the economy in aid of the claims, demands, and interests today subsumed under the heading of development. The received law largely reflects only those interests asserted under customary law and those presupposing contract as their jural postulate. To do nothing thus makes the great choice in African law by inaction.

D. Summary

Four central points of conflict between the various sets of claims, demands, and interests that seek satisfaction from the legal order, and their supporting jural postulates, may be identified. First, the rule of internal conflicts requires examination. Second, customary land law is, in any case, inadequate in its present form; the direction of change, however, requires a fundamental policy determination. Third, the extent of the control of the plan over the private sector raises important policy issues. Finally, the extent to which public enterprise will preempt any particular area of the economy must be decided. For a lawyer, these issues all raise fundamental questions of justice. Their determination requires the explicit acceptance of one set of jural postulates and the *pro tanto* rejection of an alternate set.

Whatever determination is made about these issues, plainly the several legal orders of Africa are necessarily in the midst of a vigorous transformation blown up by the winds of change. The function of law in part is to carry out the social engineering required to

---

[241] See Harvey, *The Challenge of the Rule of Law*, 59 MICH. L. REV. 603, 606 (1961): "[L]aw is a tool, a technique. It can be deemed good or bad by this amoral test of utility, or appropriateness to whatever end may be postulated, to which the law is merely a means."

[242] HANSON, *op. cit. supra* note 211, at 185-86.

solve the manifold problems thus raised. But it is also the function of law to provide relative stability to the individual during this period. How satisfactory is the law in Africa to fulfill that function?

VII. THE MAINTENANCE OF LEGALITY

Development cannot proceed save in a reasonably stable political and legal environment. Private capital will not invest in a country whose legal order does not possess a high degree of predictability. The public sector cannot advance unless long-range planning can be made effective, and effective long-range planning requires the same degree of predictability as does the private sector. The demand for legality is common to all the various sets of claims made.

The conditions of political stability are functions of constitutional arrangements. Therefore, a complete discussion of the received law for development properly requires a discussion of the extent to which the received Westminster model was apt to achieve political stability. However, the focus will be on a more limited issue—that of legality. It will be examined under two headings: the sufficiency of the norms controlling the actions of administrators, and the institutional devices purporting to guarantee the effectiveness of the norms. Finally, certain areas to which constitutional arrangements ought to address themselves if the various claims and demands that relate to development are to be sufficiently met will be suggested.

A. The Norms of Constitutional and Administrative Law

1. ADMINISTRATIVE LAW

The minimum requirement of the "rule of law"—no matter how defined—is that state power only be applied pursuant to a rule. The very nature of a rule in this sense is that it gives some advance notice of the way in which state power will be used on a given occasion.[243]

Dicey[244] and his modern follower, Hayek,[245] assert that the necessary implication of this obvious proposition is that discretion of any sort is the negation of the rule of law. Since planning requires many discretionary acts by administrators, Hayek concludes that planning is necessarily inconsistent with the rule of law. If that be so, then the Declaration of New Delhi[246] states an impossible contradiction, for its substantive goals could not be attained without violating its adjectival propositions. Without some scope

---

243 Cf. HART, op. cit. supra note 209, at 121.
244 DICEY, THE LAW AND THE CONSTITUTION (1885).
245 HAYEK, THE ROAD TO SERFDOM (1944). The issue is discussed in Harvey, The Rule of Law in Historical Perspective, 59 MICH. L. REV. 487, 492 (1961).
246 See text accompanying note 1 supra.

for discretion, development may well grind to a bureaucratic halt. At the other extreme, if state power is to be applied on an *ad hoc* basis, there can be no sense of stability in the society.[247]

The resolution of the contradiction must lie in requiring that every grant of discretion to administrators be limited by supplying them with some standards for decision, some statement of purpose, or some operative facts that must exist before the discretion can be exercised.[248] The administrators must then be required to observe those standards in making their decisions. English-speaking Africa still looks to English norms of administrative law to solve this problem. These norms were forged in a country without a written constitution, a country in which Parliamentary supremacy was absolute, and a country in which the administration was nominally an arm of Parliament. Moreover, for reasons peculiar to England, they arose in a country that places great reliance upon the probity of its civil servants. Finally, they were developed in a society in which the state's economic function was relatively limited.

As a result of these historical antecedents, English administrative law—to American eyes[249]—contains relatively few norms of administrative behavior. Absolute Parliamentary supremacy implies that administrative officers are frequently granted completely unrestricted power over the subject matter, without any rule or guide to provide boundaries for discretion. It is extremely difficult, although not altogether impossible, to challenge an administrative decision on the ground that it is motivated by reasons not related to the grant.[250] In the common law, there is no requirement that administrative officers give the reasons for their decisions, thus making it dubious that an appeal can succeed, save on the vague grounds of "unreasonableness."[251] Since Parliament has the power to delegate authority as it chooses, there may be no requirement for hearings or for other procedural protections. The common-law invocation of natural justice as a requirement has suffered from serious erosions, so that today it is prob-

---

[247] This appears to have been the issue that has determined the development of Soviet jurisprudence. See generally BERMAN, JUSTICE IN THE U.S.S.R. (rev. ed. 1963); HAZARD & SHAPIRO, THE SOVIET LEGAL SYSTEM—POST-STALIN DOCUMENTATION AND HISTORICAL COMMENTARY (1962).

[248] This is the result reached in the United States. See, *e.g.*, SCHWARTZ, AN INTRODUCTION TO AMERICAN ADMINISTRATIVE LAW 33-34 (2d ed. 1962).

[249] SCHWARTZ, AMERICAN ADMINISTRATIVE LAW 114-15 (1950).

[250] See GRIFFITH & STREET, PRINCIPLES OF ADMINISTRATIVE LAW 230-34 (1952).

[251] *Id.* at 234. See Associated Provincial Picture Theatres Ltd. v. Wednesbury Corp., [1948] 1 K.B. 223, 234; Roberts v. Hopwood, [1925] A.C. 578; Prescott v. Birmingham Corp., [1955] Ch. 210. The Franks Committee in England recommended that all administrative tribunals be required to give "reasoned decisions" as an essential reform. COMMITTEE ON ADMINISTRATIVE TRIBUNALS AND ENQUIRIES, REPORT, Cmnd. 218 ¶ 98 (1958).

ably possible in English law to withdraw a license without a hearing.[252]

One may question whether the preconditions that made English administrative law what it is today obtain in the independent African states. All have written constitutions—or did until the recent wave of *coups d'etat*. In none is there absolute parliamentary supremacy; indeed, the very existence of a written constitution usually implies that there are certain areas beyond parliamentary competence. In none are there the same traditions of rectitude in public life as exist in England. Finally, the state's role in the economy is very great, so the importance of administrative norms is correspondingly large. Nevertheless, English administrative law remains the principal body of norms for English-speaking Africa.[253] For example, despite a constitutional requirement that there be a hearing "in the determination of his civil rights and obligations,"[254] the Nigerian Supreme Court held valid a statute that authorized a minister to withdraw a bank's license to do business without holding a hearing. The right to do business is a "privilege" and not a right[255]—a classical example of the jurisprudence of concepts in action. The use of the formula that administrative action cannot be challenged where the minister is "satisfied" that action ought to be taken has effectively barred judicial review.[256]

The result of adhering exclusively to English administrative law decisions in English-speaking Africa has been to place administrators in the same position in which they are in England. Completely unrestricted grants of discretion are frequently made and seem beyond effective challenge. Statutes, by their terms, more frequently than not bar any judicial or administrative review. In particular disputes, there is no requirement for a hearing, and, if held, there are no detailed rules concerning its content. In formulating delegated legislation, there are also no requirements for public hearings or even consultation of interested parties. If there are to be some reasonable norms for administrative behavior in Africa, the formulation of codes of administrative law is desirable. But such codes are not self-enforcing; without institutional devices to support them, they become meaningless.

---

[252] Nakkudi Ali v. Jayarane, [1951] A.C. 66 (Ceylon); The Queen v. Metropolitan Police Comm'r, [1953] 1 WEEKLY L.R. 1150.

[253] See McAuslan, *Administrative Law in Kenya—A General Survey*, in EAST AFRICAN LAW TODAY, 5 COMMONWEALTH LAW SERIES 23, 55-65 (1965); Seidman, *Constitutional Standards of the Judicial Review of Administrative Action in Nigeria*, 2 NIGERIAN L.J. 232 (1965).

[254] CONST., FED. REP. NIGERIA § 22(1).

[255] Merchants Bank Ltd. v. Federal Minister of Fin., [1961] 1 All N.L.R. 598.

[256] See McAuslan, *op. cit. supra* note 253, at 59; Seidman, *supra* note 253, at 248.

2. THE ENFORCEMENT OF THE REGIME OF LEGALITY

If the tone of public life is sufficiently honest and fair-minded, formal norms are relatively unneeded. That is not the position in Africa; on the contrary, there is a notable lack of restraints upon the exercise of state power. This betrays itself most blatantly in the widespread corruption that seems to exist, especially in West Africa.[257] When corruption permeates the entire fabric of government, legality is the first sufferer, for state power is exercised on grounds unrelated to its nominal purposes.

In English-speaking Africa, the devices for the enforcement of the few standards of administrative probity that exist are in the common-law tradition. In some cases there are internal administrative appeals. Resort to the courts for relief is theoretically available if an ascertainable norm has been violated. Relief can be sought in a civil action brought by the individual affected by an administrative decision, or, in the extreme cases, in a criminal action brought by the director of public prosecutions.

The civil remedies for administrative wrongdoing thus depend upon the action of individual citizens. In such an action, the individual is pitted against the state—always an unequal contest. The individual does not have even the few procedural devices that the common law imports into criminal actions to try to redress the balance. At his own expense, he must challenge the vast panoply of state power, with all its resources in personnel, money, and legal talent, by a civil action for a declaratory judgment or for an extraordinary remedy—injunction, writ of mandamus, or writ of prohibition. Aside from the manifold technical insufficiencies of these forms of action,[258] the financial impediments to such an action are staggering. As a result of these impediments, in the United States, where almost the sole institutional protection against administrative error or arbitrariness is such an action, usually only great corporations or individuals who are supported by large voluntary associations have been able to carry through litigation. To rely upon such individual actions as the primary means of policing administrative action in Africa is to rely upon what is nonexistent.

The criminal action against fraudulent public officers in Africa is an equally weak reed. Even in the United States it is notoriously difficult to persuade the majority party to prosecute itself or its representatives; the great exposures of government corruption invariably come from the opposition. In Africa, where opposition parties are either weak or nonexistent, it is plainly bootless to

---

[257] On corruption generally, see WRAITH & SIMPKIN, CORRUPTION IN DEVELOPING COUNTRIES *passim* (1963). See also Ley, *What is the Problem about Corruption?*, 3 J. MODERN AFRICAN STUDIES 45 (1965).

[258] GARNER, ADMINISTRATIVE LAW 140-42, 152 (1963); WADE, ADMINISTRATIVE LAW 81 (1961).

think that the ruling party will expose its own corruption. In a very rare demonstration of independence, Nigerian newspapers attacked Minister of Aviation Mbadiwe for a peculiarly corrupt transaction. He was never prosecuted. Instead, Prime Minister Balewa permitted him to retain his ministerial post but made him return the plot of land at issue to the government. In Ghana, when the Commission of Enquiry into Trade Malpractices reported fraud and profiteering by high government and party officials, the report was rewritten by a committee of the cabinet before it was released to the public.

Although exhortations for honesty and integrity in public life have their place, no sufficient attack upon the manifold violations of legality in Africa will succeed unless there are institutional devices to remove the causes of corruption and to police the norms. One central cause of corruption has been the need for party financing. In Ghana, this was institutionalized. NADECO, a corporation whose shares were apparently wholly held by President Nkrumah, was set up with the main function of collecting "commissions" on all public contracts. Nominally the commissions were to be used to finance the party. Without any sanction in law, the entire operation was run with cloak-and-dagger secrecy. There can be no doubt that vast sums of this illegally garnered money did not reach the party and was siphoned into private pockets. In Nigeria, and especially in the western region, much the same procedure apparently obtained.

It is not enough simply to assert that such devices for obtaining party funds be stopped. Political parties in Africa cannot be expected to find adequate finances in voluntary contributions; the great masses of the population do not have the cash. If the sole support for the party were to come from the moneyed elite, the party programs would be warped in their favor even more than they already are. Moreover, in the one-party states of Africa, the governing party assumes a quasi-public role. In Nkrumah's Ghana and Nyerere's Tanzania, the party has (or had) formal constitutional status. In other countries, such as the individual regions of Nigeria before the coup and Kenya before the recent split in the Kenya African National Union, it had *de facto* governmental status. Yet the received law treats political parties as private voluntary associations. As a result, there are no provisions for governmental financial support. Thus, they have been forced to use governmental power illegally to acquire necessary financial sinews. The resulting corruption has been a pervasive poison in public life. Some reasonable device for financing and policing the fiscal affairs of political parties would make a long stride towards removing one source of corruption.

A second source of corruption arises out of the very fact of state intervention into the economy. Many of the activities of the state require it to contract with private business. The sums involved are large, the opportunity for cheating enormous, the incentives for corruption overwhelming. The same problem has been faced elsewhere. Government contracts are a familiar point of corruption in the United States. The problem has mainly been attacked in terms of regulations for contract procurement, open bidding, renegotiation in case of excess profits, and the like. To the extent that institutions can be devised to regularize contract procedures between government and private enterprise in Africa, a potent source of corruption might, to a degree, be eliminated.

Finally, it is useless to expect private individuals to police the corridors of power. Elsewhere, institutional devices have been invoked to do so: The *ombudsman* in Scandanavia, New Zealand, and other places; state procurators in the socialist countries; the *Conseil d'Etat* in France. Some analogous institution, fashioned to the African requirements, might prove useful.[259] Tanzania has included in her new interim constitution a Permanent Committee on Enquiries.[260] Suggestions have been made in Ghana that the new constitution should contain a similar provision.

Corruption and illegality are not unknown outside Africa. Government financing of political parties, regularized contract procedures, and *ombudsmen* will not create the millennium. But they might help.

B. Constitutional Arrangements

This analysis of the plural nature of the claims, interests, and demands that struggle for recognition in African law and of the several systems of value-acceptances which they imply suggests four principal issues to which constitutional arrangements ought to address themselves.

In the first place, if the legal order is to be responsive to the interests and values of the population, there must be adequate devices for the articulation of the claims, demands, interests, and values held by the population. The Westminster model meets this requirement on paper by a popularly elected Parliament. That a one-party state has evolved *de facto* or *de jure* in most African societies is an indication of a felt insufficiency in Western-style elections. Whether party or other institution, some surrogate must be found to act as a conduit of popular demand. But a solution cannot be found by contemplation of nineteenth-century constitutional models only. There must be an examination of the facts of African life in the light of the problem posed. One may well doubt that the requirements of a continent whose peoples make strident demands for the transformation required in the

[259] See the exchange of correspondence concerning the desirability of an ombudsman for African states: Sargeant, 1964 J. AFRICAN L. 195; Mittlebeeler, 1965 J. AFRICAN L. 184.

[260] INTERIM CONST., TANZANIA, 1965, cap. VI.

twentieth century, but who are largely incapable of communicating them through press or radio, can be met by a mechanical insistence upon bills of rights and classical concepts of freedom of speech and press as the sole guarantee that popular claims will be articulated.

Secondly, the constitution ought to address itself to the problems of African governments, not the problems that were pressing governments of England in the nineteenth century. England then was concerned with problems of representation, police, army, taxation, judiciary, and the civil service. Most constitutions in Africa address themselves to these problems and provide carefully shaped institutional forms to meet them. But not one of the English-speaking African constitutions, so far as one can determine, addresses itself directly to the issues of economic development, although they are by far the most important problems faced by African governments. One hopes that some day the constitutional arrangements of African states will include some detailing of institutions to accomplish the planning function and its implementation.

Thirdly, a principal role of government in Africa must be to maintain legality. One would like to see the constitutions address themselves directly to this issue by providing some institution seised continuously of the problem.

Finally, as we have seen, government must constantly make choices among the pluralistic jural postulates of a pluralistic society. So far as possible, the constitution ought to provide institutions by which a government that makes choices against the interests of the majority of the population could be replaced by measures short of a military coup. However, one cannot be sanguine. The nature of power in countries without deep-seated traditions of peaceful political change is fairly epitomized in the slogan "One Man, One Vote—Once." Whatever devices are designed, these countries ought to consider the problem as it emerges in Africa, not solely in the slogans of textbooks on English or American democracy.

VIII. Conclusion

This brief overview of the sufficiency of the law in independent, English-speaking, sub-Saharan Africa suggests that there are two principal sorts of problems to be faced. The law of the private sector seems adequate on the whole to meet the demands placed upon it, although it needs modernization, codification, and adaptation. The law of the plan is notable by its absence, and the law guaranteeing legality of administrative decisions is remarkable for its insufficiency. To improve these areas of law requires no normative choices; there can hardly be serious disagreement about the necessity for the changes required, although their form is highly controversial. But these are largely technical adjustments. The claims made under the several legal orders conflict at many points. Status, contract, and plan struggle for dominance as the principal jural postulate to determine the order of priority of claims. How can this struggle be resolved?

The pragmatic theory of justice requires that the legislative or judicial authority adopt the jural postulates accepted by "most" of the people. When "most" of the people do hold such postulates in common, the role of the state is merely to assign specific serial numbers to claims, interests, and demands in accordance with them. In such a case, the state is truly impartial. But where a society is so wracked with pluralistic value systems that there is no set of jural postulates commonly held, the choice between the jural postulates is the central policy decision that the state must make. In selecting status, contract, or plan as the central theme for structuring the legal order, those who control the state necessarily make the most important choice between the claims that seek legal support. Absent common value-acceptances, that choice can only be politically determined. The decision made will be one that is agreeable to those pro tempore in control of state power. In Africa the ultimate question—justice—is necessarily a question that will not be answered in the lofty halls of academe or in the writings of philosophers. It will be answered in the messy political wars that today shake the continent. Professor Bretton has said that "especially in the poorer societies of the world, economic development takes place under the general control and supervision of political forces . . . [S]ubstantive and directional choices are made on political grounds, and . . . generally, in the decolonization process, the political 'kingdom' precedes the economic one."[261]

Thus these political wars are not merely sordid arguments of tribes or disputes between placemen for the golden fruits of office. Upon their result depends the fate of the "African Revolution." If the people who control the state leave the law as it was on independence, and in the main as it is today, they will leave the economies and the societies of Africa structured as they were while under the British imperium. That structure did not produce the sort of development that African states assert is their objective.

Law is a value-neutral tool of social ordering. Lawyers alone ought not to make the policy decisions that must be made if the law is to become functional to the demands of development. Law can only discharge its function if the lawmakers make use of all the empirical information that social science can supply about the fact-milieu in which the law must function and about the value-acceptances of the society. Only then can the policy decisions that underlie many, perhaps most, legal choices in Africa (as elsewhere) be

---

[261] BRETTON, POWER AND STABILITY IN NIGERIA 3 (1962).

pragmatically sound. But to avoid making the policy decisions leaves the institutions of Africa as they were at independence. That plainly contradicts the substantive command of the rule of law. Equally plain, it contradicts the historical meaning of the "African Revolution."

LAND LAW IN KENYA

ANN P. MUNRO*

Political realities in the 1960's virtually demand that scholars and national leaders alike be concerned with and understand the interaction of law with the mechanics of social change. In stable societies the complex and variable means by which law acts to give cohesion to a social system often prove difficult of analysis. In new nations struggling to create a national identity and a unified social system, however, the evolution, creation, and function of law and its relation to society stand out with more clarity. This article will discuss one specific example of the interaction of law and society—the development of land law in Kenya.

One of the most complex and serious problems faced by colonial powers in Africa was that of land tenure. For most native Africans land has always formed the matrix of man's existence. In these primarily agricultural areas, land is usually the visible symbol of status in the community. Its protection, perpetuation, and beneficial use provide a family, clan, or tribe with basic cohesion and unity of purpose and the elder, headman, or chief with the sanctions on which his powers rest. Thus, one of the basic administrative decisions of any colonial government was its position on the nature of indigenous land tenure and the desired direction and extent of permissible evolution. These decisions spelled out in many cases the nature of indigenous political development at a later period.

A common decision as to land tenure was to provide separate systems of substantive law for Africans and settlers. In fact, colonialism has placed at least one similar stamp on each of the new African nations, namely the legacy of a pluralistic law and legal system. Two or more legal systems existed side by side during the colonial period, and the degree to which these disparate streams fused prior to independence depended upon the geographical and historical circumstances surrounding the establishment of a colony, the nature of the colonial policy espoused, and the perception of the colonial authorities as to the ultimate goals and purposes of imperial rule. A discussion of the effect of such disparate systems on social change and the developments in Kenya in reaction to this will follow.

I. HISTORICAL PERSPECTIVES: BRITISH POLICY AND AFRICAN LAND LAW

Decisions on the form which land law should take are made within the wider context of the overall goals of a colonial government. It is a historical truism that the goals of most colonial governments, or at least their priorities, have changed as different

---

* B.A., 1954 Wellesley College; M.A., 1960, Columbia University.

pressures have been brought to bear from both inside and outside the colony. Kenya was no exception. The basic aim of the colonial Kenya Government was to establish a political and economic structure in which settlers could retain power through legal and constitutional means. To assure this sort of power structure, a technique had to be found which would counteract African numerical supremacy. By creating reserves and by choosing to deal with Kenya's diverse peoples on a communal rather than an individual basis, the government felt it had found a suitable answer. True, some in the colonial service supported or opposed this policy in the interests of the Africans involved; but the primary concern in Kenya was the European settler, not the native inhabitant. The court structure, substantive law, and colonial land policy of Kenya were fashioned to implement this basic objective.

A. Structure of the Judicial System and Substantive Land Law

Court structure in Kenya has passed through several stages of development, each stage reflecting dominant attitudes in colonial government circles toward the merits of an integrated system of courts for both Africans and Europeans. Policies on court integration have resulted in changes in the direction of substantive land law development.

From the statutory recognition of traditional tribunals in 1897 until 1930, African courts were fully integrated with the main judicial system in that, though Africans and settlers had separate systems of lower courts, there "was a normal avenue of appeal from them to the Magistrates' Courts and the Supreme Court."[1] In 1930, however, the main channel for appeal from lower African courts was switched from judicial personnel to administrative officers. The change in the appeal structure seems to have been a reaction to rather compelling African opinion that too many well-informed judgments given by district commissioners and other authorities at the local level were being overturned in Nairobi on legal technicalities by judges who knew nothing about native law and custom.[2] In traditional society the law

> was not enthroned as an absolute objective standard by which the validity of any decision could be tested; it was simply what the group, acting through its representatives, and constrained by the "weight of custom" decided. An individual could not appeal to "the law" in defence of his "rights"; for it did not guarantee such rights. In many native languages there is no word for "law".[3]

---

[1] Carson, *Further Notes on the African Court System in Kenya*, J. African Admin., Jan. 1958, p. 34.

[2] REPORT OF THE COMMITTEE ON NATIVE LAND TENURE IN KIKUYU PROVINCE 40 (Kenya 1929).

[3] PHILLIPS, REPORT ON NATIVE TRIBUNALS 276 (1945).

In other words, there was a difference in outlook on the nature of justice and the part to be played by the machinery of justice in maintaining social order. The African juridical process was more concerned in bringing a disrupted social situation back to some sort of new equilibrium. It was arbitrational in form and restitutive rather than punitive in motive. Consequently, an administrative officer would, it was believed, have far less trouble in reconciling these variations in his approach than would a European trained in the efficacy of European legal concepts and procedures. Fear of disrupting the entire social organization during a transitional period was thus a factor in the 1930 change to a quasi-integrated court hierarchy.

By 1951 Kenya had a completely dual system of courts and consequently of substantive land laws. The African Courts Ordinance of 1951 institutionalized the separation by creating a fully parallel pattern of courts in Kenya. It specified that African courts should consist of benches of elders appointed by the provincial commissioner concerned and should have jurisdiction only over Africans. The 146 African courts were mainly located in the native lands, although there were urban courts in Nairobi Extra-Provincial District and in each larger township in the more settled areas. In civil matters the African courts administered native customary law, but they also had fairly extensive criminal jurisdiction and were authorized to hear charges under a considerable number of ordinances. The African courts were supervised by administrative—not judicial—officers, the district officer and the provincial commissioner. However, after the late 1950's some central legal control was attempted by Nairobi when the Provincial African Courts Officer and the African Courts Officer for the colony as a whole—who was a member of the Ministry of African Affairs of the Kenyan Government—were given joint jurisdiction with these local officers to revise and transfer cases to other courts. The monthly case review duties of the African Courts Officer provided an automatic appeal on behalf of every convicted African in the colony. Procedures particularly adapted to native law and custom were followed. For example, rules regarding use of a jury and rules of evidence were different than those in traditional English courts. Judgments were made on the basis of traditional African principles of land tenure and use.[4] However, the crucial provision of the

---

[4] Lawyers' rules and an important independent judiciary were foreign to older African methods of adjudication. A decision was either rendered by supernatural means or arbitrated by agreement—the sanctions being "socially approved violence, self-help back[ed] by public opinion, rather than constraint by established authority . . . ." Professor Evans-Pritchard on the Kipsigis, as quoted in Rowlands, *Notes on Native Law and Customs in Kenya*, 6 J. AFRICAN L. 200, 201 (1962). The aim was to balance conflicting claims in order to restore social equilibrium. In modern Africa, ordeals given judicially by a court of African elders are rare, according to Rowlands, *supra*, at 201.

1951 Ordinance was the change in the path of appeal to be described below.

Europeans, instead, used their own system of lower courts whose structure was based on a typical, English derived court system. These subordinate courts were presided over by magistrates, that is, administrative officers of the Government of Kenya who, however, acted in the subordinate courts in their judicial, not their executive or administrative, capacity.

During the colonial period the theoretical apex of the two court systems was the Supreme Court which had full jurisdiction, both civil and criminal, over all persons and all matters in the colony.[5] The Supreme Court and its laws were the ultimate sanctions in Kenya Colony. Appeal from the decisions of this court lay to the Court of Appeal for Eastern Africa and thence to the Privy Council in London.

The 1951 Ordinance made provisions for a new hierarchy of appeal. A case in the first instance between Africans would go to the African court as before. However, here the path changed. African cases now went to an African Appeals Court, then with certain restrictions to the district officer and finally to the Court of Review which was the highest and final appeal in the African court system, and therefore, the highest point of review for most Africans. The Chairman of the Court of Review was a person who had held, but did not then hold, a high judicial office. Thus, unlike Tanganyika where the Central Court of Appeal was at least presided over by a judge of the High Court of Tanganyika, in Kenya, there was an absolute severance between the African courts on the one hand and the Supreme Court and its subordinate courts on the other.

Thus Kenya had a dual court system which created certain conditions under which its two dominant cultural and legal traditions could meet and which also placed certain limitations on the evolution of the subordinate legal system. It is not strange, therefore, that the two very separate systems of substantive law which existed, especially substantive land law, also developed—if at all—on separated paths. In Kenya until 1959, the law which governed land held by Europeans was totally different from that regulating African landholding. For non-Africans the basic territorial land law was the Indian Transfer of Property Act as supplemented by local ordinances, and having its background in the English common law of 1897.[6] This was, in effect, a "colonial" land law which differed

---

5 COLONIAL OFFICE REPORT ON KENYA FOR 1958, at 69 (1959).
6   The enacted law of the Colony consists of Imperial Orders in
    Council relating to the Colony, certain English and Indian Acts ap-
    plied wholly or in part, and Ordinances of the local legislature and
    regulations and rules made thereunder. . . . In all civil and criminal
    cases to which Africans are parties, every court is guided by native
    law so far as it is applicable and is not repugnant to justice and
    morality or inconsistent with any Order in Council, Ordinance, reg-

from, but was ultimately drawn largely from, English law, especially in its provision for individual leasehold or freehold tenure in areas specifically set aside for European occupation.

The basis of Bantu land tenure was that the individual had inheritable rights as a *user* of his arable lands; but with regard to grazing lands, forests, and salt licks, he shared with the clan or tribe the beneficial use of such natural sources of wealth that had come into the possession of the tribe either by conquest or by original occupation.[7] This does not imply individual ownership of fields, nor individual rights to misuse land. Ownership, insofar as there was such a concept, was usually vested in the ancestor spirits who played a very real part in the life of the African and who symbolized his community past, present, and future. Every clan member had the right to claim support from the clan land, either through the "shifting agriculture" based on individual shambas, or among pastoral tribes through the unrestricted individual right to run stock on what was regarded as communal land; but this right was more a preemptive, possessory right than one of property. Sale was normally unthinkable, if not forbidden.

It is important to note also that, even during the time when the courts were integrated rather than parallel, there was a different substantive land law for Africans and for non-Africans. There was no procedure by which an African who so desired could include himself under British oriented land law.[8]

That different communities will have different laws, at least at the beginning of their contacts with each other, is natural. The degree to which they continue to maintain separate traditions is influenced greatly by the nature of the imposed legal structure, including the court hierarchy. And the point of main concern here is the path of appeal. It is the visible manifestation of an answer to the question of whether the colony will have an integrated or a parallel system of courts, with all the resulting implications for the legal and cultural evolution of its people; that is, whether the non-indigenous courts and legal concepts will be superimposed at the

---

ulation or rule made under any Order in Council or Ordinance, and decides all such cases according to substantial justice without undue regard to technicalities or procedure.
Id. at 70.
   [7] HUMPHREY, THE LIGURU AND THE LAND 23 (1947).
   [8]   There is no procedure in British territories whereby an African could make a formal and total renunciation of his original "personal law", so as to bring himself for all purposes within the operation of the general law (*i.e.* non-native law). It is not open to him, by his own act, to accomplish a complete change of legal status corresponding (for example) to *immatriculation* in the Belgian Congo. The most he can do is to manifest his intentions by his mode of life and associations and by the transactions and relationships into which he enters.
Phillips, *The Future of Customary Law in Africa*, in THE FUTURE OF CUSTOMARY LAW IN AFRICA 88, 95-96 (Afrika-Instituut 1956).

top of the system, with open legal channels down to the lowest tribal court, or whether the nonindigenous and indigenous systems will exist side by side in splendid isolation. Clearly an integrated system will foster more direct and immediate changes in the nature of the law administered throughout the entire hierarchy. If one's aim were total legal assimilation, or very consciously directed evolution, some degree of court integration would be sought even though this might mean acute social disorientation at the lower levels in the transitional stages.

It might be argued that the other alternative, parallel structure, with—or as some envisioned, without—ultimate evolution towards integration, is more immediately suitable to the tightly interwoven political-juridical-social African conditions. There may be wisdom in a cautious approach towards integration, but *only if* the framework is expressly stated to be transitional and *if* latitude and direction can be given to the inevitable evolution of the indigenous law in some other way. Without this freedom, the end result will certainly be stagnation of native law. But much more important, juridical chaos will result from the simultaneous pursuit of various policies by different administrative officers and native councils. This will be accompanied by native frustration which arises when actual evolutionary changes in customary land law—often undertaken in emulation of the colonial-introduced legal system—are arbitrarily denied recognition by that same colonial system for fear of the economic and political repercussions. Blocking an evolutionary approach in one field will not insure social stability, for economic, political, and psychological factors cannot all be contained.

Social disintegration is a legitimate concern, but all culture contact gives rise to complex reorientation and reinstitutionalization of norms, and wisdom would seem to lie in providing channels for directed evolution. Tension may and does become very great in the event that seeming racial overtones are added to the continued circumscription of a majority segment of the population by the power of a colonial minority. Thus, the nature of the court structure in Kenya during a crucial period placed the burden for the guidance of native law and custom—especially land law—on the more indirect channels of decisions by subordinate administrative personnel.

The policy of parallel systems in post-World War II Kenya led to frustration and was open to at least two other criticisms. Retention of a parallel legal structure meant that one very effective tool for fashioning an integrated, or even unified multiracial society in Kenya—a clearly desirable as well as forseeable goal—was being neglected by the colonial government. Moreover, such a policy was, at the time, too often used in other parts of Africa to support a colonial or settler disinclination for change. When the African Courts (Amendment) Ordinance No. 50 of 1962 gave effect to the government's latter-day policy of progressively integrating the two parallel court systems in Kenya, the day had already long passed when this technique could have served as an effective instrument for creating a unitary land law or the possibility of a unified country within a colonial framework.*

B. Colonial Land Policy

Throughout most of the period of British colonial control in Kenya, it was Britain's consistent policy not to interfere with or encourage change in customs and manner of native life, unless they were repugnant to Western concepts of justice or morality. The policy on landholding was that native communal or tribal tenure of land should be and could be retained by creating land reserves isolated from all dangers of the effects of white settlement. Indeed, this did prevent agricultural indebtedness by Africans to other races. But such negative security, however well-intentioned, was shortsighted and economically naive. It was sure to prove unsound when the land reserved became inadequate to support the shifting agriculture and growing population and when fragmentation of holdings caused by the traditional inheritance system proved uneconomical.

In reality, British policy in Kenya regarding African rights to lands was rarely well-intentioned. In fact, "if there is one conclusion to be drawn from a study of British policy in Kenya, it is that all policy has been guided and directed by the one aim of establishing a white colony there."[9] The Kenya Government was under extreme pressure from settlers to satisfy their often fluctuating demands. "Settlers did not wish to shut natives in Reserves thus removing them from white contact and from white farms. Neither did they wish to limit their own chance to expand by reserving land for the exclusive use of natives."[10] In addition, there was a "fear of labor shortages for industry, commerce, and European-operated plantations if too many Africans turned to market production,"[11] and thus subsistence agriculture was perpetuated and Africans were prohibited from growing cash crops until late in the colonial period.

Five native reserves were established in 1906,[12] but continued alienations were made with the approval of the Colonial Secretary.[13] Reaction to alienations by the African community was, however, so severe that in 1915 the colonial government issued the Crown Lands Ordinance. Crown lands were to include "all lands reserved

---

* See Appendix A infra.

[9] DILLEY, BRITISH POLICY IN KENYA COLONY 275 (1937).

[10] Id. at 249.

[11] EAST AFRICA ROYAL COMMISSION 1953-1955, REPORT, 65-66 Cmnd. 9475 (1955).

[12] The reserves were the Kikuyu, Masai, Ulu, Kikumbuli, and Kitui.

[13] E.g., European impingement on Kikuyu land in the early 1900's and on land of the Kavirondo tribes in Nyanza Province after the discovery of gold in the 1930's.

for the use of any native tribe."[14]   However, their protection was
naturally subject both to legal manipulation and to the vagaries
of interpretation of the term "Crown Lands."   It was also subject
to the fact that none of the varieties of traditional African tenure
under native law and custom were admitted as a "recognized
private title" of English land law which would have given such
land the protection of colonial law.

In 1939 the Crown Lands were specifically stated to include native
lands by several Orders in Council and were declared to be "set
aside for the benefit of the Native tribes for ever" under the jurisdiction of a Native Lands Trust Board.[15]   At the same time the
Native Lands Trust Ordinance provided for the formal extin-
guishing of all native rights in land outside the boundaries of the
native areas.   This was done despite the findings of the Kenya Land
Commission of 1933 that many Africans living on European-owned
farms had occupied this land long before the farms were allotted
for European settlement.[16]   With only slight amendment in 1944,
these laws defined the status of native land law and custom, the
rubric within which African tenurial concepts were viewed until
1959.

In contrast to its fluctuating policy regarding African land holdings, the British Government's position on the areas reserved for
European settlement was consistent over a long period of time.
As early as 1908 Lord Elgin established government policy in his
administrative rule that as a "manner of administrative convenience" no grants of land in the uplands should be made to Asiatics.[17]
When the reserves were drawn up this restriction was extended
"for convenience" to cover the African population.   For fifty years,
the settlers themselves were generally in agreement on their two
paramount aims: preservation of their land, referred to often as
the "White Highlands"; and maintenance of European political
domination.   By the technique of legal manipulation, the economic
and political levers of power were secured to them until the "wind
of change" began to blow in the middle 1950's.

During the 1950's a number of factors coalesced to create a situation ripe for changes in these policies by the Kenya Government.
The Mau Mau emergency in 1952 precipitated a series of measures
aimed at ameliorating the long-festering land problem.   One of the
roots of Mau Mau was surely native land hunger.   For historical

---

[14] HAILEY, AN AFRICA SURVEY 717 (1957).
[15] Orders in Council of 1938-39: Kenya (Highlands) Order in Council,
1939; Kenya (Native Areas) Order in Council, 1939; Crown Lands (Amendment) Ordinance No. 27 of 1938; Native Lands Trust Ordinance No. 28 of
1938.
[16] REPORT OF THE KENYA LAND COMMISSION, 1933, Cmnd. 4556 (1934). See
also MEEK, LAND LAW AND CUSTOM IN THE COLONIES 87 (1946).
[17] TENURE OF LAND IN THE EAST AFRICAN PROTECTORATE 25, Cmnd. 4117
(1908).

and geographical reasons, the Kikuyu felt these desires most acutely. Indeed it was among the Kikuyu that the most sophisticated changes in customary land law were emerging. A more detailed discussion of the evolution in land tenure practices among the Kikuyu and other tribes will follow this section, but it is clear that many changes had already taken place by 1950 without official recognition by the Kenya Government. These changes constituted a subtle adaption by many Africans to the realities of an authoritarian colonial power structure, an attempt to consolidate their own position in terms that they felt the European would accept.

The Colonial Office had procrastinated on land policy decisions, but Mau Mau made it impossible for the Government to postpone making decisions any longer. In 1954 the Swynnerton five year plan "To Intensify the Development of African Agriculture in Kenya" was submitted by the Assistant Director of Agriculture.[18] The rubric was still one of "tribal" development, but the aim was more revolutionary. The intent was to raise the output, especially in African areas of high potential, by improving farming methods and raising cash crops.[19] This involved tackling one of the basic land problems—fragmentation. Economically, the plan called for recognition and encouragement of the evolution from communal to individual land tenure. Consolidation and registration of landholdings were made the basis for issuing "individual" freehold titles to these new parcels of land. Titles were to be negotiable, creating a new mobility in land transfer and disposition, and obviously also introducing the twin dangers of land alienation to nontribal and nonracial buyers or lessees, and the emergence of a landless class. These changes went hand-in-hand with the institution of modern techniques of farm planning both for mixed farming and predominantly stocking areas to achieve the best economic use of the available land in Kenya.

Recognizing these historical land frustrations and the economic stagnation of the colony as a whole, the Government grasped the opportunity presented by the emergency to force consolidation and registration of lands, especially in the Kikuyu districts of the Central Province and in other areas where voluntary consolidation was slow in making headway.[20]

---

[18] A PLAN TO INTENSIFY THE DEVELOPMENT OF AFRICAN AGRICULTURE IN KENYA (1954).

[19] Hitherto, in most cases African farmers had been prohibited from growing cash crops. With the introduction of coffee and pyrethrum especially, the African was introduced to the vagaries of fluctuating international market prices. Just before independence Kenya acceded to a restrictive coffee quota under an International Coffee Agreement; moreover, the demand for pyrethrum has not lived up to expectations.

[20] The first movement toward land consolidation had come in 1948 from the people themselves, not the government. Under the leadership of their chief, some people in a location of the North Tetu Division of the

While the Swynnerton plan was in its initial stages, the now
famous East Africa Royal Commission[21] was meeting to prepare a
report which, since its publication in 1955, has been both widely
praised and widely tested. One of the really significant colonial
papers in recent times, the Royal Commission Report achieved no-
toriety by its fresh approach to the complex economic problems of
the region, and by its refusal to be bound by the older agricultural
concepts which had notably failed to solve the land dilemma. It
called for a complete economic reorientation. It gave prime importance to a basic alteration of the existing pattern of land tenure
among Africans, to be achieved by gradually breaking down the
stultifying restrictionism that is implicit in a land reservation policy based on racial exclusiveness.

> We think that there is no hope of progress for Kenya
> except by its development as an integrated economic unit.
> By the present policy of exclusive tribal reservations, and
> under the various obligations by treaty agreement and for-
> mal declaration of which we were instructed to take ac-
> count in our deliberations, Kenya in particular has been
> divided up into a number of watertight compartments, none
> of which is or can be made economically self-sufficient, and
> the frustrations of the last twenty years have been largely
> due to the failure to recognize that fact. It is therefore
> that we think it necessary to encourage the breaking down
> of tribal and racial boundaries, and to replace them by
> confirming individual titles to land where they exist and to
> encourage their acquisition where they do not.[22]

Land *need* for subsistence production was no longer to be the
criterion on which claims to land would be entertained. Instead
access to land was to be granted upon the criterion of economic
use.[23] The Commission felt that the rigidities of African tribal
society were, in the last resort, political rigidities; and that this
political authority, where obstructive, should not be allowed to
hamper the fullest possible development of modern economic institutions. Economic rationality demanded policy changes in the legal
basis of political power in Kenya.

Finally in 1959 the colonial Government made its decision. With
Ordinance Nos. 27 and 28 of 1959,[24] the Legislative Council gave the

---

South Nyeri District reallocated their land so that improved organization
and production would be possible. MacArthur, *Land Tenure Reform and
Economic Research into African Farming in Kenya*, 8 EAST AFRICAN ECON.
REV. 80 (1961).

[21] Sir Hugh Dow, Chairman; Sally Herbert Frankel; Arthur Gaitskell;
Rowland S. Hudson; Daniel T. Jack; Frank Sykes; Sir Frederick Seaford;
and Chief Kidah Makwaia.

[22] EAST AFRICA ROYAL COMMISSION 1953-1955, REPORT, 56, Cmnd. 9475
(1955).

[23] *Id.* at 346.

[24] Native Lands Registration Ordinance No. 27 of 1959; Land Control
(Native Lands) Ordinance No. 28 of 1959; Land Titles (Amendment)
Ordinance of 1959.

first official recognition to a process of evolution in African customary land law and usage which had been going on for several
decades. Statutory provision was made for the registration of consolidated landholdings and for the acquisition of individual negotiable titles to such pieces of land. A further move was taken when
on October 13, 1959, the Kenya Government sent to the Legislative
Council a highly controversial proposal to open the "White Highlands" to Asians, Africans, and any others of proved competence
as farmers.

Thus much of economic and legal import happened in Kenya
between 1954 and 1959. The Royal Commission Report played a
pivotal psychological role, bringing in its wake not only the Ordinance Nos. 27 and 28 but also the opening up of the "White Highlands." The political pressures and requisites which had held up
official government sanction for so long had not been able to stifle
the continuous informal acknowledgement in both the African court
structure and British administrative circles of the trend towards
individual land tenure. The perception of legal, economic, social,
and ultimately political rights as within the purview of only group
—communal rather than individual—national concern was fast
crumbling. The economic and legal levers, once inserted, set the
rest of the social fabric aquiver.[25]*

C. Conclusion

Now the political and social implications of these legal-economic
changes had to be faced. When it opted for a policy of creating
land reserves and a "parallel"court structure, with what these implied for Kenyan development, the colonial Government had made
certain implicit, if not explicit, decisions about the desired nature
and basis of political control in the colony. Tinkering with the
economic and legal underpinnings of this land-centered culture
would certainly not be a game played for its own sake. The
stakes were much larger. The 1959 "legalization" of the previously
unrecognized but nonetheless evolving individualization of African
land tenure spelled the breakdown of the reserve system which had
been built around a communal (meaning both group-tribal and
racial) view of legal, cultural, economic, and political relations
among Kenyans of various racial backgrounds. The opening of the
"White Highlands"—symbol of the exclusive white power position—
embodied the core of the revolution that was occurring. In fact
the changes in court structure, when they finally came in 1962, were
little more than a nicety and a British gesture to a tradition of

---

[25] For a more detailed description and analysis of the legal and economic
revolution of 1954-59 and the permissive atmosphere it engendered which
enabled more flexibility in political and constitutional evolution, see Ann
P. Munro, The Land Tenure Revolution in Kenya, 1954-59: Legal and Political Implications (unpublished Masters Essay, Columbia University 1960).
  * See Appendix B infra.

logical constitutional development. That these basic legal and economic changes were made in the late 1950's was evidence of the recognition—by at least some key figures in the Colonial Office and Kenya Colony itself—that further evasion of very basic economic and political changes was probably not possible even under a pretext of legal orthodoxy. The problems facing Kenya today and the range of choices open to it are a product jointly of the British policy just described and of African land law at a particular point in its evolution.

II. THE RESULTS OF BRITISH POLICY: EVOLUTION IMPEDED

A. *Impeding the Development of African Law*

Contrary to some opinion, native law and custom regarding land had not been static. Instead, development towards individual land holding under native law had progressed to varying degrees in different areas. The effect which British legal and economic policy had on the evolution of that law presents a notable study in the interaction of society and the law.

It should be remembered that virtually all actual or potential changes in Kenya's economic, political, social, or legal structure were viewed by the colonial Government within a group framework and evaluated in terms of what effect they might have on the position and power of one community vis-à-vis another. The adoption of the reserve policy in the early twentieth century by the Government signalled its decision to view and deal with the Kenya population on a communal as opposed to an individual basis. This institutionalized racial separation of the European, Asian, and African as well as tribal isolation one from another. The intent was to compartmentalize and thus more easily control any changes in the *status quo*.

By mid-twentieth century, the land situation was complex and chaotic. Impetuses for change in Kenya have been economic and demographic pressures, the blatant disparity between African and European political power, and the indirect and more subtle influence of the native courts and native councils directed along one line or another by the administrative policies of district officers. Historically, the colonial regime had actually done two things at once on the local level: it had, both inadvertently and consciously, introduced individualizing values which weakened traditional communal ties; and, concurrently, restricted the framework for African development to that of native law and custom. Thus it had weakened one base and refused to regularize a new one. No official machinery was empowered to recognize and implement the changes in tenure and usage which had taken place. Nor was any African able to obtain consideration of his particular claims concerning land title or any other matter on the basis of English law.

It is among the Kikuyu that traditional land law evolved farthest
from the concept of group tenure and beneficial usufruct toward
that of individual freehold tenure and irredeemable sale. The
Kikuyu land unit consists of five main districts of the Central Province: Embu; Meru; Fort Hall; Nyeri; and Kiambu. The Kikuyu
tribe itself inhabits the last three districts. And even among the
Kikuyu, those in Kiambu have moved farthest toward individualization and the breakdown of the *githaka* system, the customary system of land tenure. The Kiambu Kikuyu claim to have bought
their land by an irredeemable purchase in a series of transactions,
begun prior to European arrival, from the Ndorobo hunters who
previously inhabited the district.[26] It has been suggested that
this claim, made before two Kenya land commissions, was a deliberate falsification.[27] At stake was the basis of their claim that their
own individually owned land had been alienated by European settlement in the highlands. Under these circumstances they might
well have felt that it was necessary to claim that outright sale of
land was customary in Kiambu because of the Kikuyu purchase
from the Ndorobo. Nonetheless their claim has convinced one
eminent scholar in the field.[28]

Whatever the legal or practical status of land in Kiambu Kikuyu,
all the commissioners could at least agree that individual tenure
was well in sight by 1933, and that it would be neither wise nor
practicable to try and prevent it. But the Kenya Government
failed to take any effective position, and ten years after the Commission met, a district commissioner could still say:

> The idea of private ownership, combined with outright
> sale and purchase of land, has for many years been taking
> shape in the minds of the Kiambu Kikuyu. . . . Hundreds,
> possibly even thousands of acres have changed hands by
> "irredeemable sale" during the past 10—15 years, and most
> of this has gone into the hands of a very few people, includ-
> ing chiefs, tribal elders and the educated minority. . . . Na-
> tive law and custom is not codified, nor is it static, nor is
> there any authority duly empowered to adjust it to chang-
> ing conditions. It purports to be administered by the na-
> tive tribunals, but the judgments of the tribunals have
> never been recorded—merely the effect—and their fre-
> quent departure from the old law has too often passed un-
> noticed.[29]

---

[26] The Kenya Land Commission of 1933 was unconvinced; however, it
did agree that "by a process which consisted partly of alliance and partnership and partly of adoption and absorption, partly of payment, and
largely of force and chicanery," the Kikuyu had already absorbed or dis-
placed the Ndorobo by 1887. REPORT OF THE KENYA LAND COMMISSION, 1933,
at 92-93, Cmnd. 4556 (1933).

[27] LAMBERT, THE SYSTEMS OF LAND TENURE IN THE KIKUYU LAND UNIT
79 (1950).

[28] LEAKEY, MAU MAU AND THE KIKUYU 8 (1952).

[29] PHILLIPS, REPORT ON NATIVE TRIBUNALS 59 (1945).

Private ownership was becoming more common in other native areas, also, under the encouragement of native councils. As we have seen, the position of the local native councils and native tribunals in the evolution of traditional land law was ambivalent. Although the councils did not legally have rule making powers as to land tenure, some did pass resolutions which, despite the governmental refusal to confirm them, were nevertheless accepted as valid and welcomed by the local native tribunals faced with a deluge of land litigation. Many native councils, both in this Kikuyu district and in others, passed resolutions encouraging or recognizing the evolution of land law in the direction of individual tenure and the possibility of outright sale.[30] Regardless of the nonlegal status of such changes, they must be acknowledged as one of the avenues of informal evolution of the law.

Furthermore, the administrative officer in his appellate judicial and less formal supervisory roles effected the shaping of new native law. "Clarifications" were drawn up for the benefit of native tribunals in districts which were flooded with litigation arising from the transfer of land rights.[31] Lacking any central governmental direction, a variety of policies were espoused by district officers throughout the colony as a result of personal preference and inclination. The impact of these informal policy choices did not point in any single direction regarding the evolution of land law.[32]

In one district we see customary law being reshaped by public opinion and powerful interests without either encouragement or hindrance; that is what is happening when there is a purely *laissez-faire* policy, and the result seems invariably to be a trend towards individualism. In another district we find a policy in force which seeks neither to accelerate nor to retard the spontaneous individualistic movement, but which does attempt to guide and regularize it [Nyeri] . . . . In yet another district we see a policy which, whatever its vision of the distant future may be, is based on the deliberate aim of applying a brake to what are regarded as—at the present stage, at any rate—dangerous individualistic tendencies. In each of these cases law is, consciously or unconsciously, being made—whether by tacit acquiescence, by administrative guidance, or by refusal to recognize any departure from the principles of the indigenous system.[33]

---

[30] For specific details see HAILEY, NATIVE ADMINISTRATION IN THE BRITISH AFRICAN TERRITORIES 193, 785 (1950); MEEK, *op. cit. supra* note 16, at 98; PENWILL, KAMBA CUSTOMARY LAW 37 (1951); PHILLIPS, *op. cit. supra* note 3, at 209.

[31] See HAILEY, NATIVE ADMINISTRATION IN THE BRITISH AFRICAN TERRITORIES (1950); PENWILL, KAMBA CUSTOMARY LAW (1951).

[32] For broad coverage of this aspect, see the excellent material in PHILLIPS, REPORT ON NATIVE TRIBUNALS (1945).

[33] *Id.* at 286-87.

Prior to 1959, therefore, customary law had evolved, even in the absence of legal machinery for its recognition, regularization, or control. However, the accretions to African land law, which had become or were becoming established native custom, were in the awkward position of possibly differing from the native custom which official government policy was willing to uphold.

But the evolutionary process was inevitably halted short when its logical implications appeared to challenge the exclusive land basis of European power in the country.[34] It seems reasonable to suggest that pressure from the settlers was one vital facet of the official willingness to allow the evolution in native law and custom to go unrecognized. A significant change in the indigenous communal land pattern would have implications which could lead to a political and psychological, as well as legal and economic, diminution of European power. In effect, African law was not allowed to bring whatever flexibility it possessed into full play. Thus, its effectiveness as a social foundation, perhaps capable of mitigating racial—or at least tribal—land tensions by imperceptible but steady degrees, was never tried.

B. Conclusion

From a study of the development of native land law under the above described conditions, some questions can be answered. It seems clear that the basically European concept of individual freehold tenure met a favorable response among certain African groups for some very specific reasons. The benefits seen to accrue to individual freeholders were constantly before the eyes of Kenya Africans. It seems equally clear that the influence of these legal land patterns did not operate directly through legal channels of the courts and judicial action. Rather it was through a more informal personal administrative medium, especially through the district officer, that the evolution of native law and custom found its recognition. Nonetheless, even here, though the preponderance of administrative encouragement was toward individual tenure, the lack of central authoritative guidance made it possible for some officers to lend their support to a rather static backward-looking form of communal land tenure and use. Whatever the virtues of either approach, the *laissez-faire* governmental attitude led, by the 1950's, to chaos, apprehension, uncertainty, and ill will.

---

34 *E.g.*, though the report of the Kenya Land Commission of 1933 recommended that native custom "should be progressively guided in the direction of private tenure, proceeding through group and the family towards the individual holding," the Kenya Government did not take any effective position at that time on the desirable directon of the evolution of African land law. REPORT OF THE KENYA LAND COMMISSION, 1933, at 420-21 Cmnd. 4556 (1934).

III. PROBLEMS AND CHOICES: LAW IN A MODERN AFRICAN STATE

A. *The Problems Presented*

In most African countries post-colonial legal trends have moved
in the direction of adoption of the imported nonindigenous legal
system. The tendency is to adopt the European law not just in
such fields as commercial and tort law but also eventually—though
at slower speeds it seems—in the less tractable areas of land law,
marriage, and succession.[35] If Kenya should follow this path, it
would not be surprising, given the nature of its pre-independence
authority structure. Perhaps for that very reason, the immediate
post-independence Kenya leaders have chosen to operate within
the framework of nonindigenous law. However, by holding in
abeyance any decision on the role law is to play in their new African nation, the Kenya leaders have obviously not narrowed the
options so as to eliminate the possibility of building on the communal spirit of traditional native law and custom as a way of in-
fusing their version of African socialism with indigenous flavor.

Nonnative land law in Kenya is now a colonial-British-Indian
adaptation of the English common law of 1897. Still operative over
large areas are varieties of native law and custom in various stages
of evolution. Where individual freehold tenure has taken hold
among African farmers, the synthetic statutory Kenya land law is
applicable. But even here, land once registered may still run into
legal snarls concerning property inheritance.[36] Customary land law
remains unwritten save for a number of "guides" for African tribunals and the more recent efforts by lawyers and anthropologists
with the help of "assessors" to assemble and generalize tribal custom into a more "unified" written statement.*

There were Africans in the Kenya Legislative Council in the
late 1950's and there surely are others now who, for various reasons, would like to see British common law excluded from Kenya
and reliance placed on native law and custom. They emphasize its
adaptability to meet social and economic changes. There are others
who feel that land tenure is an area in which change toward non-

---

[35] Certain institutions even in sophisticated areas remain almost un-
touched: the leviratic inheritance of a "brother's" widow, bride-price, polygamy, circumcision, the sharing by sons of a father's inheritance. These
customs were stabilizing in old societies and are attacked last because of
their intimate connection with cultural and social identity. Rowlands, *supra*
note 4, at 200.

[36] The registration procedure as envisaged in 1957-58 is reported as
working well in practice. However, some titles are still registered in the
names of deceased person's, perhaps from unfamiliarity with the new title
procedure but also perhaps tied to the unwillingness of second sons to
report death of the landowner where a "one owner, one farm" policy
would disadvantage them. For details see Homan, *Succession to Registered
Land in the African Areas of Kenya,* J. of Local Admin. Overseas, Jan.
1963, pp. 49-54.

* See Appendix C *infra.*

indigenous patterns might be desirable but not essential. Though native law and custom should not be extended, neither, they argue, should it be excluded unless there is sufficient evidence of a desire for change and adequate preparation to counter inevitable social disruption.[37] As the social order changes, the argument goes, it is important for the law to be sufficiently flexible to adapt to new circumstances and yet retain its cohesiveness, believability, and effectiveness as an efficient instrument for adjudication of disputes and preservation of social equilibrium.[38]

On the other hand it was the consensus of a 1960 conference on African law in London that African customary law should be "rejected as the basis of a general legal system; [because] it would be incapable of application as such, since it is too imprecise, has too many gaps, and is not adaptable for modern commercial matters."[39] Implicit in this argument is the view that private ownership is more efficient than customary tenure in attaining the goal of intensive economic development. The cost in terms of the social disorientation of the peasants is ignored, and could perhaps be vitiated, they say, or even substantially solved in the natural course of economic betterment.

> Such a solution corresponds to the interests of capitalist development. But for the majority of peasants it may lead to dispossession of their land and final ruin. Even the International Bank Mission does not conceal that the transition to private land ownership "raises the risk of excessive indebtedness, eventual concentration of ownership of land in the hands of those who have money to lend, and the creation of a destitute landless class." This course leads to the rapid and deep class differentiation of the peasantry, the emergence of rich farmers, and the conversion of the bulk of the peasantry into landless farm lands.[40]

Recent Ghanaian development provides an interesting and instructive parallel situation.[41] Ghana, too, inherited a pervasive legal dualism from Britain: English derived law coexisted with several varieties of customary tribal law, though the laws were applied in a separate but integrated court system. Since independence, the "old starting presumption of the applicability of customary law has been replaced by a presumption that common law prevails . . .

---

[37] Hannigan, *The Imposition of Western Law Upon Primitive Societies*, in 4 COMPARATIVE STUDIES IN SOCIETY AND HISTORY 1, 7 (1961).

[38] See Fallers, *Customary Law in the New African States*, 27 LAW & CONTEMP. PROB. 605 (1962) for a description of a court case showing the flexibility and effectiveness of modern customary law in Busoga, Uganda, just prior to independence (October 1962).

[39] THE FUTURE OF LAW IN AFRICA 24 (Allott ed. 1960).

[40] Potekhin, *Land Relations in African Countries*, 1 J. MODERN AFRICAN STUDIES 39, 57-58 (1963).

[41] HARVEY, A VALUE ANALYSIS OF GHANAIAN LEGAL DEVELOPMENT SINCE INDEPENDENCE (Gov't Print. Office; Accra, Ghana 1963).

[though this] common law . . . need not be entirely the English law which has been received but may include certain rules of customary origin."[42] These common-law rules have been basically altered as to the "scope of their application and their future treatment in the legal order" in the transition to a national common law. Further, "one of the most persistent value competitions in legal theory and in the practical orientation of a legal order is that between the individual and the community. . . . While the evolving legal order of Ghana is certainly not directed by rampant individualism, it seems quite clear that a shift in favour of individual values has occurred."[43] Harvey characterized the legal developments as of 1963 as "pragmatic", "eclectic", and "peculiarly nondoctrinaire."[44]

Nonetheless, the significance of Ghana's experience is not just in the trend itself, but in the background consideration of her concern with African socialism. For in his address to the First All-African Peoples' Conference in 1958, Kwame Nkrumah said:

> In the vast rural areas of Africa the people hold land in common and work it on the principle of self-help and co-operation. These are the main features still predominating in African society, and we cannot do better than bend them to the requirements of a more modern socialistic pattern of society.[45]

Though Dr. Nkrumah's pronouncements in succeeding years pushed Ghana's socialistic revolution more and more progressively in the direction of "scientific socialism" of the doctrinaire Marxist variety, the body of the law in many areas seems not to have been bent in quite the same manner, but instead has retained some of the common law devotion to individual ownership and to the form—though not always the spirit—of legalized change.

B. The Choice for an African Socialist Kenya

The colonial legacy within which Kenya must solve her present-day problems is a mixed one. Side by side with widespread retention of the customary patterns of communal land holding is an ever-widening agricultural sector dedicated to individual private freehold tenure and the manipulation of land as a more flexible economic asset. In the past, legal, official, and operational measures and restrictions combined with the African shortage of capital to reinforce the dominant position of the European producer and in turn the dominant prestige position of the nonindigenous land use and tenure patterns within the pluralistic legal hierarchy. On economic, if not other, grounds some commentators have criticized latter-day colonial policy for following the recommendations of

---

[42] *Id.* at 13.
[43] *Id.* at 16.
[44] *Id.* at 15, 19.
[45] Quoted in Potekhin, *supra* note 40, at 58.

various commissions to accelerate the process of "individualization
of land rights and registration—thus altering the indigenous system
of tenure in order to encourage foreign capital investment—as the
only solution of economic ills."[46]

Perhaps this path seemed the only way to break down the re-
sistance of the white settlers to change—though to credit this as
the reason for the official decision to encourage private tenure
would seem to be more devious than necessary. The colonial Government was doubtless less interested in coaxing the white settlers
to accede to the inevitable than it was in preserving the status of
nonindigenous land law or improving the economic position of
Kenya. And, indeed, to those who were concerned with the
transfer of power to Africans, it was clear that the ease and smooth-
ness of this inevitable transfer might be closely linked to the extent
to which an African farmer had adopted the central socioeconomic
values and patterns of the expatriate farmer.[47] Here in Kenya, the
role of "modernizers" would fall not just on the members of the
civil service bureaucracy and the professional elite but also on the
growing number of small and also large-scale "advanced" African
farmers.

Thus in making a choice for Kenya, leaders have to reckon with
the existence of two loci of pressures for retention of European-
introduced models. While some of the politically oriented elite may
see value for themselves and for Kenya in preservation of the
British-implanted constitutional models, there is also a slowly growing segment of an agricultural elite which is eager to retain the
prestige and pecuniary rewards accruing to adepts in the new land
tenure and use patterns.

Now an independent Kenya must decide whether the present
"mix" of land law patterns is either acceptable or expedient given
the current state of Kenya-African economic development and especially the pressures for implementation of African socialism and
its elevation to the level of a coherent ideology. Thus a search for
an ideological consensus is often juxtaposed against the need to
deal with Kenyan economic realities. Obviously the African leadership of Kenya is not monolithic, nor is it united in its perception
of national needs. Conflicts will naturally arise from competition
between different segments of the elite for control over the nature
and speed of modernization. There is one group within the ruling
Kenya African National Union (KANU) party, for example, that
is committed to an ideological approach, whether it be pro-socialism
or anti-colonialism. It is not unreasonable to suppose conflict between this group and representatives of the growing African land-

[46] Elias, Government and Politics in Africa 192 (1963).
[47] For an interesting article on political change and modernization, see
Kilson, *African Political Change and the Modernization Process*, 1 J. Modern African Studies 425 (1963).

lord capitalist class eager for the extension of individual tenure
and private property. Indeed, the March 1966 resignation from
KANU of Mr. Oginga Odinga and the formation of a new political
party, the Kenya African Party of Electors (KAPE),[48] now the
Kenya People's Union (KPU), make explicit some of the existing
discontent. In addition, there are the interests of the Kikuyu, with
their historic desire for landholding.

Some decisions seem to have been made, at least temporarily, in
the "White Paper," *African Socialism and its Application to Planning in Kenya*, published by the Government of Kenya in July,
1965.[49] The paper is illuminating for more than just the flexibility
and realism of its approach. In this first explicit statement on the
subject by the Kenya Government, it speaks of "two African traditions which form an essential basis for African socialism—political
democracy and mutual social responsibility."[50] Those features of
traditional political democracy which deserve to be translated into
the modern Kenyan state are those which "hedge against the exercise of disproportionate political power by economic power groups";
assure that "political rights [do] not derive from or relate to economic wealth or status"; and regard age, citizenship, and allegiance
to the country as the only criteria required for political participation. A party of the elite is specifically disallowed. "Mutual social
responsibility is an extension of the African family spirit to the
nation as a whole"; the duty of a citizen to work is matched by his
reciprocal right to have the products and benefits of society shared
among its members.[51]

Tom Mboya, who was largely responsible for this present document, pointed out several years ago that

> the challenge of African socialism is to use these traditions
> to find a way to build a society in which there is a place
> for everybody, where everybody shares both in poverty and
> in prosperity, and where emphasis is placed on production
> by everyone, with security for all.
>
> .   .   .   .   .
>
> The question becomes [a little] more complicated when
> we interpret African socialism in terms of ownership of
> land. I have already said that the possession of individual
> land title is an idea foreign to Africa. . . . Land titles are
> bound to come, and in some places such as Kenya's Central
> Region, where the process of consolidating land fragments
> revolutionized the tenure system, they have come in great
> numbers. But it would be a mistake to adopt this as the
> standard system for all parts of Kenya or for all of Africa.

---

[48] South China Sunday Post-Herald (Hong Kong), April 17, 1966, p. 9,
cols. 5-6.
[49] REPUBLIC OF KENYA, AFRICAN SOCIALISM AND ITS APPLICATION TO PLAN-
NING IN KENYA (Gov't Printer, Kenya 1965).
[50] *Id.* at 3.
[51] *Id.* at 4.

Among other agricultural tribes, like the Meru of Abaluhya
or Luo, it would be difficult to introduce land titles uni-
versally without destroying the sense of values which the
communal system provides. Some may, no doubt, take the
view of the Kikuyu, to whom the possession of a title means
a good deal in terms of personal security. But this merely
sets the government the challenge of finding a formula by
which people could be given title without destroying the
communal system.[52]

The "White Paper," however, in spite of its apparent acceptance
of individual land ownership as perhaps both inevitable and economically desirable, concentrates on the regulation of land acquisition and use rather than on the specification of acceptable types of
land ownership and the role of law in this behalf. Theorizing on
the function—ideological or pragmatic—of law in society is absent.

Nonetheless, it *is* in agriculture that government plans "provide
perhaps the best example of African Socialism at work."[53] A wide
range of organizational forms for production and marketing are
suggested for use: national farms, cooperatives, companies, part-
nerships, and individual farms probably coupled with cooperative
marketing techniques. The colonial priority of land settlement and
transfer is to be replaced by the priority of land development,
where idle or mismanaged land will not be tolerated. The "need
and practicality" of limiting individual property ownership may
also be investigated. Further, the existing legislation will be strictly enforced to ensure that the few laggards in an area of prospective land consolidation will be "made to comply" and that "those
few who refuse to cooperate in a major cooperative farming scheme
are made to do so or lose their land."[54] Underlying all this seems to
be a legal pragmatism similar to that which Harvey described in
Ghana and to that which is evolving in Guinea and Senegal.

For many internal political reasons, the Kenya Government has
so far chosen to act within the nonindigenous constitutional framework inherited from the colonial era. Decisions affecting land use
have been made within the legal "given" of Western parliamentary
democratic procedures, with some neglect perhaps at the essential
lower levels of policy consultation. However, in their efforts to en-
list law to the cause of guiding change, Kenya politicians have made
some constitutional changes where needed. As in Ghana, in response
to national needs a semifederal constitution adopted just before independence has given way to a presidential constitution adopted in
December 1964.* The pre-independence constitution retained the
vestiges of communal thinking. It "safeguarded land on a regional
and tribal basis and sharply restricted the authority of the central
government to introduce planned redistribution of population out-

---

[52] MBOYA, FREEDOM AND AFTER 168, 171-72 (1963).
[53] REPUBLIC OF KENYA, *op. cit. supra* note 49, at 50.
[54] *Id.* at 38.
* For changes in the Constitution of Kenya, see Appendix C *infra*.

side the former European-owned areas."[55] This communal policy
during colonial days had allowed for and tolerated a certain independence of action *within* tribal frameworks, while supporting
white control. The present drive for a national identification and a
national strength and purpose considers such tribal restrictions on
legislative action as impediments to progress. The clarion call is
for national strength.

The new presidential constitution gives the central government
powerful tools to use in the intensive development of agriculture
throughout the country. Mismanaged or unused farms can be ex-
propriated in the national interest (with compensation to owners)
by the Ministry of Agriculture for redistribution of the population
to achieve optimum use of arable land. Clearly these economic
changes will have grave social consequences, especially to the Masai
and other pastoral tribes to whom much land which has been idle
or underused and hereto protected by law belongs. Given the pre-
cariousness of tribal relations in Kenya, such a decision to favor national goals over tribal ones is of great importance. One hopes that
the decisionmakers in Nairobi will come to represent all of Kenya
on a nontribal basis.

One also hopes that the flexibility and pragmatism expressed in
the "White Paper" will continue to represent the course of action
in an African socialist Kenya. The fragility of the "stability" of
many African governments has again been evidenced in the February 1966 coup in Ghana, the most recent of a series of military take-
overs in the Congo, Dahomey, the Central African Republic, Upper
Volta, and Nigeria. Unfortunately, reason and pragmatism cannot necessarily be counted on to satisy the post-independence expectations generated among not only the unemployed, landless, and
discontented (of which Kenya has many) but also the second eche-
lon, dispossessed bureaucrats. In this context, it might have been
sounder politically for the Kenya Government to have arrived at
the final form, or at least the major ideas of this "White Paper,"
after some sort of consultation with people at all levels of the
party organization, rather than having it promulgated from the
height of ministerial wisdom.[56] In any case, up to now many of
the colonial lessons in the art of legal manipulation and power consolidation can be seen to have been well learned in Kenya.

IV. The Functions of Law in Society

Law plays various roles in societies. It generally is regarded as an
instrument to attain other ends, as "value-neutral," and as "merely
a technique of social ordering."[57] In its instrumental role law can

---

[55] Segal, *The Problem of Urban Unemployment*, Africa Report, April
1965, p. 20.
[56] Sanger, *Some Reflections on Leaving East Africa*, Africa Report, Oct.
1965, p. 30.
[57] HARVEY, *op. cit. supra* note 41, at 2.

be seen as a stabilizing factor in society, as a means for planning and directing change, and as a mechanism for consolidating political power or furthering economic development. And often it cannot be so neatly analyzed but must be seen as accomplishing several of these purposes.

Traditional tribal societies in Kenya used law—or more accurately the adjudicative mechanism—to provide a means for maintaining order and restoring social equilibrium after a rupture. Indeed Western society searches for a like kind of stability when it tries to control the future and eliminate the arbitrary and unpredictable with a "rule of law" rather than a "rule of men."

But law can also be used as a purposive instrument for shaping the social environment. It can make manifest the goals and priorities of a society. "The law should be the legal expression of the political, economic, and social condition of the people and of their aims for progress,"[58] said Kwame Nkrumah. In this sense it spells out the desirable or permissible political, economic, and social relationships or patterns of interaction between persons.

In colonial Kenya a clear example of the delineation of the authority structure in a country by legal means is provided. Colonial law set out the political and economic framework of the colony; it was an undergirding for the political and economic privilege of the Europeans in Kenya. It defined the rules for playing the political game and made certain that the prerequisites for political power—landholding, economic power, and personal social status—remained beyond the reach of all but a handful of nonwhites until colonialism was in its last days. The transition from communal to individual land tenure went unacknowledged for fear of its economic and political ramifications.

Law as an instrument for creation and consolidation of national power is not unique to the colonial era. Creating a new nation is much like creating a new myth. Those clever at the manipulation of symbols are at a distinct advantage. The new myth to be created concerns a new unit—the national unit—a unit which has barely emerged from the welter of local peculiarities comprising the colonial territory. But mythmaking often needs sterner sanctions than an appeal to symbols. For example,

> Since the advent of responsible African government [in Ghana], legal devices and techniques have been consistently used to neutralize sub-national power centres, particularly the traditional authorities, and to organize all legitimate power on a national basis. This is seen clearly in the successful struggle for a unified and not a federal government, in the concentration in Parliament of plenary sovereignty except where expressly limited by a reservation of

---

[58] Allott, *Legal Development and Economic Growth in Africa*, in CHANGING LAW IN DEVELOPING COUNTRIES 200 (Anderson ed. 1963).

power to the entire people.[59]

Too little is known about the effectiveness of law as an instrument for planned change: whether law is the cause or the result of new situations, or "to what extent law . . . act[s] as a brake on economic progress, or alternatively stimulate[s] or harness[es] such progress."[60] The East Africa Royal Commission felt that the advances in agriculture which were absolutely essential to Kenya's economic health would necessitate a complete break with the past, a reorientation of African techniques of land use and land tenure, and a rationalization of economic practices. It also felt that the end justified the change, and that there was a logical and perhaps even necessary causal relationship between the proposed changes and the goal. Of course what has happened is that where the traditional communal system of land tenure and use was thought to inhibit the efficient use of land, the African farmer has been legally enabled to adopt individual freehold tenure. The legal changes are permissive, not obligatory; and the degree to which the legal change has become an effective guiding norm is problematical.

In socialist countries the connections between economics and law have been particularly close. The legal system has played a role supportive of economic goals. Surely economics is one of the pivotal reasons for the appeal of socialism in new African countries. Like the American Negro, the African is searching for ways to mend the psychic split in his personality: for ways to be both modern and African in cultural identification. In looking for ways to make socialism particularly responsive to and representative of the African milieu, many national leaders have turned to the communal landholding patterns of native law and custom as an aspect · of the Negro cultural heritage worthy of preservation. "The African socialist idea is that traditional farms can be transmuted readily and directly into large-scale, technologically advanced farms if the government supplies managerial direction and mechanized equipment."[61] The 1963 election manifesto of KANU pledged itself to a "democratic African socialist society"; and the 1965 "White Paper," while failing to specifically mention communal tenure and leaving it perhaps to a prospective working party to investigate land tenure policy, certainly envisages group production and marketing —if not ownership—as a vital part of Kenya's African socialist economy. In the words of one of African socialism's leading theoreticians, Leopold Sedar Senghor, the aim of a socialist development plan is

to organize production rationally. Our plan will include

---

[59] HARVEY, op. cit. supra note 41, at 16.
[60] Allott, op. cit. supra note 58, at 194.
[61] Drew, How Socialist Are African Economies?, Africa Report, May 1963, p. 13.

three sectors: a socialized sector—agriculture; a mixed
sector—public utilities and semigovernmental societies; and
a free sector—banks, commerce, [and] industry . . . which
will be oriented toward the objectives of the plan and, to a
certain extent, controlled.[62]

Senghor goes on to say that, fortunately, agriculture in Negro-
African society has traditionally been socialistic, that is communal
in nature. This communal pattern was animated by a religious
feeling, a concern for the total man—body and soul—and for ordering his relationships harmoniously. In this sense, he sees African
socialism as essentially political—concerned with man operating
within his environment—and derivatively economic in satisfying
man's needs. Sekou Toure, too, views the political structure, goals,
and priorities as setting the framework for the economic structure.
This puts Kenya on the horns of an ideological dilemma, for the
"present economic structure of Kenya cannot remotely be termed
'socialistic.' "[63] Colonial patterns of individualistic enterprise
and land exploitaton still loom large in both the African and European productive centers of the economy. However, Potekhin points
out that this may not necessarily prove incompatible with an
African socialism. For, though in the transition to socialism the
communal system of peasant ownership may have its advantages, it "need not by any means be a binding pre-condition for the
socialist way of development."[64]   *135920*

Thus the possible functions of law in a society are multiple: it
can be a stabilizer, a technique for social ordering, a manifestation
of the economic and political structure or goals of a nation, an
instrument of planned change, a mechanism for the consolidation
of political power, a means for maximizing economic potential, and
an expression of a value system. The exact combination of the
above for Kenya has yet to be worked out.

---

[62] SENGHOR, ON AFRICAN SOCIALISM, 58-59, 108 (1964).
[63] Rosberg, *Independent Kenya: Problems and Prospects*, Africa Report,
Dec. 1963, p. 7.
[64] Potekhin, *supra* note 40, at 38. On the other hand, if social and political control and guided evolution are the desired goals, it is possible to by-
pass the legal court structure in the ways the Chinese experimented with
in the late 1950's and thereafter. This meant introducing more communist
party control of political development through the building up of a system
of informal nonlegal sanctions against undesirable behavior.

APPENDIX A

The statutory provisions for the structure and operation of the court system in the Kenya of 1967 are found in two chapters (ten and eleven) of the 1962 revised edition of the *Laws of Kenya*.

The Courts Act, LAWS OF KENYA cap. 10 (rev. ed. 1962), which was originally enacted in 1931, provides for a Supreme Court and for subordinate courts presided over by magistrates. Within this hierarchy are the Muslim subordinate courts, presided over by liwalis, kahdis, or mudirs (Muslim officials with either wholly judicial or combined executive-judicial functions). The African courts, previously beneath this system, are now being integrated into it by various devices.

The African Courts Ordinance No. 65 of 1951 has been replaced by the African Courts Act, LAWS OF KENYA cap. 11 (rev. ed. 1962; rev. 1963). The basic changes that this act brought into effect in the African court structure in 1963 reflect the intent of the African Courts (Amendment) Ordinance No. 50 of 1962. For civil cases and for criminal cases arising under the unwritten law and originating in the African courts, the appeal channel has been altered. A magistrate and a provincial African courts officer have replaced the district officer as the link between the African Court of Appeals and the Court of Review. For such cases the Court of Review is the final appellate tribunal. Section 50 of the African Courts Act, *supra*, contains the reintroduced appeal to the Supreme Court for criminal cases arising under the written law. Moreover, the Court of Review now includes an incumbent judge of the Supreme Court.[65]

The Kenya Government has recently stated that it plans to eliminate the African courts entirely from the system and replace them with lay magistrates as part of a unified court structure (as Tanzania has done). The relevant legislation—the Kadhi's Courts Bill, the Judicature Bill, and the Magistrate's Courts Bill of 1967—was introduced into the National Assembly in March, 1967.[66]

APPENDIX B

The crucial period in the late 1950's can be clarified and extended by reference to the changes in land law in the 1960's. The 1962 revised edition of the *Laws of Kenya* provides a starting point. For statutory purposes, all the land in Kenya is divided into two categories: (a) Special Areas, basically Trust Land (including the old Native Land Units) and private freehold, totaling 50,000 square

---

[65] For additional details, see Watts, *The Court of Review, The Appeal System: African Courts, Chapter 11 of the Laws of Kenya*, 2 E. AFRICAN L.J. 151 (1966).

[66] See Kenya Gazette, Supp. No. 17 (Bills No. 4), March 10, 1967, and Supp. No. 19 (Bills No. 5), March 11, 1967.

miles of territory; and (b) Crown Lands, that is, special reserves, alienated and unalienated land, and private freehold, constituting the remaining 174,000 square miles of territory.[67]

The Special Areas are governed by two laws: (a) the Trust Land Act, LAWS OF KENYA cap. 288 (rev. ed. 1962) (formerly the Native Lands Trust Ordinance, 1939), which defines the Special Areas and provides for agricultural and township plot leases of up to thirty-three years and mining leases of up to twenty-one years; and (b) the Land Registration (Special Areas) Act, LAWS OF KENYA cap. 283 (rev. ed. 1962), which was enacted as the Native Lands Registration Ordinance No. 27 of 1959, and which provides for the ascertainment of rights and interests in land, the consolidation of land holdings, and the registration of land titles in these areas. In addition, it provides for the control over subsequent transactions involving such land through the Land Control (Special Areas) Regulations, 1961, which replaced the Land Control (Native Lands) Ordinance No. 28 of 1959.

The Crown Lands are governed principally by three laws. First, the Crown Lands Act, LAWS OF KENYA cap. 280 (rev. ed. 1962), which provides for 999-year leases for agricultural land and 99-year leases for township and "special purpose" plots. The English form of conveyancing was introduced to Kenya through its predecessor, the Crown Lands Ordinance, 1915. The second law governing the Crown Lands is the Registration of Titles Act, LAWS OF KENYA cap. 281 (rev. ed. 1962), which was enacted in 1919 and which has provided a Torrens-type title registration system for all land outside the Special Areas. The third law governing Crown Lands is the Land Titles Act, LAWS OF KENYA cap. 282 (rev. ed. 1962), which was enacted in 1908 and which provides for the certification and registration of titles or interest in immovable property within certain prescribed coastal areas.

Two occurrences in 1963 are significant. The Registered Land Act No. 25 of 1963 came into force on August 16, 1963.[68] The provisions of this act, consummating the integration process formally begun in 1959, are intended to obliterate the distinction between Special Areas and Crown Lands by providing a single system of land-title registration and land transfer. This system will gradually be extended to cover all land previously covered by other laws. Section 164 of the act essentially repeals the Indian Transfer of Property Act, 1882. Part of the Land Registration (Special Areas) Act, LAWS OF KENYA cap. 283 (rev. ed. 1962), has been superseded by the Registered Land Act, *supra*, and the remainder has been

---

[67] COLONIAL OFFICE REPORT ON KENYA FOR 1962, at 41 (1964).

[68] See Kenya Gazette, Supp. No. 66 (Ordinances No. 5), Aug. 27, 1963. For more details about the act, see Maini, *An Outline of the Land Law of Kenya, and the Registered Land Act,* 2 E. AFRICAN L.J. 145 (1966).

renamed the Land Adjudication Act.[69] Thus, the Land Adjudication Act is the vehicle for converting African interests into freehold
statutory estates, which then can be registered.

Kenyan Independence on December 12 was the second significant
occurrence of 1963. Chapter XII of the Constitution of Kenya,
promulgated by the Kenya Independence Order in Council, 1963, is
concerned with land. Briefly summarized, chapter XII set up a
Central Land Board to buy land for resettlement schemes, established Divisional Land Control Boards to control transactions in
agricultural lands, and vested title to land substantially as follows:
Crown Land titles in the seven Regions, and Trust Land titles in
county councils (instead of in the Trust Land Board).

There have been constitutional changes since December 12, 1963,
that can only be sketched here. The "Constitution of Kenya" now
means the document described in the Kenya Independence Order
in Council, 1963, as amended by the following: Constitution of
Kenya (Amendment) Act No. 28 of 1964; Constitution of Kenya
(Amendment) (No. 2) Act No. 38 of 1964; Constitution of Kenya
(Amendment) Act No. 14 of 1965; Constitution of Kenya (Amendment) Act No. 16 of 1966; Constitution of Kenya (Amendment)
(No. 2) Act No. 17 of 1966; Constitution of Kenya (Amendment)
(No. 3) Act No. 18 of 1966; Constitution of Kenya (Amendment)
(No. 4) Act No. 40 of 1966. Not all of these acts are relevant to
landholding; for example, No. 17 of 1966 specifies that a Member of
Parliament must resign his seat if he resigns from the parliamentary
party. However, the main effect of these changes has been to create
a strong, centralized, republican government in place of the limited,
federal structure bequeathed by the British Colonial Office. All
land previously vested in the Regions (primarily Crown Land) is
now vested in the central government, and the Central Land Board
has been abolished in favor of the Settlement Fund Trustees, which
was established by the Agriculture Act, LAWS OF KENYA cap. 318, §167
(rev. ed. 1962). Finally, the provisions for the control of land transactions, chapter XII, part 3 of the Constitution of Kenya, have been
repealed and reenacted in statutory form.

The national interest in land rights has been forcefully stated.
Land in Kenya today is vested either in the Government, in county
officials, or in individuals. In the Special Areas, tenures and interests
under customary law are being investigated and recorded (after
consolidation and adjudication) under the Land Adjudication Act
and then registered under the Registered Land Act No. 25 of 1963.
Crown Land is also registered and systematically brought under the
single unified legal code governing all real property subject to
conveyancing and epitomized by the Registered Land Act, *supra*.

---

[69] See Registered Land Act No. 25 of 1963, § 165. This has now become
chapter 300 of the 1964 revised edition of the *Laws of Kenya*.

Strong central authority permits the granting of land on whatever terms seem desirable, though the Constitution guarantees land rights in an area to everyone "ordinarily resident" in that area. Until now, customary law regarding extratribal land sales has been extremely recalcitrant. Likewise, Government attempts at multiracial resettlement programs, such as the Shimba Hills Settlement Scheme in Coast Province, have met with scant and delayed approval. Nonetheless, the authority to press for nontribal use of agricultural land clearly exists, though the decision to use it forcefully will involve political risks.

APPENDIX C

The Restatement of African Law Project of the University of London School of Oriental and African Studies, at the invitation of the Government of Kenya, has recently finished recording the basic customary civil law of marriage, divorce, succession, and family relations now accepted by the various tribes and administered by the African courts. Under the same auspices, Eugene Cotran, with the assistance of Law Panels, has studied the surviving customary offenses recognized by the Kenya tribes (some ten of which were not criminal under the Kenya Penal Code) and made recommendations to the Government on their restatement and unification.[70] Under the Constitution of Kenya, legislation codifying the customary offenses must have been introduced by December 12, 1966, if the courts were to continue to apply the rules of the customary criminal law.

---

[70] See COTRAN, REPORT ON CUSTOMARY CRIMINAL OFFENCES IN KENYA (Gov't Printer, Nairobi 1963).

POST-NKRUMAH GHANA: THE LEGAL PROFILE OF A COUP†

William B. Harvey*

I. Introduction

The *coup d'état* in Ghana on February 24, 1966, carried out by the army with police support, ended the fifteen year old government of Dr. Kwame Nkrumah. Of that period, almost nine years had elapsed since the British colonial power withdrew and granted sovereign independence to the former Gold Coast on March 6, 1957. Ghana was the first of the colonial territories of black Africa to achieve independence, and Dr. Nkrumah's government carried the hopes and aspirations not only of the Ghanaian people but of many others. Colonial apologists awaited the justification of a century's bearing of the white man's burden. Critics of imperialism welcomed the cutting of political bonds as a first step toward complete economic and cultural emancipation. More ominously, the cold war antagonists began to marshal their forces for encounters in a new theater.

The Nkrumah government achieved the remarkable feat of disappointing everyone. Ghana's economy was shattered by a disastrous drop in the international price of cocoa, by the waste of resources on nonproductive prestige projects, and by increasing corruption among governmental officials. The massive popular support Nkrumah had enjoyed at independence was eroded steadily by the economic disappointments of the people and by governmental mismanagement. Dr. Nkrumah's reaction to growing signs of political discontent was increasing authoritarianism. He alienated fellow African leaders by his compulsive drive for dominance and by his support of subversion in their territories. The Western powers endured his shrill denunciations without major retaliation but grew more reluctant to provide the aid that he sought for bolstering the limping economy. To the Eastern powers he was hardly more satisfactory. Though his government was officially committed to socialist development, economic plans usually were ignored at the implementation level, the private sector of the economy was harassed but not eliminated, and misconceived government enterprises dissipated public resources. Nkrumah's Ghana was clearly not an Eastern satellite; at best it was a sympathetic, but unpredictable, supporter.

In these circumstances, the coup of February 24 provided no surprises. Fighting was brief, and the few casualties incurred were

---

† This article is based upon developments through July 19, 1966, the date of National Liberation Council Decree No. 65.

* Dean of the School of Law and Professor of Law and Government, Indiana University. A.B., 1943, Wake Forest College; J.D., 1949, University of Michigan.

largely among the President's personal guard. The army's action was greeted by widespread rejoicing. Though the inadequacies and misdeeds of the Nkrumah regime were great, even the army's delay in intervening was predictable: it had maintained the strong non-political imprint of its British parentage.

It seems most improbable that Dr. Nkrumah will be able to re-impose his control on Ghana, despite his fulminations from Guinea, where President Sekou Toure has accorded him the ambiguous status of co-President. The new government is peacefully and firmly in control, and it is to the structure, powers, and policies of that government that we will now direct our attention. This article will sketch briefly the legal profile of a *coup d'état* and seek in its subsequent enactments clues to the future legal and governmental development of Ghana.

II. POST-NKRUMAH CHANGES

A. The Executive

Two days after the coup its leaders formally declared the structure and powers of the new government. A proclamation established the National Liberation Council with Lieutenant General J. A. Ankrah as chairman and Commissioner of Police J. W. K. Harlley as deputy chairman. As originally constituted, the Council consisted of four army officers and three police officials, but today the membership is balanced between them.[1]

The Proclamation also suspended the Republican Constitution of 1960, dismissed Dr. Nkrumah from his offices of President and Commander-in-Chief of the armed forces, dissolved the National Assembly, dismissed all ministers, and abolished the Presidential Commission that had been set up to exercise the powers of the President during Dr. Nkrumah's absence from the country. Nkrumah's Convention Peoples' Party, the only lawful political organization since 1964,[2] was dissolved, and membership in it prohibited.

Into this governmental vacuum stepped the National Liberation Council. It reserved to itself plenary legislative power, to be exercised by decree,[3] as well as the full competences granted by any preexisting law to the President, the cabinet, or a minister.[4] Thus

---

[1] The Council's first decree added another member from the police. National Liberation Council Decree No. 1 (1966)   [National Liberation Council Decree will hereinafter be cited as N.L.C.D.].

[2] Republican Constitution, 1960, art. 1A. This article was added by the Constitution (Amendment) Act, 1964, Pub. Act 224 (Ghana).

[3] Proclamation For The Constitution of a National Liberation Council for the Administration of Ghana and for Other Matters Connected Therewith § 3   [The Proclamation For The Constitution of a National Liberation Council for the Administration of Ghana and for Other Matters Connected Therewith will hereinafter be cited as Proclamation].

[4] Proclamation § 7; National Liberation Council (Proclamation) (Amendment) Decree (1966); N.L.C.D. No. 1, § 2 (1966).

the Council became the government of Ghana, merging in itself all legislative and executive powers. In practical operative effect, this consolidation of powers in the Council probably did not differ from that previously enjoyed by Dr. Nkrumah and his close advisors. Nevertheless, the "Proclamation for the Constitution of a National Liberation Council for the Administration of Ghana and for Other Matters Connected Therewith" stripped away the legal facade of separation of the powers and functions of the President from those of the National Assembly and abandoned the theory of minimally limited government that the Republican Constitution had preserved by reserving to the people the power to amend the Constitution in certain respects.[5]

Though the Council assumed all ministerial powers, it showed a marked reluctance to distribute portfolios among its members. Apparently fearing that such a move would cast Council members in an unduly "political" role, it undertook to act only in its corporate capacity. Since this ideal was not fully practicable, the Council initially delegated to senior civil servants acting as the principal secretaries or heads of ministries the numerous ministerial functions laid down by statute. In the exercise of these functions, however, the civil servants were made subject to such directions as the Council might give.[6] By a later decision, ministerial portfolios were assigned to the various members of the Council.

In a search for greater insight into the existing administrative machinery of government and for ways in which it might be improved, the Council has established an Administrative Committee.[7] The duties of the Committee include advising the Council on all matters of central and local government administration and making recommendations on organization, staffing, and training. Prior to the establishment of this Committee, however, basic changes in the structure of local government had been decreed. Provision was made for the replacement of the elective councils at various local government levels by "management committees" to be appointed by the Council. These committees are to perform all functions previously exercisable by the elective councils, and they, like their predecessors, are governed by the Local Government Act of 1961. The membership structure provided for the management committees further reflects the reliance by the Council on technicians and its effort to depoliticize government at all levels.[8]

---

[5] For a discussion of the Republican Constitution, 1960, see HARVEY, LAW AND SOCIAL CHANGE IN GHANA *passim* (1966).

[6] Ministers' Functions (Delegation) Decree, N.L.C.D. No. 11 (1966).

[7] National Liberation Council (Administrative Committee) (Appointment) Decree, N.L.C.D. No. 31 (1966).

[8] Illustrative is the composition of a city or municipal committee: (a) the senior medical officer, (b) the regional education officer, (c) the assistant chief planning officer, (d) the regional engineer of the Ghana National Construction Corporation, and (e) a private person nominated by the senior police officer of the region.

B. The Judiciary

Of the basic governmental structures of Ghana, the judiciary was affected least by the coup. The Proclamation provided that, despite the suspension of the Constitution, the courts should continue to function with the same powers as before. Judges and all others holding posts in the judicial service were continued upon the pre-coup terms and conditions of service.[9] The judges were required to take a new oath, however, swearing to act not only in accordance with the "laws and usage,"[10] but also in accordance with the "decrees" of Ghana.[11]

Nevertheless, the judiciary still bore the scars of the Nkrumah period. In 1961, legislation had been enacted to create special criminal courts to deal with offenses against the safety of the state.[12] In late 1963, the government's inability to procure from such a court the conviction of three defendants accused of treason brought the dismissal of Sir Arku Korsah as Chief Justice, the resignation of Sir Arku and Mr. Justice William B. Van Lare from the Supreme Court, and legislation authorizing the President to void the special court's judgment of acquittal.[13] A more fundamental consequence of the acquittal, however, was a constitutional amendment granting the President summary power to dismiss any judge of the superior courts.[14] Dr. Nkrumah promptly exercised this power in dismissing one High Court judge and three judges of the Supreme Court, including the sole survivor of the special criminal court.

After the coup, the National Liberation Council acted promptly to remove these impingements on the judiciary. A Judicial Service Commission of six members was established, consisting of the Chief Justice as chairman, the most senior judge of the Supreme Court, the Attorney General, the Chairman of the Civil Service Commission, and two nominees of the National Liberation Council, who must be retired judges of the superior courts.[15] Important functions in the selection and discipline of judges and judicial officers are assigned to the Commission. The Chief Justice and other

---

[9] Proclamation § 2(3).

[10] Oaths Act, 1960, Constitutional Act 12, First Schedule.

[11] National Liberation Council (Oaths) Decree, N.L.C.D. No. 6, § 1 (1966).

[12] The Criminal Procedure (Amendment) Act, 1961, Pub. Act 91 (Ghana), later replaced by the Criminal Procedure (Amendment) Act, 1964, Pub. Act 238 (Ghana).

[13] The Criminal Procedure (Amendment) (No. 2) Act, 1963, Pub. Act 223 (Ghana).

[14] The Constitution (Amendment) Act, 1964, Pub. Act 224, § 6(c) (Ghana).

[15] Judicial Service Act, 1960 (Amendment) Decree, N.L.C.D. No. 39, § 2 (1966), as amended by Judicial Service Act, 1960, (Amendment) (No. 2) Decree, N.L.C.D. No. 58 (1966). As originally constituted by N.L.C.D. No. 39 (1966), the Commission included two representatives of the bar and did not include the Chairman of the Civil Service Commission.

judges of the Supreme Court and High Court are to be appointed by
the National Liberation Council acting on the advice of the Judicial
Service Commission.[16] The Council has similar appointive powers
with respect to lower court judges, but it may delegate these powers
to the Judicial Service Commission.[17] Protection of judicial tenure
has been reinstituted. Judges of the Supreme Court and High
Court may be removed only by the National Liberation Council,
acting on the advice of the Judicial Service Commission, for either
stated misbehavior or infirmity of body or mind. Their salaries
cannot be diminished while they remain in office.[18] Lower court
judges still do not enjoy these usual safeguards of judicial independence, but the power to discipline them has been removed from
the President or his designee[19] and vested in the National Liberation
Council. However, its action is subject to the binding advice of the
Judicial Service Commission.[20]

One of the most typical expressions of authoritarianism is the
creation of special courts to deal with criminal prosecutions in particular cases or series of cases, frequently those involving political
opposition to the incumbent regime. The *Working Paper on The
Rule of Law in a Free Society,* prepared for the International Commission of Jurists meeting in New Delhi in 1959, declared, with
justification, that "the trial of accused persons must take place before an independent court. Special courts created *ad hoc* for a
particular case or series of cases endanger fair trial or at least create
pursuance [*sic*] of instructions given by the Executive."[21] The special criminal court in Ghana amply illustrated these dangers. It
operated under summary procedures and modes of proof established by the President and with a jury selected from a special
list.[22] Its judgment was final and unreviewable. When one such
court resisted executive pressure and acquitted the accused, the
judgment was voided and the defendants re-tried. On retrial,
a conviction was predictably returned.

---

[16] Judicial Service Act, 1960, (Amendment) Decree, N.L.C.D. No. 39,
§ 1(3) (1966).
[17] Judicial Service Act, 1960, (Amendment) Decree, N.L.C.D. No. 39,
§ 3(a) (1966).
[18] Judicial Service Act, 1960, (Amendment) Decree, N.L.C.D. No. 39,
§§ 1(4), 7 (1966).
[19] Judicial Service Act, 1960, Constitutional Act 10, § 18.
[20] Judicial Service Act, 1960, (Amendment) Decree, N.L.C.D. No. 39,
§ 3(c), (d) (1966).
[21] INT'L COMM'N JURISTS, THE RULE OF LAW IN A FREE SOCIETY 318 (1959).
[22] The original special courts legislation excluded jury trial. The Criminal Procedure (Amendment) Act, 1961, Pub. Act 91, § 3(3) (Ghana);
Criminal Procedure Code, 1959, Pub. Act 30, §§ 242-45 (Ghana). After the
acquittal of three defendants in late 1963 the constitution of a special
criminal court was revised by substituting for the former three-judge court
a judge of the superior courts sitting with a jury of twelve persons drawn
from a special list of jurors. The Criminal Procedure (Amendment) Act,
1964, Pub. Act 238, § 1 (Ghana).

Treatment of the special criminal court by the National Liberation Council was prompt and decisive. The court was abolished, the legislation authorizing it was repealed, and the retrial conviction of the five defendants charged with treason was declared null and void.[23] However, three of the defendants, who long had been associated with Dr. Nkrumah's government, were retained in "protective custody."[24]

C. *Public Service*

To assure the necessary continuity of government, the initial Proclamation of the National Liberation Council continued the public services of Ghana as they existed before the coup.[25] The Council in fact has been inclined to rely heavily on the senior civil servants for various quasi-political or policy-oriented roles. As has been noted, ministerial functions were delegated to the principal secretaries.[26] Public service technical personnel dominate the management committees that are to replace the local government councils.[27] The Economic Committee, the first appointed by the Council and surely the most important, is composed predominantly of senior civil servants. The committee is charged with responsibility for studying the present state of the economy and recommending ways of rehabilitating it.[28]

D. *Law of Ghana*

Despite the revolutionary change effected by the *coup d'état*, the legal order of Ghana remained remarkably stable. The original Proclamation of the National Liberation Council continued in force all enactments and rules of law as they existed prior to the coup, subject, of course, to the plenary legislative power of the Council.[29] In this body of law, decrees of the National Liberation Council have effected a number of significant amendments. In addition to those discussed under other headings, several merit brief mention. The offense of unlawful exportation of cocoa has been reduced from a second degree felony to a misdemeanor, with a consequent reduction of penalty.[30] The Criminal Code was further amended to make punishable violent entry into any building or onto land,

---

[23] Criminal Procedure (Special Criminal Division) (Abolition) Decree, N.L.C.D. No. 43 (1966).

[24] National Liberation Council (Protective Custody) (Amendment) (No. 4) Decree, N.L.C.D. No. 44 (1966).

[25] Proclamation § 5.

[26] Ministers' Functions (Delegation) Decree, N.L.C.D. No. 11 (1966).

[27] See Local Government (Interim Administration) Decree, N.L.C.D. No. 26 (1966).

[28] National Liberation Council (Economic Committee) (Appointment) Decree, N.L.C.D. No. 4 (1966).

[29] Proclamation § 3(2), (3).

[30] Criminal Code, 1960, (Amendment) Decree, N.L.C.D. No. 28 (1966).

even by a person entitled to possession.[31] The 1959 enactment that
provided for suspending any pension or allowance upon the detention of the entitled person under the Preventive Detention Act
was repealed retroactively, thus entitling the pensioner to all
payments withheld.[32]

The prospect of a broad review and revision of the body of law
appeared when the Council appointed a Legal Committee composed
of certain judges of the Supreme Court, the principal government
lawyers, four leading practitioners, and a representative of the law
faculty of the University of Ghana.[33] The Committee has been
given responsibility for examining the existing law, recommending
revisions, and making other suggestions on legal matters, "including
matters preparatory to the setting up of a commission to consider
a new constitution for the country."[34] The activity of the Legal
Committee thus far has been disappointing. It appears doubtful
that it will become a significant force for either law reform or the
development of new legal institutions.

The inadequacies of the Legal Committee are illustrated by a
decree that it recommended to the Council. The proposed decree,
which the Council promulgated,[35] repealed rent stabilization legislation enacted in 1962 and 1963.[36] Regulations issued under this
legislation had imposed a nominal rental of one shilling per year on
cocoa land held by a member of the owning stool and five shillings
per acre if the landholder was not a member of the owning stool.[37]
Repeal of the 1962 legislation restored the effect of customary law
rules applicable to such tenancies, which, in the main, provided for
substantially higher rentals. My criticism of the repealing decree
is not now directed at its substantive effects. Rather, it is directed toward the Legal Committee for recommending and the
Council for legislating on such a vital subject without adequate
study of the effects of the controls and the consequences of their
removal. Illustratively, what were the economic and political
implications of the rent control measures? Who are the principal
beneficiaries of their removal, chiefly landowners or the public
treasury? How does the repeal affect the politically sensitive status
of the chiefs and other traditional rulers? My personal inquiries
reveal no evidence that the Legal Committee considered these questions or advised the Council on them before recommending the

31 Criminal Code, 1960, (Amendment) Decree, N.L.C.D. No. 47 (1966).
32 Pensions (Special Provisions) Act, 1959, (Amendment) Decree, N.L.
C.D. No. 55 (1966).
33 National Liberation Council (Legal Committee) (Appointment) Decree, N.L.C.D. No. 38 (1966), as amended by N.L.C.D. No. 56 (1966).
34 National Liberation Council (Legal Committee) (Appointment) Decree, N.L.C.D. No. 38, § 3 (1966).
35 Rents Stabilization Acts (Repeal) Decree, N.L.C.D. No. 49 (1966).
36 The Rents (Stabilization) Act, 1962, Pub. Act 109 (Ghana); The
Rents (Stabilization) Act, 1963, Pub. Act 168 (Ghana).
37 The Rents (Cocoa Farms) Regulations, 1962, L.I. 186.

repeal of the rent stabilization acts. Rather, the only professed basis for the recommendation was the unpopularity of the controls in the affected areas.

E. Political Controls

The enactments discussed under this heading reflect the efforts of the National Liberation Council to move against the ousted Nkrumah regime as well as to provide curbs against political activity generally. The former may be divided into provisions to neutralize politically individuals and associations that supported Dr. Nkrumah and measures to publicize and punish various corrupt practices of the former government and its members and supporters.

The initial Proclamation of the National Liberation Council not only dismissed Dr. Nkrumah, his ministers, and the National Assembly; it also dissolved the Convention Peoples' Party and prohibited membership in it.[38] Later decrees began the process of removing the imprint of the Party and of Dr. Nkrumah from various features of national life. No longer is the Party flag the national emblem; the original design was readopted for the national flag.[39] The title of Kwame Nkrumah University of Science and Technology lost its reference to the former President.[40] More significantly, certain wing organizations of the Convention Peoples' Party were dissolved and organizational acts with respect to them prohibited under criminal penalties.[41]

The most extreme sanction applied to members and supporters of the ousted government has been detention. The Preventive Detention Act, probably the most hated and feared enactment under Nkrumah, originally was kept in force,[42] but soon was repealed.[43] Even before repeal, however, the Council had laid the legal foundation for its own detention powers under the euphemism of "protective custody."[44] The protective custody net has been sweeping. Many persons have been held as part of a class, e.g., all members of the dissolved Parliament or all district commissioners.[45] Subsequent decrees have authorized protective custody

---

[38] Proclamation § 2(2)(e).

[39] National Liberation Council (Proclamation) (Amendment) Decree, N.L.C.D. No. 1, § 3 (1966).

[40] National Liberation Council (Kwame Nkrumah University of Science and Technology) (Amendment) Decree, N.L.C.D. No. 33 (1966).

[41] National Liberation Council (Dissolution of Ghana Moslem Council and National Council of Ghana Women) Decree, N.L.C.D. No. 15 (1966).

[42] Proclamation § 3(2).

[43] Preventive Detention Act, 1964, (Repeal) Decree, N.L.C.D. No. 30 (1966).

[44] National Liberation Council (Protective Custody) Decree, N.L.C.D. No. 2 (1966).

[45] National Liberation Council (Protective Custody) Decree, N.L.C.D. No. 2, Schedule (1966).

for 446 named individuals.[46] Descriptions of the detained persons
rarely suggest the basis for their detention; they range from "Financial Advisor to the Presidency" to "Lorry Driver" and "C.P.P.
Activist." There are some familiar names: Tawia Adamafio, Ako
Adjei and Cofie Crabbe, first imprisoned by Dr. Nkrumah under the
Preventive Detention Act, were later convicted of treason on retrial in the special criminal court. After the voiding of this judgment by the National Liberation Council and the repeal of the Preventive Detention Act, they continue their confinement in protective custody.

Dr. Nkrumah's government was not only oppressive; it was
appallingly corrupt. A major part of the post-coup activity has
been directed toward ferreting out official wrongdoing, laying the
basis for criminal prosecutions, and tracing assets that can be returned to the public coffers. The Ollennu Commission has been
inquiring into official misconduct connected with the issuance of
import licenses; another commission under Mr. Justice Apaloo has
been investigating the former President's property. Pending the
reports of these commissions, legal tools have been devised for
immobilizing assets and in some cases forfeiting them to the government.

By decree, the National Liberation Council has forbidden numerous persons and organizations to withdraw funds from bank accounts or remove valuables deposited with a bank as security or
for safekeeping.[47] Bankers similarly are forbidden to pay out funds
or return valuables and are obliged to provide information to the
Council concerning accounts or other valuables. Persons with accounts affected include Dr. Nkrumah and his wife, all members of
Parliament and ministers, all regional commissioners, and many
persons named as individuals. The organizations include the Convention Peoples' Party and wing organizations such as the Young
Pioneers' Movement and the National Council of Ghana Women.
When an individual account is blocked, the decree always includes
the named person and his wife. As to whether a woman is the wife
of a person named in a decree, whether a particular account belongs
to a named person, and other critical factual issues, a certificate
signed by the Chairman or Deputy Chairman of the National Liberation Council is made conclusive. There is no provision for hearing interested parties before the certificate is issued. The prohibi-
tions of the decrees are enforced by substantial criminal sanctions.

---

[46] N.L.C.D. No. 37 (1966); N.L.C.D. No. 41 (1966); N.L.C.D. No. 42
(1966); N.L.C.D. No. 44 (1966); N.L.C.D. No. 45 (1966); N.L.C.D. No. 53
(1966).

[47] National Liberation Council (Bank Accounts) Decree, N.L.C.D. No. 7
(1966), as amended by N.L.C.D. No. 9 (1966); N.L.C.D. No. 13 (1966);
N.L.C.D. No. 21 (1966); N.L.C.D. No. 24 (1966); N.L.C.D. No. 32 (1966);
N.L.C.D. No. 35 (1966); N.L.C.D. No. 57 (1966); and N.L.C.D. No. 60 (1966).

By another series of decrees,[48] the Council has authorized the Auditor General to investigate the accounts of a number of organizations and to report to it his findings, as well as "such comments and recommendations as appear to the Auditor General to be in the public interest to make." For these purposes, the Auditor General has been given extensive investigatory powers. Affirmative obligations to provide him information on the nature and extent of property belonging to the scheduled organizations have been imposed on persons in possession or control of it. These obligations, as well as the prohibition of disposition of property without the Auditor General's direction, are enforced by criminal sanctions. Fifteen organizations have been scheduled for investigation, including the Convention Peoples' Party and its wing organizations, the Cocoa Marketing Board, and both the African Affairs Centre and the Bureau of African Affairs.

The earlier decrees freezing the assets of persons or organizations associated with Dr. Nkrumah applied only to bank accounts and deposits of valuables with banks, for security or safekeeping. Later the net was cast more widely. A subsequent decree prohibited the transfer of other assets such as land, buildings, bonds, shares of stock, motor vehicles, and jewelry.[49] All post-coup transfers by the scheduled organizations or persons were voided unless approved by the Council, except those transfers made pursuant to a court order or authorized by an enactment. Again the affected owners included Dr. Nkrumah and his wife, a number of categories of individuals, forty-eight other named persons, and three organizations.

The decrees thus far considered have frozen assets pending the auditing of accounts and other investigations. For a number of organizations, however, summary forfeiture of all assets has been decreed.[50] Ownership of the forfeited assets was vested in the Council subject to disposition "in such manner as the National Liberation Council may direct."[51] The organizations whose assets were scheduled for such forfeiture are the Convention Peoples' Party, the Ghana Farmers' Co-operative Council, the Young Pioneers Movement, the Ideological Institute at Winneba, the African Affairs Centre, the Bureau of African Affairs, the Moslem Council, and the National Council of Ghana Women. A later decree similarly forfeited all assets of two other organizations, the Market

---

[48] National Liberation Council (Auditor-General's Functions) Decree, N.L.C.D. No. 12 (1966), as amended by N.L.C.D. No. 22 (1966); N.L.C.D. No. 46 (1966); and N.L.C.D. No. 48 (1966).
[49] National Liberation Council (Prohibition of Transfers of Assets) Decree, N.L.C.D. No. 40 (1966).
[50] National Liberation Council (Forfeiture of Assets) Decree, N.L.C.D. No. 23 (1966).
[51] National Liberation Council (Forfeiture of Assets) Decree, N.L.C.D. No. 23, § 3 (1966).

Women's Union and Nkrumah Kurye Kaw, and, in addition, dissolved the organizations.[52]

The foregoing measures were directed at persons and groups closely identified with the ousted regime. The National Liberation Council has made clear, however, that it seeks a general moratorium on political activity. In his radio address at the end of the first one hundred days, General Ankrah, Chairman of the National Liberation Council, declared that "we cannot at this stage afford to indulge in Party political wrangles when we are confronted with the spectre of economic bankruptcy . . . . Until the preparatory work [for eventual return to civilian administration] has been satisfactorily completed, the Council will not tolerate any form of Party political activities and will take drastic steps against persons trying to defy its decrees."[53] Within a week of the coup, this posture had been given legal effect.

By a decree for the "preservation of public peace," the Council prohibited the formation or operation of *any* political party.[54] It also prohibited, under criminal penalties, "all activities whatsoever likely to assist in the formation or operation of a political party."[55] Under such a broad prohibition with such lack of definiteness, virtually any group activity could be in jeopardy. As a potential political force, the Ex-Political Detainees Organization has been dissolved and organizational activities connected with it prohibited under severe penalties.[56]

The present effort to depoliticize the country does not, in General Ankrah's words, "imply that the Council intends to remain in power indefinitely. At the opportune time, the country will revert to civilian rule, and the Council is taking appropriate steps to prepare the grounds for that."[57] The first of these steps is the appointment of a Political Committee.[58] Under the chairmanship of Mr. Edward Akufo-Addo, a distinguished lawyer who was dismissed from the Supreme Court by Dr. Nkrumah, the Committee covers a wide political spectrum. Not surprisingly, supporters of the dissolved Convention Peoples' Party have been excluded. Functions of the Committee include making proposals to the Council on

---

[52] National Liberation Council (Dissolution and Forfeiture of Assets) Decree, N.L.C.D. No. 3 (1966).

[53] "First 100 Days," broadcast speech by Lt. General J. A. Ankrah, June 3, 1966.

[54] National Liberation Council (Preservation of Public Peace) Decree, N.L.C.D. No. 3 (1966).

[55] National Liberation Council (Preservation of Public Peace) Decree, N.L.C.D. No. 3, § 2 (1966).

[56] National Liberation Council (Dissolution of the Ex-Political Detainees Organization) Decree, N.L.C.D. No. 34 (1966).

[57] "First 100 Days," broadcast speech by Lt. General J. A. Ankrah, June 3, 1966.

[58] National Liberation Council (Political Committee) (Appointment) Decree, N.L.C.D. No. 59 (1966).

changes in laws or policies to serve better the public interest and the interests of the people of Ghana and advising the Council on matters referred by it to the Committee. All doubt as to the nature of the Committee is removed, however: It "shall act solely as an advisory body to the National Liberation Council and . . . the Council is not obliged to accept any proposal, suggestion or advice submitted."[59]

F. Economic Reform

No concern of the National Liberation Council has been more pronounced than that relating to Ghana's economy. With the ravaging effects of an unfavorable international market for its primary export compounded by official waste, mismanagement, and corruption, the economy urgently demands reform. Yet thus far this pressing concern has been reflected relatively little in the formal enactments of the Council. An Economic Committee has been appointed to study and recommend,[60] certain taxes have been reduced,[61] the penalties for certain currency offenses have been revised,[62] and customs and excise tariffs amended.[63] The enactments discussed in the preceding section may be viewed appropriately not only as political weapons against the Convention Peoples' Party but as a concerted attack against the pervasive official corruption that has drained off public funds. The Council also has announced plans to turn over a number of unprofitable state enterprises to the private sector of the economy and to invite private participation in several others.

While the Council pledged its immediate preoccupation with the economy, its actions have not been precipitate. Thus far it has decreed only minor adjustments. Presumably studies currently proceeding will suggest more fundamental reform. There is little evidence as yet, however, to indicate the new routes on fundamental policy that the Council proposes to follow.

III. Assessment and Conclusion

It is premature to assess the accomplishments or failures of the National Liberation Council. Having ousted a corrupt, oppressive, and ineffective government, the Council understandably is preoccupied with moving against the malfeasants, removing the most blatant expressions of political oppression, and rationalizing basic governmental administration. The Council has pledged itself to

---

[59] National Liberation Council (Political Committee) (Appointment) Decree, N.L.C.D. No. 59, § 4 (1966).

[60] National Liberation Council (Economic Committee) (Appointment) Decree, N.L.C.D. No. 4 (1966).

[61] Ghana (Reduction of Taxation) Decree, N.L.C.D. No. 5 (1966).

[62] Currency Act, 1964, (Amendment) Decree, N.L.C.D. No. 8 (1966).

[63] Customs and Excise Tariff Regulations, 1966, (L.I. 504) (Amendment) Decree, N.L.C.D. No. 63 (1966).

humane, honest, and effective government; to "a strong and progressive welfare society in which no one will have any anxiety about the basic needs of life . . . a society in which the individual Ghanaian will be able to enjoy a modern standard of living based on gainful employment"; to "the suppression, repeal or amendment of those obnoxious laws, Nkrumah's instruments of tyranny and oppression with which he reduced the people of Ghana to virtual slavery and abject misery"; and to restoration of "the rule of law and basic human rights to the people of Ghana." These measures are to be taken, however, without "resort to indiscriminate acts of vengeance against those who were associated with the discredited party."[64] There is no reason to doubt the dedication of the Council to these objectives, and it deserves the patience and understanding of its own people and the world as it pursues them.

Forbearance from condemnation, however, should not foreclose an expression of concern when remedial measures adopted by the Council follow discredited patterns employed by the ousted regime. The euphemism of "protective custody" does not conceal the fact that without charge or trial large numbers of persons have been deprived of their liberty. Some have been released, but many remain in prison. Serious infringements of property interests have been decreed without affording affected parties an opportunity for a fair hearing. Ex parte official determinations of factual issues crucial to the application of sanctions have been made conclusive. Total legislative and executive power has been consolidated in the eight members of the Council, and steps for the validation of that power by the consent of the governed lie in the unforseeable future. Certain modifications have been made in the law without the careful antecedent study that could assure a rational relation of enactment to social needs and governmental purposes.

As a result of the *coup d'état* Ghana now has a new opportunity, unencumbered by the euphoria of newly gained independence, to restructure public power and reshape legal institutions. Difficult, indeed tragic, though the last decade has been, it can provide the new constitutional and legal order with useful insights into the nation's needs. This essay will conclude with a few suggestions of the most important of these needs.

A. Executive Domination

The cardinal feature of the Nkrumah government was the progressive consolidation of power in the executive. Initially by his great political skills and popularity, and later by legal and extralegal measures, Dr. Nkrumah decimated his political opposition and reduced the National Assembly to complete inconsequence and irrelevance. The constitutional amendments of 1964 gave him ul-

---

[64] "First 100 Days," broadcast speech by Lt. General J. A. Ankrah, June 3, 1966.

timate power over the judiciary. This one-party, indeed one-man, domination of all fundamental organs and powers of government predictably produced a corrupt tyranny. Arguments for the concentration of governmental powers and against a system of checks and balances rely primarily upon the undoubted shortage of qualified manpower and upon the widely perceived need for a vigorous, effective response to demands for economic and social development. The Ghanaian experience of the past decade seriously compromises the persuasiveness of these arguments for the consolidation of unlimited governmental power in the hands of a small revolutionary elite. No better example than Dr. Nkrumah need be offered of the corroding and corrupting effect of total power. Whatever the price in speed and efficiency of governmental action exacted by dispersion of power among governmental organs that check and control each other, that price is justified if it provides safeguards against the authoritarianism, the pervasive fear, the insecurity of the Nkrumah regime.

Ghana's experience does not suggest that a system of checks and balances must be based in any major way upon the recognition and use of divisive, sub-national power centers with their attendant loyalties, such as chiefs or other traditional rulers. A prominent Western diplomat suggested to me after the coup that the chiefs should play an important role in the new constitutional order of Ghana. I would regard any such development as serious retrogression. Vital though some of the stools may be as religious and cultural forces, they are ill-fitted to play significant roles in modern government. Adequate safeguards against a dangerous concentration of power can be achieved by the allocation of limiting and balancing roles to legislative and judicial organs under constitutional and legislative norms. The objective is not to fragment fragile national entities nor to immobilize government. It is rather to provide sufficient assurance against that monopolization of all government powers in the same hands that invites tyranny.

B. Creation of the New Institutions

The easiest task of the National Liberation Council will be the elimination of these offensive aspects of the constitutional and legal order associated with the Nkrumah regime. The equally important but far more difficult task will be the creation of new institutions to avoid dangers and meet needs starkly revealed by recent experience. Three kinds of institutions may be mentioned briefly for illustration.

1. LEGISLATIVE

If legislative innovation emerges full-blown from the brow of a Jovian executive, it has enormous potential for both social disruption and ineffectiveness in attaining its stated or assumed objectives. Even the laudable eclecticism of African leaders may create grave

problems. Foreign legislative models, highly successful on their
native soil, may be entirely inappropriate to African circumstances.
Legislative initiatives should be based on a careful study of the
social, economic, and political facts obtaining in the country and a
careful choice of techniques to serve clearly conceived goals. One
of many illustrations of Nkrumah's failure in this connection was
the abortive Marriage, Divorce and Inheritance Bill of 1963. A
similar failure of the National Liberation Council may be found in
the decree restoring customary law rules to tenancies of cocoa
lands.[65]

Procedures should be devised and institutionally assured to re-
duce the frequency of such failures in the future legislative program of Ghana. Among the possibilities deserving consideration
are the establishment of substantive standing committees of a restored Parliament to study legislative proposals, more frequent
use of specialized *ad hoc* commissions to investigate problems and
recommend legislative solutions, the establishment of an adequately
staffed and financed Law Revision Commission, and the support of
more active and more relevant social research in the universities.
The procedures adopted should include both resort to competent
social, economic, and legal research by specialists and regularized
opportunities for those affected by legislative proposals to urge
their views in open hearing.

2. ADMINISTRATIVE

Professor Hayek's contention that any official discretion is incompatible with those decencies of government commonly subsumed by the "rule of law" cannot be sustained.[66] It reflects a
yearning for governmental passivity that current conditions, particularly in the underdeveloped parts of the world, render unthinkable. Official action under grants of discretionary power is inevitable and, in fact, desirable. It is equally desirable, however,
that the discretion of officials be circumscribed by standards that
permit a review of their actions and a determination whether they
have acted within the proper scope of their authority. A common
phenomenon under Dr. Nkrumah was a grant of broad discretion to
an official to take action, and to take it at such times as he believed
the public interest required. This should be replaced by norms
that articulate the policy goals, specify the official with authority
to act, and indicate the standards that are to control his discretion.

The establishment of such a pattern in granting official powers
is an indispensable first step toward responsible and decent government. The true villain is not discretionary power; it is official
action unauthorized by any legal norm, or authorization to act
within an uncontrolled discretion. It is also the absence of an ef-

---

65 See text accompanying notes 36-38 *supra*.
66 HAYEK, THE ROAD TO SERFDOM *passim* (1944).

fective system of administrative review that can be invoked by the
citizen who is adversely affected by the acts of officials. Therefore,
the architects of the new constitutional and legal order of Ghana
should give careful attention to the development of a body of administrative law permitting the citizen to demand effectively that
the officials justify their action in a legal norm, and curbing actions
that a competent tribunal cannot find to be related rationally to
the standards guiding discretion.

3. ECONOMIC PLANNING

The action of the National Liberation Council in withdrawing the
state entirely or in part from certain enterprises suggests that
future governmental intervention in the economy may be less than
in the past. More generally, many development economists today
are questioning attempts to devise overall economic plans and are
urging greater reliance on specific project planning and implementation. Whether such a trend will develop in Ghana is now unpredictable. It is predictable, however, that the continuing role of
the government in the economy will be substantial and that some
effort to plan development will be continued.

It is unnecessary now to assess Ghana's past efforts at general
economic planning. Whatever the merits or defects of the plans
themselves may have been, it is clear that at the level of implementation they were almost total failures. Even in the planning phase
itself, the planners were unable to rely on the active cooperation of
ministers and civil servants. Once the plan was prepared, it had
no determinate legal status, and the guidelines it provided in allo-
cating scarce resources and coordinating government actions were
ignored frequently at the ministerial and presidential levels. The
resulting pattern of *ad hoc* decisions, in league with international
market conditions, accelerated the deterioration of the economy.
It is difficult to believe that even the staunchest advocate of planning would contend that the Ghana variety under Dr. Nkrumah
was better than the untrammeled play of market forces.

If Ghana's economic development is to be planned, the lawmakers
must devise legal institutions for the improvement of both plan
formulation and implementation. Assured access of the planners
to all governmental data is an indispensable minimum. Formal
legal status for a planning commission, including not merely specialists but also representatives of the executive and legislative
body as well, would be desirable. Granting it power to review and
coordinate all ministerial budgetary requests also might be considered. Providing the planning commission with its own legal
staff might help to assure continuing adaptation of the legal order
to the needs of development.

C. *Political Participation*

In conclusion, a brief word on the most important aspect of the legal order—that which structures the citizen's participation in his government. Aside from the indeterminate potential role of the Political Committee, no such participation now exists in Ghana. The desire of the Council for a respite from politics until it sets the government's house in order is understandable. I believe, however, that the structuring of a wider participation by the people and their leaders is among the most urgent tasks before the new government. Basically democratic institutions characterized the indigenous order of Ghana. Even under Nkrumah the formal facade of a representative democracy was preserved, and the Party, with its wing organizations, provided minimal channels of communication between the people and those in power. The people greeted the ouster of the Nkrumah government with general approval. Within the populace there is now no evidence of deep cleavages, tensions, or hostilities that would make the return of a more open political society dangerous to the public peace. I doubt profoundly that any people has ever become adept in the art of democratic government solely through the tutelage of a self-appointed military junta. The constitutional and legal machinery for popular participation in solving the problems left by the Nkrumah regime and in building a secure and humane society in Ghana calls for early attention.

LAW AND SOCIETY IN GHANA†

S. K. B. ASANTE*

Few would deny that the evolution of the nation-state in formerly
dependent Africa is one of the most challenging political developments in the second half of the twentieth century. The growing
pains of this evolution and the distressing signs of political instability have often provoked facile, if not pejorative, pronouncements
by politicians, journalists and scholars; but they have also stimu-
lated more perceptive observers like Professors Arthur Lewis,[1] S. A.
de Smith[2] and David Apter[3] into serious and engaging studies of
the complex forces at work in that part of the world. Professor
Harvey's *Law and Social Change in Ghana* clearly belongs to the
latter category.

This work deals primarily with those aspects of Ghanaian public
law that "structure, channel, allocate and control public power and
define the role of the citizen in relation to the power structure."[4]
The accent is on developments under the Nkrumah regime (1951-
1964); and Professor Harvey's central thesis is that the basically
democratic legacy of the British was ultimately distorted by the
emergence of autocratic tendencies in this period.

The analytical jurist, as well as the orthodox legal historian, will
find this book invaluable. It is regaled with a masterly, if too
rigorous, analysis of an impressive body of what the Austinian
would term "law properly so called"; the Nkrumah Constitution of
1954, the Ghana (Independence) Constitution of 1957, the Republican Constitution of 1960, a host of statutes and executive instruments, and the major judicial decisions on public law are all subjected to a searching examination in the process of diagnosing the
value preferences of the ruling elite. But this study has even
deeper significance for the legal philosopher, for Professor Harvey
himself declares that this study grew

> not out of a specialized area interest in Africa, but out of pri-
> mary concern with some of the perennial problems of legal
> philosophy. What is law or, more appropriately, what do
> we mean when we talk about law? Does it imply a neces-
> sary value content? If not, what is the source or sources
> of the value acceptances discernible in various legal orders?
> How does a particular value acceptance achieve such a de-

---

† This article is based upon LAW AND SOCIAL CHANGE IN GHANA, by
William B. Harvey. Princeton, New Jersey: Princeton University Press.
1966. Pp. xiii, 453. $10.00.

* Lecturer in Law, University of Leeds. LL.B., 1956, University of
Nottingham; LL.M., 1958, University of London; J.S.D., 1965, Yale University.

[1] LEWIS, POLITICS IN WEST AFRICA (1966).

[2] DE SMITH, THE NEW COMMONWEALTH AND ITS CONSTITUTIONS (1964).

[3] APTER, THE GOLD COAST IN TRANSITION (1955).

[4] HARVEY, LAW AND SOCIAL CHANGE IN GHANA ix (1966).

gree of articulation and strength that it can call upon the
technique of law for support and implementation?[5]

These philosophical perspectives are evident throughout the
book. In elaborating upon the philosophical underpinnings of this
study, Professor Harvey offers a working definition of law as "a
technique of social ordering deriving its essential characteristic from
its ultimate reliance on the reserved monopoly of systematically
threatened or applied force in politically organized society."[6] He
emphasizes that law is only a technique of social ordering; where
values are concerned it is essentially neutral and can be used to
implement the value assumptions of nazism, communism, or Western democracy. This avowedly positivist definition of law clearly
has its merits, for by drawing a distinction between law as it is
and law as it ought to be, Professor Harvey avoids the invidious
task of adjudging the enactments of the Nkrumah regime as null on
the ground that they violated some hallowed, immutable postulates. The popular view that the ex-President's dismissal of Sir
Arku Korsah as Chief Justice was unconstitutional probably stems
from the notion that the act offended some norm of a higher law,
for the barest acquaintance with the Republican Constitution will
disclose that it was technically unimpeachable.[7] However, Professor Harvey is quick to concede that the effort to view law as
essentially value-neutral and as deriving its value content from
extrinsic sources "perhaps cannot be entirely successful," for "certain values are so commonly associated with its use that they
may come to appear as inevitable concomitants."[8] He cites as an
example the principle that a legal standard must be promulgated in
advance of its application.

The importance of this qualification was graphically demonstrated by the phenomenon of "The Presidential Command" that
became a distinctive feature of the Nkrumah regime. This was a
much-favored technique consisting in the frequent issue of imperi-
ous presidential edicts outside the normal legislative processes,
usually in defiance of well-entrenched norms but often self-con-
tradictory. They invariably threw the administration into a state
of near anarchy. By presidential command, university departments
were abolished or transferred to a different campus with scant regard for the provisions of the appropriate charter, chiefs were de-
posed and new chiefdoms created in defiance of established law,
lavish appropriations were made without prior legislative approval,
and public corporations were dissolved notwithstanding elaborate
statutory guarantees. One may question whether these edicts can

---

[5] Id. at vii.
[6] Id. at 343.
[7] "The appointment of a Judge as Chief Justice may at any time be
revoked by the President by instrument under the presidential seal."
REPUBLICAN CONST., GHANA (1960) art. 44, para. 3.
[8] HARVEY, op. cit. supra note 4, at 345.

be properly characterized as law. Formal authority for these edicts could probably be derived from article 55 of the Republican Constitution of 1960, which empowered the President to issue, by legislative instrument, directions having the force of law and taking precedence over all except the fundamental law of the land. But in any case there is no denying that these edicts had the essential characteristic of law stipulated by Professor Harvey, namely, the ultimate backing of the force of the politically organized society. Yet a technique of social ordering must surely mean something more than this erratic and capricious signification of presidential pleasure.

To say this is not to subscribe to any natural law philosophy or to Fuller's idea of inner fidelity to law, but merely to underscore the truism that the essential characteristic of a technique of social ordering is to ensure social order. To those who regard law as a process of authoritative decisionmaking, this positivist definition poses a number of problems. A study in law and social change must necessarily range over the whole spectrum of decisionmaking at all levels—national, regional, and local. The Nkrumah regime, in fact, made its most telling impact on the Ghanaian people through the agency of regional and district commissioners—local executive functionaries who, in effect, operated a regime of social ordering quite distinct from and virtually independent of the norms promulgated by organs of the central government. These functionaries dispensed their own summary "palm tree" justice, intimidated the courts, bullied law enforcement officers into compliance with their wishes, harassed civil servants with orders to depart from established procedures, issued edicts depriving citizens of lands or houses under unauthorized zoning and planning schemes, and, not infrequently, ordered the imprisonment of "political undesirables" without trial. If, as Professor Harvey maintains, the essential characteristic of law is ultimate reliance on a reserved monopoly of systematically threatened and applied force, then the regime of the regional and district "commissars" was indeed law, for the law enforcement agencies were undoubtedly at their beck and call, and their *diktat* prevailed as the dominant norm in every locality under their jurisdiction. Yet Professor Harvey's analysis of the legal tools of political monopoly makes only a passing reference to this phenomenon. If these local edicts be denied the status of law for want of ultimate basis in the fundamental law of the land, the question arises whether a study concerned with law and social change can dismiss as "extralegal" norms which actually and intimately governed the lives of ordinary Ghanaians. This unorthodox regime of local edicts that substantially blunted the formal prescriptions of the central government is at least pertinent to an inquiry into the interaction between the articulation of value acceptances and their implementation by law. It is undoubtedly relevant to Professor Harvey's central thesis that, whatever may have been the value orientation of the basic structuring of public power in Ghana, autocratic values in fact determined the realities of political life.

Professor Harvey's description of the legal tools of political monopoly is one of the most illuminating essays in his work; it is extremely well-documented and eminently convincing. After portraying the essentially democratic orientation of the representative institutions and the franchise system which formed the baseline of the Nkrumah regime, he carefully exposes the formidable armory of legal devices by which the regime systematically eliminated effective political opposition. The failure of the Republican Constitution to guarantee civil liberties, the statutory restrictions on access to elective office, the outlawry of free expression through potent sedition and treason laws, the proscription of free association, and, most notorious of all, the Preventive Detention Act that allowed imprisonment without due process are all thoroughly analyzed to demonstrate the all-pervading theme of autocracy.

That the charge of autocracy is sustained is undeniable. However, Professor Harvey does not make clear whether the ruling elite was committed to autocracy as an end or as merely an inescapable technique of dealing with the peculiar problems of an emergent African country. This raises the crucial political question raging over the whole of emergent Africa: Are the problems facing the ruling elites in newly independent African countries so complex, so peculiar, and so formidable as to warrant the establishment of authoritarian regimes? The apologists for the Nkrumah regime, for instance, sought to justify authoritarian rule on the grounds that it was necessary to ensure rapid economic development and to contain the turbulence unleashed by radical, social and economic changes; that it was the only effective technique of eliminating tribalism, localism and regionalism and of welding the heterogeneous communities into a united nation; and that the security of the infant liberty of the new nation against the sinister forces of "imperialism, colonialism and neo-colonialism" demanded the detention of "subversive elements" without the luxury of a trial hedged about with elaborate technicalities. A variation of the authoritarian argument was that the multiparty system was inherently divisive in a society still characterized by tribal sensitivity and that, in any case, it was wasteful of manpower, relegating to opposition benches able men who could participate in the urgent task of nation building. Furthermore, there was nothing in the African political process to warrant the importation of this peculiarly Western system. Party-political warfare was alien to the traditional political mechanism, and the post-independence era was not bedeviled by deep ideological cleavage. Public criticism of the government was a destructive indulgence because it distorted well-intentioned government policies and measures to a gullible public. In Ghana, the authoritarian philosophy was consummated in the inauguration of a monolithic one-party state, dedicated to Nkrumahism—a local version of Marxist Socialism—and claiming the unquestioning loyalty of all Ghanaians. Professional bodies, industrial and labor organizations, educational institutions, the universities, literary and scientific societies, the press, Parliament, the judiciary, and even religious bodies were all obliged to adhere to the tenets of the party's ideology. Dissent was treason.

There can be no meaningful discussion of autocracy without reference to these fundamental presuppositions. A rigorous appraisal of the Nkrumah regime will undoubtedly sustain the thesis that autocracy was a dominant value per se; nevertheless, the fashionable arguments usually advanced in defense of autocracy cannot be ignored, if only because they are still crucial in shaping the destiny of practically all other African states.

A most stimulating analysis of the interaction between law and society is to be found in the chapter on value competition in the Ghanaian public order. Professor Harvey identifies a number of basic antinomies as critical determinants of the scheme of values in the Ghanaian legal order. His theoretical premise is that antinomic competition is to be found in any legal system, and that a legal system is viable to the extent that antinomic tensions are controlled by processes of compromise and adjustment among the members of the social group and the elite who exercise the greatest power in shaping the law. Professor Harvey diagnoses the following basic antinomies as the value determinants in the Ghanaian public order; traditional localism and nationhood, African unity and nationhood, individualism and collectivism, autocracy and democracy, social change and stability.

This exercise is a valuable contribution to sociological jurisprudence; Professor Harvey displays great dexterity in tracing the basic presuppositions permeating the legal order and demonstrates a profound insight into the structure of Ghanaian society. However, the process of identifying basic antinomies in a legal order implies certain intellectual assumptions which are by no means axiomatic in Africa. It is an established Euro-American tradition to discuss social and political phenomena in terms of general ideological postulates or principles connoting articulate value systems— individualism, collectivism, democracy, right-wing, left-wing, conservative, liberal, progressive, and the like. The first intellectual assumption that this schematic view of social ordering implies is that by a clinical examination of social phenomena one can diagnose the inexorable unfolding of these principles in the social process. Tied up with this is the assumption that these principles resolve themselves into opposing pairs and, further, that one can identify distinct social groups as the rival champions of these principles.

The first question that may be raised is whether the political, legal and social developments in Africa are susceptible to such tidy generalizations. In any particular politico-legal situation in Africa, the forces at play may be so complex, so multifarious, so fluid, and so encumbered with expedient makeshifts and compromise as to defy any attractive rationalization in terms of sweeping philosophical postulates. Take, for example, the assertion that opposition to the Nkrumah regime emanated from social groups wedded to traditional localism. In fact, a close examination of the motivations of the main opposition groups[9] will reveal that the dominant factors were revulsion at the totalitarian excesses of the government, disillusionment over corruption and nepotism, exasperation with erratic policy determination, political frustration, especially among the disappointed adherents of the ex-President's Convention Peoples' Party,[10] and, most important of all, genuine economic grievances—particularly those provoked by discriminatory taxes on cocoa produce. True, in the face of the undoubted organizational superiority of the C.P.P., localism and traditionalism were exploited and pressed into the service of the opposition. In Ashanti, for example, the traditional loyalty to the Golden Stool[11] was cleverly manipulated by the National Liberation Movement as an effective catalyst of the opposition. But this was essentially a matter of strategy, not commitment to traditionalism as a substantive end in itself. Thus, although the N.L.M. loudly proclaimed its preference for a federal constitution before independence, its concern was not so much to set up regional governments as to use the bogey of secession in securing effective guarantees against totalitarian rule. Little wonder that it dropped the federation idea as soon as the Ghana (Independence) Constitution of 1957 promulgated what it regarded as adequate brakes on autocracy.

The analyst, wedded to the schematic conception of social phenomena, is bound to experience considerable difficulty in tracing the ideological basis of the political alliances of the Asantehene (King of Ashanti) within the last fifteen years. This venerable custodian of the Golden Stool and the embodiment of traditionalism first assumed a posture of benevolent neutrality at the beginning of the Nkrumah regime. He did not resist the enthusiastic reception of the C.P.P. among the Ashanti; he stood by when his capital elected, as its first representative to the National Assembly, Mr. Casely Hayford, who was both a member of the C.P.P. and a

---

9 The United Gold Coast Convention, the Independents, the Ghana Congress Party, the Muslim Association, the Northern Peoples Party, National Liberation Movement, and the Anlo Youth Association.

10 The C.P.P. was the ruling party in the Nkrumah regime. In 1964 it was proclaimed the only legal political party in Ghana.

11 The Golden Stool is the traditional symbol of the Ashanti nation. Its incumbent is the Asantehene (King of Ashanti), and legend has it that the Golden Stool embodies the soul of the Ashanti people. Therefore, it has a deep emotive significance among the Ashantis. This was dramatically demonstrated at the turn of the century when the Ashantis declared war on the British for desecrating the Stool.

Fanti.[12] From this position of neutrality, the Asantehene became a bitter opponent of the C.P.P. when he joined forces with the N.L.M. in the middle 50's. Immediately after independence (1957), he performed a complete political somersault, declaring his loyalty to the C.P.P. and fiercely denouncing his former colleagues in the N.L.M. His ardent support for Nkrumah persisted until the ouster of the ex-President, at which time he enthusiastically hailed the new military regime.

Even where these ideological postulates are identifiable as political and legal determinants, it is still hazardous to designate pairs as engaged in antinomic competition. Pan-Africanism, for example, was not opposed to Ghanaian nationhood, as Professor Harvey maintains. At least Nkrumah, who vociferously propagated both ideas, regarded African unity as the consummation of Ghanaian nationhood. Both were but aspects of the major political preoccupation throughout Africa, namely, the acquisition of "black power" in Africa and the world.

Perhaps the most serious shortcoming of the essay on value competition is the inadequacy of the criteria used. Instead of delving into the political and legal order of Ghana to discover the peculiarly Ghanaian sources of political and legal determinants, Professor Harvey came to Ghana with the legal philosopher's armory of predetermined value criteria and sought to verify them by reference to local experience. This exercise is unobjectionable in itself, but, by purging these criteria of local content, Professor Harvey is compelled to rely on high-level abstractions that are patently inadequate for unraveling the full depth of Ghanaian value acceptances. Such well-worn terms as autocracy and democracy, individualism and collectivism, change and stability, localism and nationhood, can only give but a general impression of the intricate forces shaping the political and legal order in Ghana. Thus, the dichotomy between autocracy and democracy fails to portray in depth two crucial ideas vying for supremacy in the structuring of African legal systems. On the one hand, it is argued that the all-important goals of high standards of living and rapid economic development are best realized under a regime in which a highly centralized and authoritarian government, immunized against the excesses of opposition factions, has unfettered power to mobilize the resources of a united country into achieving the quickest results in social and economic development. On the other hand, it is stressed that there can be no meaningful concept of progress in Africa that does not ensure respect for human dignity and encourage the widest possible participation in the decisionmaking process, and, further, that the baffling problems of economic and social development can only be solved by utilizing all available intellectual resources, not by autocratic regimes intolerant of sensible criticism.

---

[12] One of the four principal tribes of Ghana.

The danger of using high-level abstractions is particularly demonstrated in Professor Harvey's discussion of the collectivism-individualism antinomy. At one stage the learned author declares: "The decline of the collectivist values supporting the traditional order has been more than balanced however by a new collectivist orientation toward the nation-state."[13] By using the term "collectivist," an attractive ideological formula, he glosses over the distinction between two essentially different ideas: First, the "collectivism" of the traditional African order—essentially a technique of social insurance sustained by an intricate system of reciprocal obligations and rights and revolving principally around the extended family unit but assuring security and dignity to individual members of the family. Second, the "collectivism" of the nation-state, which, under Nkrumah, was an authoritarian state machinery, sustained by a monolithic party, that deprived the individual citizen of human dignity without any firm assurance of material security. Under the traditional African order individualism was synonymous with the pursuit of self-interest at the expense of social obligation, whereas individualism under the Nkrumah regime was identifiable with the assertion of human dignity against the harsh encroachments of the state. Thus, traditional African "collectivism" and collectivism in Nkrumah's Ghana have little in common beyond an arbitrary philosophical classification.

The question may be raised whether the foregoing criticism of the application of universal value-criteria to the Ghanaian situation is fair in view of Professor Harvey's declared interest in the perennial problems of legal philosophy. Two points may perhaps be made in answer to this question. First, there is no necessary inconsistency between a value analysis primarily rooted in Ghanaian circumstances and a professed interest in general legal philosophy. An empirical examination of the political and legal order of Ghana would probably yield results of general jurisprudential significance even though the conclusions may have been reached by the inductive method. Second, the use of predetermined value-criteria inevitably betrays a prior ideological commitment that tends to detract from the objectivity of the study of a foreign legal system. By comparison with most studies of Ghanaian developments, Professor Harvey's work is eminently fair and refreshingly objective. Yet even Professor Harvey betrays his own value preferences when he asserts that "the individualism-collectivism antinomy is closely related to the competition between democracy and autocracy."[14] Again he displays the bias of a Western liberal when, in assessing the status of the individual in modern Ghana, he declares that "one of the customary approaches to such an assessment is in terms of fundamental private rights and the machinery for their . . . protec-

---

[13] HARVEY, *op. cit. supra* note 4, at 359.
[14] *Id.* at 360.

tion against the state or its functionaries."[15] His analysis of the absence of legal guarantees for security of property rights, for independence of the judiciary, and for freedom of speech, movement, and association unmistakably points to an adherent of American constitutional principles. These values are not irrelevant to Africa, but the postulates of human dignity in Africa need not necessarily follow Western or Eastern formulations.

Professor Harvey's conclusions on the changes in value acceptances in pre-independence days would seem to support Sir Henry Maine's theory about the movement of progressive societies from status to contract. Professor Harvey maintains that the traditional order in Ghana was dominated by collectivist values: "It would hardly be an overstatement to say that in this order there was no operative concept of the individual. The family or lineage was the basic unit of social organization."[16] He goes on to say that in the colonial era this collectivism was eroded by individualism until by the time of independence a disintegrating traditional order could hardly resist the "accelerating development of law-government predominantly grounded on individualistic values."[17]

The so-called progression from collectivism to individualism in African societies may be viewed from at least three angles—the legal, the economic, and the philosophical or social. From the legal standpoint, the criticial question is whether the group or the individual is the primary juridical unit. Spelled out more fully, this aspect of the progression poses, *inter alia*, the following questions: Is land ownership vested in the individual or in some corporate entity as the state, the family, or the lineage? Has the individual criminal responsibility, or does an individual's criminal act necessarily attract the corporate or collective responsibility of the group? Does the individual owe any civic duty as a distinct entity or only as a part of a group? From the economic standpoint, the enquiry is directed to the central question whether the social order admits of private enterprise in the form of individual farming, fishing, or other economic activity or whether the order irresistibly impels corporate or collective economic activity. As far as the philosophical aspect of the progression is concerned, the crucial question is whether the society is dominated by the concept that the community interest must prevail over self-interest. In other words, does the social ordering ensure a sort of social insurance system with a heavy accent on the individual's obligation to the community, or does it lean in favor of the unbridled pursuit of self-interest as the essential precondition of a just and productive system?

There is no necessary congruence of these three aspects of the collectivism-individualism phenomenon. Thus legal "individual-

---

[15] *Id.* at 359.
[16] *Id.* at 357–58.
[17] *Id.* at 358.

ism" is perfectly compatible with philosophical "collectivism"; that
is, a legal order which revolves around the individual as the basic
juridical unit is clearly compatible with a philosophical value system which proclaims the paramountcy of the public interest. Nor
does an order that emphasizes the corporate entity as the primary
juridical unit necessarily preclude robust individual economic activity.

In the traditional order the accent was on the group as the basic
juridical unit. Political organization, for instance, emphasized the
clan, the lineage, and the family as vital legal personae. Marriage
was not a voluntary union of one man and one woman to the exclusion of all others, but an alliance of families in which the bride
and bridegroom served as representatives of two groups. In the
law of succession, the group interest was again predominant; freedom of testation was strictly tabooed, and even self-acquired property of the decedent devolved on the family as a group. The scheme
of land ownership again emphasized the group as the basic juridical unit, especially in the highly centralized states. Criminal responsibility, however, was basically individual. Civic duty to the
state, such as the payment of customary tribute and liability for
military service, was also basically individual. This emphasis on
the group as the primary legal persona did not necessarily preclude
private enterprise, a fact not often realized. At first blush, the
traditional schema in the distribution and incidence of landed interests appears to deny any significant status to the individual.
But the concept of stool or family ownership of land, for instance, admitted of exclusive, individual rights known as the usufruct. The
usufruct assured to the usufructuary full, exclusive, and transmis-
sible rights of possession and beneficial use, but not the right
to alienate the land itself. Within this framework of individual
usufruct there was ample scope for economic individualism. True,
traditional social process employed cooperative endeavor to accomplish the formidable tasks of clearing and cultivating large
tracts of impenetrable forest lands, and the collective efforts of
kinsmen invariably resulted in the creation of family property.
But there was nothing to prevent an enterprising individual from
establishing his own private concern by his own unaided efforts.
That legal doctrine did not preclude individual economic activity is
borne out in the colonial era by the robust growth of the cocoa
industry, which was largely owned and run on an individual basis.
This momentous economic transformation from subsistence to commercial farming was achieved without any prior overhaul of the
ownership patterns in traditional law. In short, the idea of corporate ownership was often a doctrinal myth, rigorously asserted
and respectfully acknowledged, but bereft of all significant economic content.

Philosophical "collectivism" has, of course, been the distinctive
feature of African social ideas. The group interest undoubtedly

prevailed over the individual interest in traditional Ghana. But by group interest one refers to a sort of social insurance system which at once emphasized the individual's obligation to the community and assured him social security and human dignity. Ultimately, therefore, the group interest was identifiable with the individual interest. That the traditional order showed scrupulous concern for the individual is demonstrated by the elaborate ceremonial rituals that accompanied the birth and the death of an individual. These events brought to a stop all activity, economic or otherwise; members of the community were required to reflect upon the addition or loss to the race of a human being. A traditional saying states that "it is man, not wealth, that counts."

How far did these values change in the colonial era? From the legal standpoint the individual achieved an enhanced status as a juridical unit. Land law provides a good example. Under the impact of new economic and social conditions, such as the introduction of commercial farming, the decline in traditional political authority, and the interaction with English juristic ideas, the usufruct matured into a "freehold" interest that assured the individual full rights of beneficial user, including the right of alienation. However, judicial pronouncements still paid lip service to the concept of communal ownership. The English concept of free testation imperceptibly crept into the Ghanaian law of succession. Furthermore, nearly all colonial regulatory laws presupposed the individual as the basic juridical unit.

In the economic sphere, the colonial era saw the inauguration of flourishing private enterprise in commercial agriculture. Cash crops, being perennial crops, led to regimes of permanent cultivation that enhanced the usufructuary's individual economic activity.[18] Other forms of commercial activity, especially retail trade, also reflected the phenomenal growth of private enterprise. Thus legal individualism was, on the whole, accompanied by economic individualism.

But these developments did not substantially detract from the Ghanaian commitment to philosophical or social collectivism. In short, the emergence of the individual as a primary juridical unit and the growth of private enterprise have not significantly changed the average Ghanaian's attitude about his basic obligation to support and assist members of his extended family or his village. Take, for example, the case of a family member indicted for a criminal offense. Undeniably, such an individual has sole criminal responsibility at law for his acts. Yet his indictment involves the whole extended family in frantic efforts to retain counsel and to ensure the best available defense in order to avoid the stigma of a conviction. Here legal individualism fails to arrest the full implica-

[18] See Asante, *Interests in Land in the Customary Law of Ghana—A New Appraisal*, 74 YALE L. J. 848, 857 (1965).

tions of philosophical collectivism. This persistence of philosophical collectivism in the face of individualistic pressures in the economic and legal spheres is one of the most fascinating social developments in present-day Ghana. Neither Oxford nor Harvard has succeeded in extricating the educated Ghanaian from the intricate web of obligations implicit in the traditional family system. In short, economic and legal individualism has been pressed into the service of philosophical collectivism. Moreover, traditional institutions tend to assume new forms in the sustained struggle for survival. Members of one village who have migrated to distant urban areas have kept the social insurance idea alive by organizing themselves into mutual help associations that go to the assistance of needy members. No state institution has offered a comparable mechanism of social security. What the Nkrumah regime attempted to do was to accentuate obligation to an authoritarian state machinery without assuring any of the social insurance benefits and the edifying attributes that the traditional order offered to individuals. It would not be an exaggeration to assert that the Nkrumah regime collapsed because it lost sight of the basic tenets of African humanism.

Modern developments in Africa have shown that the process of social change is far more involved than the rash pronouncements of the ruling elite would suggest. In Ghana, a colonial regime imbued with Western individualistic values did not succeed in effecting a radical change in the basically collectivistic attitudes of the Ghanaians. The time lag between formal prescriptions and social acceptance of the value underpinnings of these prescriptions proved an imponderable factor. Likewise, the Nkrumah regime, for all its loud advocacy of Eastern socialist values, hardly changed the solid attitudes instilled by a hundred years of contact with the British. Thus, while the Republican Constitution of 1960[19] proclaimed a one-party, socialist state, the courts continued to be administered by British-trained judges, who not only wore grey wigs and scarlet gowns, but who also looked to English decisions for inspiration. The Republican Constitution made no reference to a bill of rights, but the essential ingredients of the English concept of the rule of law were sufficiently rooted in Ghanaian public life to generate a revulsion against wanton totalitarianism.

---

[19] As amended by Constitution (Amendment) Act, 1964, Pub. Act 224 (Ghana).

THE SOURCES OF LAW IN THE NEW NATIONS OF AFRICA: A CASE STUDY FROM THE REPUBLIC OF THE SUDAN

Cliff F. Thompson*

I. Introduction

The decline of colonial empires and the ascendancy of independent nations in Africa opens a formative era for the sources of African law, an era in which the new nations will attempt to fashion legal structures in their own image. Legal pluralism, "the co-existence of a number of legal systems within a given area,"[1] is a major characteristic of the existing legal structures. By focusing attention upon the pluralistic sources of law in the Republic of the Sudan, we can examine the nature of an existing legal structure and the possibility of important transitions.

The Sudan, geographically the largest country in Africa, is primarily supported by the immense cotton crop of the Gezira, which is located to the south of the confluence of the White and Blue Niles.[2] At the confluence are situated the "Three Towns"—Khartoum, Khartoum North, and Omdurman. Together they constitute the major urban and administrative center in a predominantly rural nation.

Within the frontiers of the Sudan, the Nile touches the homelands of differing peoples who characterize the contrast between North Africa and sub-Saharan Africa. Simplified, this is a contrast between a northern desert, inhabited by Arab Muslims, and a south of swamp and forest land, inhabited by Negroid peoples who, except for the few educated and often converted by Christian mission schools, practice animistic religions. To bridge the stubborn dif-

---

* Associate Director, African Law Center, Columbia University; Editor, *African Law Digest*; Secretary, Sudan Law Project, 1961-1965; and Lecturer in Law, University of Khartoum, 1961-1965. A.B., 1956, LL.B., 1960, Harvard University; M.A., 1962, Oxford University.

The author expresses his thanks to members of the Sudanese legal profession for innumerable conversations concerning parts of this article and to Mr. David L. Perrott, now of Exeter University, England, who read an early draft of the article and made numerous useful suggestions.

[1] Schiller, *The Changes and Adjustments Which Should Be Brought to the Present Legal Systems of the Countries of Africa to Permit Them to Respond More Effectively to the New Requirements of the Development of the Countries*, in Legal Aspects of Economic Development—Surveys Made at the Request of UNESCO 193, 194 (Tunc ed. 1966).

[2] The most recent general study, Henderson, Sudan Republic (1965), includes a descriptive bibliography. The inaccuracies regarding the 1964 Revolution mar an otherwise meritorious book. Also useful is Said, The Sudan—Crossroads of Africa (1965), which emphasizes the relationship of the north and the south. See also Gaitskell, Gezira—A Story of Development in the Sudan (1959).

ferences between its north and south is the Sudan's gravest domestic concern.[3]

The Sudan attained full independence to deal with its problems when the Anglo-Egyptian condominium administered by the British faded peacefully from existence on January 1, 1956. In a pattern now familiar in Africa, the army seized power from a weak parliament on November 17, 1958. Nearly six years of stable but stagnant government followed. The unprecedented, and unexpected, victory of unarmed citizens against the military regime in the 21 October 1964 Revolution remains the basis of the present civilian government. This popular revolution did not give rise to new ideas about the law so much as it spun dormant ideas into a new life powerful enough to influence profoundly the sources of law.

These freshly articulated ideas often conflict with the present sources of law. Any effort to analyze the sources of Sudanese law more than half a century after the establishment of the present legal system and more than a decade after independence can, therefore, only provide an outline with many blurred edges. This outline will focus upon five interrelated topics: (1) the existing sources of law; (2) the availability of applicable legal materials; (3) significant gaps and uncertainties; (4) key issues for the future; and (5) pressures for fundamental change.

II. EXISTING SOURCES OF LAW

"Source" has a variety of meanings, such as historical or psychological origin, but our initial concern will be with the authorizing source within the legal system that gives a particular rule its validity as the applicable law. The major sources of formally authorized law in the Sudanese legal system are three: Islamic law, customary law, and general territorial law.[4]

The distinction between "personal laws" and "lawyers' laws" is

---

[3] As of July 1966, an estimated 15,000 enlisted men of the Sudan Army were engaged in the effort to eliminate the rebel activity that began in earnest in the three southern provinces in early 1964. The situation in mid-1966 remained unresolved but was greatly improved compared to the chaotic and random violence of 1965. Compare HENDERSON, op. cit. supra note 2, at 152-202, with SAID, op. cit. supra note 2. For conflicting views as to the origin of the problems in the southern Sudan, compare Abdel-Rahim, The Development of the British Policy in the Southern Sudan: 1899-1947, 1965 (mimeograph on file with the Sudan Ministry of Foreign Affairs), with ODUHO & DENG, THE PROBLEM OF THE SOUTHERN SUDAN (1963). For an excellent case study of northerner-southerner differences, see Rehfisch, A Study of Some Southern Migrants in Omdurman, 1962 SUDAN NOTES AND RECORDS 50.

[4] For an account of the Sudan's legal system, see Cotran, Sudan, in JUDICIAL SYSTEMS IN AFRICA — (Allott ed. 1962); Guttman, A Survey of the Sudan Legal System, 1956 SUDAN LAW JOURNAL AND REPORTS 7 [hereinafter cited as SUDAN L.J. REP.].

useful in describing the role of the three sources.[5] Personal laws deal with subjects such as marriage, divorce, inheritance, and other matters of the family. The content of Islamic law and customary law is primarily personal. Lawyers' laws, with which the general territorial law is chiefly concerned, deal with legal relationships arising from the complexities of modern commercial and industrial society. For example, company law is clearly lawyers' law, while torts are in the gray area where the general territorial law may overlap with customary law or Islamic rules. Unlike personal laws, lawyers' laws contain many rules that are unlikely to cause ethical controversy but that are necessary as a guide for behavior, whether in selecting a side of the road upon which to drive or in establishing corporate enterprises.[6]

The administration of the three sources of law is controlled by an independent judiciary. The hierarchy of courts is organized into two divisions, and the Chief Justice has the major supervisory power.[7] The civil division administers the customary law and the general territorial law, which includes both civil and criminal matters. The Shari'a division, presided over by the Grand Kadi, administers Islamic law between Muslims.

A. Islamic Law

The primary secular authorization for Islamic law originated in 1902 when the Sudan Mohammedan Law Courts Ordinance established the existing structure for the Shari'a courts and provided for promulgating regulations.[8] Regulation 53 of the Sudan Mohammedan Law Courts Organization and Procedure Regulations of 1916 allows the Shari'a courts to apply "the authoritative doctrines of

---

[5] See generally Twining, *Some Aspects of Reception*, 1957 SUDAN L.J. REP. 229, 232-33. Note that there may also be "political laws," *i.e.*, laws deriving from a particular political problem and with a definite political purpose, such as the Sudan's South Africa Boycott Act (No. 30) (1963).

[6] Sir Frederick Pollock emphasized that there is a "vast bulk of modern law dealing with matters of public order for which a rule of some kind is wanted, but, until the rule is made by competent authority, it is indifferent from an ethical point of view what it shall be." POLLOCK, ESSAYS IN THE LAW 266 (1922). Most lawyers' laws will not be "indifferent from an ethical point of view" in the sense that they will embody social and moral philosophies that may be highly debatable.

[7] See THE SUDAN TRANSITIONAL CONST. ch. IX (amend. 1964), in Republic of Sudan Gazette (Special Supplement 1964). The Transitional Constitution is the product of the 21 October 1964 Revolution. An outline of the hierarchy of the courts is in Cotran, *op. cit. supra* note 4, at 218-19. As a general guide, the ranking of the civil division begins with the Court of Appeal at the top, followed by the high court, the province courts, the district courts, and the local courts (chiefs' courts and native courts). In the Shari'a division, the ranking is: Court of Appeal, high court, Kadis' courts.

[8] Sudan Mohammedan Law Courts Ordinance, 1902, § 8, 11 LAWS OF THE SUDAN 2 (1955). For a description of the *Laws of the Sudan*, see note 27 *infra* and accompanying text.

the Hanafia jurists except in matters in which the Grand Kadi otherwise directs in a judicial circular or memorandum, in which case the decision shall be in accordance with such other doctrines of the Hanafia or other Mohammedan jurists as are set forth in such circular or memorandum."[9] The power of the Grand Kadi to issue such a circular or memorandum is extremely important because it is the method by which Islamic law in the Sudan may be brought into accord with the most modern views of Islamic scholars.[10]

A civil division court may also apply Islamic law to personal law questions[11] where the parties are Muslim and they all consent[12] in writing[13] to the jurisdiction of the court. In such a case, the civil division court would apply the Islamic law as modified by any custom not contrary to "justice, equity or good conscience."[14]

B. Customary Law

The most utilized authorizations for customary rules are found in the Chiefs' Courts Ordinance of 1931, which governs the three southern provinces, and in the Native Courts Ordinance of 1932, which governs the remaining six provinces.[15] The local courts established pursuant to them administer "the native law and custom" within the area of their jurisdiction.[16] However, the custom must not conflict with "justice, morality or order,"[17] the Sudanese form of the repugnancy clause found in British legislation dealing with local customary laws.[18]

Nearly 1,000 local courts handle fifty-five to seventy-five percent of the total number of cases heard in the Sudan, depending on which of several acceptable methods of calculation is used.[19]

---

9 Sudan Mohammedan Law Courts Organization and Procedure Regulations, 1916, § 54, 11 LAWS OF THE SUDAN 19 (1955). Although the majority of Muslims in the Sudan adhere to the Maliki School, the Sudan adopted the Egyptian practice of applying the Hanafia School. See FARRAN, MATRIMONIAL LAWS OF THE SUDAN 38-39 (1963).
10 See Anderson, *The Modernisation of Islamic Law in the Sudan*, 1960 SUDAN L.J. REP. 292, 295-96.
11 Civil Justice Ordinance, 1929, § 5, 10 LAWS OF THE SUDAN 12 (1955).
12 Civil Justice Ordinance, 1929, § 38, 10 LAWS OF THE SUDAN 17 (1955).
13 A judicial gloss added by Heirs of El Tayeb El Melik v. Ahmadiya Zawya, AC-REV-262-1961, 1962 SUDAN L.J. REP. 135, 138.
14 Civil Justice Ordinance, 1929, § 5(a), 10 LAWS OF THE SUDAN 12 (1955).
15 Chiefs' Courts Ordinance, 1931, 10 LAWS OF THE SUDAN 165 (1955); Native Courts Ordinance, 1932, 10 LAWS OF THE SUDAN 170 (1955). See generally Nur, *The Role of the Native Courts in the Administration of Justice in the Sudan*, 1960 SUDAN NOTES AND RECORDS 78.
16 Chiefs' Courts Ordinance, 1931, § 7, 10 LAWS OF THE SUDAN 166-67 (1955); Native Courts Ordinance, 1932, § 9, 10 LAWS OF THE SUDAN 172-73 (1955).
17 *Ibid.*
18 See ALLOTT, ESSAYS IN AFRICAN LAW 194-201 (1960).
19 See Nur, *supra* note 15, for the smaller calculation; the larger figure

Nearly all the cases involve personal law questions, but some also concern wider customary law issues like the allocation of grazing rights between tribal areas.[20]   Cases can go from the local courts, where laymen preside, into the regular civil division court structure, where professional judges generally conduct the proceedings.[21] Approximately two cases originating in the local courts reach the Chief Justice weekly.[22]

By implication from the two local courts' ordinances, the civil division courts, when hearing appeals or revisions from the local courts, are authorized to apply the customary law and to apply the test of "justice, morality or order."[23]   When deciding disputes concerning personal law questions, civil division courts have specific power to apply "any custom applicable to the parties concerned which is not contrary to justice, equity or good conscience," unless the custom has been modified by legislation or by the decision of a competent court.[24]   Civil division courts also have general power to recognize a rule of customary law even if it did not arise in a case coming from one of the local courts under the Chiefs' or Native Courts Ordinances or even if it did not relate to a personal law issue, so long as the court regards the customary rule as in accordance with "justice, equity and good conscience" and not in conflict with a statute.[25]

---

was cited by the official delegates from the Sudan to the African Conference on Local Courts and Customary Law held in Dar es Salaam, September 9-19, 1963.   The different calculations are the result of differences between the years selected, the doubtfulness of some figures in any year, and the question of how far Islamic law questions are to be considered customary law.

[20] *E.g.*, Adam Mohamed Ibrahim v. Abbaker Ahmed Kagir, AC-REV-93-1959, 1959 SUDAN L.J. REP. 45 (dispute about unregistered land remanded to province judge to hear evidence on "native custom").

[21] Chiefs' Courts Ordinance, 1931, §§ 9, 10, 10 LAWS OF THE SUDAN 168 (1955); Native Courts Ordinance, 1932, §§ 11, 12, 10 LAWS OF THE SUDAN 173-74 (1955).

[22] This figure was obtained from Chief Justice Mohamed Ahmed Abu Rannat in September 1964 and was valid for at least the five preceding years.   The current disruption in the southern Sudan has virtually eliminated the cases coming from the three southern provinces.

[23] *Cf.* Chiefs' Courts Ordinance, 1931, 10 LAWS OF THE SUDAN 165 (1955); Native Courts Ordinance, 1932, 10 LAWS OF THE SUDAN 170 (1955).   There is no specific authorization, but the conclusion is consistent with the purposes of the ordinances.

[24] Civil Justice Ordinance, 1929, § 5, 10 LAWS OF THE SUDAN 12 (1955). It is probable, but not undisputed, that "custom" in this passage includes the customary religious laws of the Coptic, Greek Orthodox, and other minority communities in the Sudan. See FARRAN, *op. cit. supra* note 9, at 87-91.

No known judgment has attached any significance to the difference between this formula and the "justice, morality or order" formula of the Chiefs' Courts Ordinance, 1931, § 7, 10 LAWS OF THE SUDAN 166-67 (1955), and the Native Courts Ordinance, 1932, § 9, 10 LAWS OF THE SUDAN 172-73 (1955).

[25] Civil Justice Ordinance, 1929, § 9, 10 LAWS OF THE SUDAN 13 (1955).

C. General Territorial Law

The general territorial law, the third major source of law, is potentially applicable to all Sudanese regardless of their ethnic group or religion. It consists of legislation and of judge-made law. The key to the authorization of this source is section 9 of the Civil Justice Ordinance of 1929: "In cases not provided for by this enactment or any other enactment for the time being in force, the Court shall act according to justice, equity and good conscience."[26]

The "enactment[s] for the time being in force" are found in eleven official volumes entitled *Laws of the Sudan*, published 1954 to 1956, and in the legislative supplements that have appeared monthly in the *Republic of Sudan Gazette* since the publication of the *Laws*.[27] Legislation has always been promulgated in both Arabic and English. The eleven volumes brought together the statutes enacted from the beginning of the condominium in 1898 that were in force at approximately the time of independence. The *Laws of the Sudan*, including the supplements, is far from comprehensive in its coverage of modern lawyers' law. Consequently, the "cases not provided for" are numerous.

The content of the general territorial law has predominantly reflected English law. For example, the Penal Code[28] was modeled upon the Indian Penal Code drafted in 1837 from English common-law principles by Lord Macaulay.[29] In the field of judge-made law, as early as 1920 a Chief Justice of the Sudan stated that he would apply English law rather than any other foreign law because it was the law understood by him.[30] A 1926 dictum that Sudanese

---

[26] *Ibid.* The original version of this section was in Civil Justice Ordinance, 1904, § 4 (Reproduction P/008 of the Central Archives, Khartoum), which is substantially identical.

[27] The Laws Commission established by the revised edition of the Laws Ordinance, 1953, 8 LAWS OF THE SUDAN 163 (1954), issued the volumes, which were prepared and arranged by Sir Charles Cumings and were edited by Cecil H. A. Bennett. Each volume indicates the date it came into force and is the authorized edition of all legislation appearing in the Gazette through a noted date. The most precise citation to the ordinances and their sections in the volumes is by page number. For an analysis of the organization of the monthly Gazette, see 1 AFRICAN L. DIGEST 3-4, 267-68 (1965). See also note 38 *infra*.

[28] Penal Code, 1925, 9 LAWS OF THE SUDAN 1 (1955).

[29] Anderson, *supra* note 10, at 294.

[30] Chief Justice R. H. Dun in Abu Fatma Sharif v. Mansour El Shouehi, AC-APP-3-1920 (unreported), where he applied the English Sale of Goods Act. In a separate judgment, Mr. Justice G. W. Williamson agreed with the point noted in the text. See also Antonious Saad v. Aziz Kroufi, AC-APP-5Q-1919 (unreported) (preference of English law to other foreign law does not imply superiority of English law); Grivas Bros. v. Nicola Pothitas, JC-APP-54/55-1910 (unreported) (English rule applied although contrary to rules of Egyptian, French, and German law). *But see* Ali Mahmoud Obeid v. Barclay's Bank (D.C.O.), Shendi, AC-APP-9-1959, 1961 SUDAN L.J. REP. 228 (American law considered in preference to English law).

courts are "guided but not bound" by English law has been re-peated often enough to have become a judicial cliché.[31]

That the cumulative heritage of Sudanese lawyers' law derives primarily from English law is due to several factors stemming from the predominance of the British administration during the condominium. First, the establishment of second-language training in English made useful the legal works of the common-law world. Second, since 1936, the earliest date for providing university legal education in tropical Africa, there has been formal training in the English common law.[32] Finally, Sudanese personnel, as well as British personnel, have been involved in the establishment and growth, since the beginning of the century, of a body of lawyers' law adopted or adapted from English common law.[33]

III. AVAILABILITY OF APPLICABLE LEGAL MATERIALS

The identification of the formally authorized sources of Sudan law unfortunately does not allow direct transit to an examination of substantive legal issues. We must first take account of the barriers that thwart access to the relevant legal materials. Access to these materials is a precondition for research and reform; absence of it can endanger even the routine operation of a legal system. The existence of substantial barriers may surprise a law-yer from a legal system where library and administrative services, such as a law reporting system, are long established and taken for granted. A review of the Sudan's efforts to build these basic serv-ices is instructive of the full dimensions of the difficulties that may confront a new nation.

Disturbing illustrations of the dangers exist in regard to both the legislative and judge-made aspect of the general territorial law. Each of the eleven volumes of the *Laws of the Sudan* contains "Instructions For Using This Edition." These instructions provide a procedure for relating new legislation to the *Laws*, but this pro-

---

[31] Heirs of Ibrahim Khalil v. Abdel Moniem, AC-APP-6-1926 (unre-ported). See, *e.g.*, Aisha Abdel Fam v. Shamboul Ahmed, BNP-HC-CS-400-1952 (unreported) (just and reasonable English law followed although not binding).

[32] The Legal Secretary of the Sudan Government opened the school of law at Gordon Memorial College in 1936, according to the information gathered from University of Khartoum records by Ustaz Natale Olewak Akalawin. Memories of the surviving members of the first class of six men place the date as anywhere from 1935 to 1938. One university catalogue, which states that the first law diplomas were awarded in 1936, probably means that the first diplomas went to the class that entered in 1936. See generally Khalil, *A Plea for a Shorter LL.B. Course in Khartoum*, 1963 J. AFRICAN L. 125; W. Twining, *Legal Studies at the University of Khartoum*, 1962 J. AFRICA L. 145.

[33] A reading of the unreported judgments in the period prior to inde-pendence indicates that Sudanese judges became consistently active in the late 1930's, chiefly at the district court level.

cedure has never been followed.[34] As a result, for more than six
years it was impossible to know if a particular section in the *Laws*
had been changed without perusing all of the unbound supplements
to the *Laws*, unless one made marginal notes in the *Laws* at the
time of the passage of new legislation. Indexing by handwritten
marginal notes is makeshift at best, and the assignment of this task
to untrained clerks meant that by 1962 no one set of the *Laws* contained all necessary notations.[35]

   To remedy this unfortunate situation, a senior legal draftsman
in the Attorney General's Chambers voluntarily prepared an index
during 1962-1963.[36] The preparation of the index lapsed from 1964
until mid-1966, when a concerned member of the faculty of law of
the University of Khartoum updated it.[37]   That the preparation of this legislative research tool has yet to be institutionalized
illustrates the unsteadiness of reform.

   The index is of little value unless a researcher or governmental
official has access to all of the monthly legislative supplements of
the past ten years because no cumulative edition of the supplements
has appeared since the publication of the *Laws*.[38] The rareness
of a complete collection of the supplements is indicated by the University of Khartoum's inability to accumulate one until 1966, after
having spent a year of intensified effort to locate missing items.[39]
The shortage of legislative materials has not disrupted the administration of justice in the Three Towns because of the closeness of
numerous personal contacts.[40] But the situation in the province

---

   [34] The instructions printed on the back of the title page in each volume
envisaged the use of cumulative leafs for amendments placed in an envelope
at the back of each volume. Devising a workable system is particularly
difficult where the work of the government printer is not dependable. The
Sudan had initiated an investigation of its official printer in 1966.
   [35] The Attorney General's Chambers had one set with most of the notations. Known omissions cast doubts upon the entries in it, making it difficult to depend upon.
   [36] See Cole, *Guide to the Laws of the Sudan*, 1962 SUDAN L.J. REP. 263.
   [37] Mr. S. J. Trueblood did the updating. The revision was duplicated
and distributed by the faculty of law of the University of Khartoum, and
its publication was planned for the 1966 *Sudan Law Journal and Reports*.
   [38] However, a reprint of volume 4 of the *Laws of the Sudan* incorporated
the relevant changes made by the legislative supplements through May 15,
1962. The difficulty of securing a complete set of the *Laws* should not be
overlooked: five of the eleven volumes are now out of stock.
   [39] The slow sequence of events is instructive as to the difficulties. The
Honorable Mohamed Ibrahim Khalil collected a core of the materials in
1963. They were supplemented in 1964-1965 by visiting Professors E. Scoles
and N. Penney. By prolonged searches and by using photo-duplication, Mr.
S. J. Trueblood was able to complete two sets in 1965-1966.
   [40] A typical example: the trial of an Indian expatriate arrested at the
airport for violation of exchange regulations was postponed in April 1966
because the appropriate amending legislation could not be located. The
defendant's advocate, Sayed Omar Abdel Aati, contacted friends in the
government and the university in an effort to locate the law and speed the
legal process.

and district headquarters is less satisfactory, although they are now adequately provided with legal treatises.[41]   There is also a wilderness of ungazetted subordinate legislation that is so difficult to obtain that even the courts of the Three Towns have been delayed in the dispatch of their work.[42]

In contrast to the uneven battle to provide access to legislative sources, the creation of a reporting system for case law is one of the great achievements of an independent Sudan.[43]   During the British administration Sudanese judges became adept in the common-law technique of evolving legal rules through a series of cases.   But the British legacy did not include the systematic reporting of cases that is an integral element of a modern common-law system.[44]

There have been four milestones in the development of the *Sudan Law Journal and Reports*.   They began with appeals by some Sudanese judges that the availability of reported cases was essential for the molding of law unique to the Sudan.[45]   The argument by

---

[41] A survey by the Sudan Law Project Trek Team (Ustaz Saeed Mohamed Ahmed El Mahdi, Ustaz Zaki Mustafa, and Mr. C. F. Thompson) indicated an acute shortage of all legal materials outside the Three Towns. The courts aggravated the problem by delaying requests for missing legislative supplements.   The Team's appeals to various institutions resulted in a grant in 1963 by the British Embassy to supply specified English law treatises to all judicial headquarters in the Sudan.

[42] See, *e.g.*, Alam Maximos v. Khadiga Hamad El Brigdar, AC-REV-73-1958, 1958 SUDAN L.J. REP. 80, where the Court of Appeal said, "delay . . . [was] caused by our inability to obtain the Local Order of the Omdurman Municipality under which the Dilapidation Order was issued."   *Ibid.*

[43] For details of the first organizational efforts, see Guttman, *Law Reporting in the Sudan*, 6 INT'L & COMP. L.Q. 685 (1957); W. Twining, *Law Reporting in the Sudan*, 1959 J. AFRICAN L. 176.

[44] The scattered and unsystematic efforts at law reporting prior to independence are listed in 1960 SUDAN L.J. REP. 334. The British administration could not have easily overcome the problems of expense and personnel, and these problems remain.   In 1952, Chief Justice W. O. B. Lindsay offered another explanation: "From the point of view of the practical administration of Justice, Circulars and Commentaries are the best medium for drawing attention of Judges and Magistrates to points of practice and established precedents arising out of the judicial interpretation of the Codes. In addition, a quarterly journal for limited circulation to the more academic minded would probably be useful."   Memorandum of November 8, 1952, attached to AC/Gen/6-1 of November 26, 1952 (on file in the Sudan Law Project collection at the University of Khartoum).   By 1955, however, the same Chief Justice wrote: "I hope my successor, the Honourable Mr. Justice Abu Rannat, will find a way to overcome the very real difficulties of regular law reporting at this critical stage in the development of the Judiciary, co-inciding, as it does, with the departure of the British members of the Judiciary."   Lindsay, *Preface* to CASES IN THE COURT OF APPEAL AND THE HIGH COURT, 1/1/53-30/6/54, at iii (Stanley-Baker comp. 1955).

[45] The earliest known appeal was by Mr. Justice Atabani in Mohamed El Tahir El Tom v. Taha Mohamed Attiya, Merowe District Court-CS-79-1941 (unreported), on retrial in 1943:   "Referring to my personal digest— and again regretting the absence of official reporting which would at least secure uniformity . . . ."

Mr. Justice Osamn El Tayeb in 1956 is particularly notable.

[I]n this [northern province] circuit we are mainly engaged in the determination of agricultural land cases.
These lands which lie on the banks of the River Nile or in
its bed when it changes its course, as it usually does
throughout the years, causes some lands to disappear and
other to emerge. We have to find for ourselves the legal
principles to be applied in litigation arising out of this state
of affairs and other matters. We have to investigate and
carefully study the local and customary notions of possession and ownership, of acquisition of title and rights of
cultivation or sharing in produce of date trees or other
profits, the right of pre-emption and how it is extinguished,
the right of specific performance of unregistered sales, the
recently recognized right of *gusad*, etc. These local and
customary notions must form the bases of our judgments,
provided they are not repugnant to any codified law, and
not contrary to justice, equity and good conscience. Many
of these seem to be firmly and finally established, but as we
see from the English Law Reports, the established rule or
principle of law when applied to a new set of facts, itself
appears as a novelty. And the application of the old rule
to new facts as they arise from time to time, adds considerable knowledge to it by new opinions as to extending or
limiting its application and expounding it according to
trends of thought and social changes in the community.

Much of the Law we now apply in this Province is peculiar to the nature of the litigation we have and we can
strictly call it Sudan Law. This Law we can find only in
our judgments, and foreign authorities seldom afford any
help. Let us collect the pieces of this law, put them together between two covers and make them available for
each one of us.[46]

The second milestone was reached in 1957. The campaign by
the faculty of law of the University of Khartoum to persuade the
government to provide funds for publishing current law reports
starting with cases from 1956, the year of independence, met with
success. Members of the faculty, working virtually without remun-
eration and between other duties, published five volumes within
five years and established the reports as an institution of recognized
value.[47] It then became possible to convince the government that

[46] Damer Province Court/Gen/2-7 of December 15, 1956 (on file with
the Sudan Law Project collection at the University of Khartoum). This
document was circulated to all district judges and resident magistrates in
the northern province and to the Chief Justice. However, Mr. Justice
Osman El Tayeb's solution was less ambitious than published reports; he
suggested that the judges pool carbon copies of significant decisions as a
start.

[47] Mr. E. Guttman began work on the first volume of the *Sudan Law
Journal and Reports* in July 1957, and it became available in the Sudan at
the end of 1958. Publication difficulties contributed to the continuance of

there ought to be a paying post for a person who would systematize the reporting and train a member of the judiciary as general editor.[48] Thus the third milestone was reached when the first full-time general editor began his duties in late 1962, and the fourth was achieved when the first Sudanese became general editor in 1965.[49]

Despite encouraging progress, law reporting in the Sudan cannot yet be taken for granted. The services of the Sudanese general editor are increasingly being used to settle cases as well as to report them.[50] The greatest danger presently is that the personnel shortage that prevented a qualified Sudanese from taking over the law reports at an earlier date will now operate to diminish the effectiveness of the general editor. Another danger is that an annual appropriation for the reports is far from certain, a problem reflecting current political antagonisms as much as the shortage of funds.[51]

---

roughly the same gap, so that the 1960 *Sudan Law Journal and Reports* became available in mid-1962.

[48] The Council of the *Sudan Law Journal and Reports* agreed to this in principle in August 1961 at the urging of Mr. W. L. Twining, who as general editor for the 1958-1960 volumes had increasingly systemized the law reporting. The most difficult aspects of implementing this policy, which was completed by the secretary of the Sudan Law Project, were: (1) convincing the government to provide a salary for the post, thereby virtually doubling the budget of the publication; (2) thoroughly reviewing the possibilities of immediate Sudanization before finally approving the use of an expatriate; and (3) balancing the expectations of the council and the various foreign programs that could supply someone. In the latter context, it is only a slight exaggeration to say that the council expected the services of a foreign chief justice and that the foreign programs expected to supply someone who would become Sudan's Chief Justice.

[49] Excellent cooperation by the Massachusetts Institute of Technology's Fellows in Africa Program, which is supported by the Ford Foundation, resulted in Mr. C. W. Brewster being appointed as general editor in September 1962. Mr. Brewster's account of his work is interestingly told in McPhee, *Fifty-Two People on a Continent,* The New Yorker, March 5, 1966, p. 101. He and the associate editor, Mr. Justice El Amien El Amien, who in 1965 became the first Sudanese general editor, brought the reports up to date with the 1962 to 1965 volumes. In April of 1966, the 1964 volume became available in the Sudan, and the 1965 volume was at the printer in England. They also reviewed all cases decided from 1956 on, in order to include any reportable decisions previously missed. Primarily because law reporting had become centered in the judiciary, the faculty of law of the University of Khartoum was planning to have its own law journal, but as of late July 1966 it was not clear what the relationship to the *Sudan Law Journal and Reports* would be.

[50] Although assisted by Miss Ihsan Fakhri, a graduate of the faculty of law of the University of Khartoum, the general editor in April 1966 found that his nearly full-time assignments as a judge imperiled the schedule of the *Sudan Law Journal and Reports.*

[51] The judiciary remains independent, but in mid-1966 many of the judges spoke privately, but frequently, of political harassment. The government's failure to grant salary increases given other departments was cited as an example.

The absence of a law reporting system at independence was symptomatic of the paucity of information or materials relating to any source of Sudanese law. An early improvement was the compilation of a legal bibliography primarily of published books or articles in English.[52] Projected bibliographies of Sudanese Government publications and published writings in Arabic remain uncompleted.[53] There were some unpublished anthropological studies that could provide useful information about Sudanese customary law, particularly those at the Institute of Social Anthropology, Oxford University.[54] The Sudan's Central Archives at the Ministry of Interior also held unpublished materials relevant to law, but the admitted incompleteness of the collection, the restrictions on access, and the use of a very general indexing system diminish their value for legal research.[55]

It was realized soon after independence that a vast supply of extremely important materials lay buried in government files and storerooms throughout the country. Alarmingly, it was equally obvious that there was constant destruction of the documents through the ravages of nature and by human neglect. The documents included judicial decisions for the more than fifty years preceding the establishment of the current series of reports and other legal documents, like reports on customary laws, land tenure, and the administration of justice by district commissioners and other governmental officials. Saving these unpublished documents was important for several reasons. In addition to providing information relevant to current legal and social science problems, they have a unique historical value.[56] They are also essential in the preparation of teaching materials grounded in Sudanese experience. A

---

[52] W. Twining, P. Twining & Nasri, *Bibliography of Sudan Law* (pt. 1), 1960 SUDAN L.J. REP. 313.

[53] See *id.* at 314. A bibliography of relevant Sudan Government publications in English was begun in 1961 but never completed. The other bibliographies were never started.

[54] Under the direction of Professor Evans-Pritchard, whose own writings on the Sudan have been prodigious (see, *e.g.*, the listing in W. Twining, P. Twining & Nasri, *supra* note 52, at 320), the Institute has been the training ground for many of the anthropologists at the University of Khartoum.

[55] An extreme shortage of personnel is the major problem; the three senior officials are so completely engaged in meeting the requests of government departments and classifying the materials already available that it is difficult for them to undertake collection treks to the provinces. One of the important services the archivists performed was the reproduction of basic legal materials that were largely unobtainable, such as the Civil Justice Ordinance, 1900 (Reproduction P/008), the Sudan Penal Code, 1899 (Reproduction P/006), and the Sudan Code of Criminal Procedure, 1899 (Reproduction P/007).

[56] Documents not suitable for published law reports, or of insufficient interest for detailed indexing, have nevertheless been preserved, partly because of the urgings of Professor G. N. Sanderson, head of the history department at the University of Khartoum. He pointed out that much of what is known of medieval England comes from law reports.

strong stimulus for saving and publishing judicial decisions came from the nature of Sudanese law practice. Because the pre-1956 cases were not generally available, surprise was the essence of the judicial process to the extent that the courts would decide a case on the basis of a decision unknown to the advocates and judges in the courts below.[57]

The Sudan Law Project was the response to the need to salvage the pre-1956 cases and other documents. Once the reporting of the post-1956 judgments became sufficiently stabilized, the faculty of law at the University of Khartoum established the Project, a co-operative venture with the judiciary and the Attorney General's Chambers that received financial support from the Ford Foundation.[58] Since 1961, the Project has succeeded in compressing the work of half a century into a few years and has provided a model for similar documentation projects undertaken or planned for other African countries.[59] Systematic searches of all parts of the country produced more than 1,500 potentially reportable cases plus other documents.[60] By mid-1966 the major accomplishments were the acceptance for publication of the 1900-1940 civil law reports[61] and the completion of an excellent documentation collection, some

---

[57] See, e.g., Kattan v. Kattan, AC-REV-47-1957, 1957 SUDAN L.J. REP. 35.

[58] For the organization and administration of the Project from 1961 to 1964, see Thompson, *Research into the Law of the Sudan*, in THE PHILO-SOPHICAL SOCIETY OF THE SUDAN: RESEARCH IN THE SUDAN 152, 179 (12th Annual Conference 1964).

[59] The Project was the first such legal documentation program in Africa; a similar undertaking was subsequently started in Tanzania. For many useful suggestions during its organization, the Project is indebted to Professor A. N. Allott and his Restatement of Customary Law Project staff at the University of London. One of the major conclusions of the Conference on Research Priorities in African Law, held on December 6, 1965, by the African Law Center, Columbia University, was the need "to assist in halting the rapid and continuous loss of unpublished materials" in Africa. See 1 AFRICAN L. DIGEST Item 373 (1965).

[60] The Sudan Law Project Trek Team between 1961 and 1963 found that conditions varied considerably from district to district. At Merowe, Sayed Ali Mohamed Ali Turki, the records keeper, had efficiently preserved nearly 50 years of land cases—the finest judicial archive anywhere in the Sudan. But the general situation ranged from chaos to catastrophe. At Berber, for example, all of the district's records, except for files actually in use, had been blended in an abandoned hut, with rain and dirt as a feeding ground for vermin. In Port Sudan, law reports were burned to clear a room for the police. Some of the Team's documentation work is described in FORD FOUNDATION, TWO AFRICAN PATTERNS 37-38 (1966).

[61] The final stage of the editing was initiated in 1964 by Ustaz Zaki Mustafa and concluded during 1965-1966 by Mr. S. J. Trueblood. Prolonged negotiations for a publisher were successfully completed in April of 1966 with Oceana Press, which did not require a prior financial commitment by the Sudanese Government. The general difficulty of finding the funds for needed legal publications in Africa is illustrated by the appeal in 1 AFRICAN L. DIGEST Item 995 (1965) by the editors of the digest of all Nigerian law reports.

eighty percent of it consisting of 12,000 select pages on microfilm.[62] An indication of the usefulness of the materials is that their availability has already made possible the first Sudanese-oriented publication for legal instruction, a publication that government officials are also using in the practical administration of the law.[63]

The achievements of the Project must realistically be viewed with the disappointments. Although the basic work of salvaging the pre-1956 cases was concluded in 1963, the remainder of the civil cases (covering the years 1940-1956) will not reach a publisher before 1967, and the work on the criminal cases has been negligible since 1964.[64] There have also been delays in completing the salvaging of the legal documentation other than judicial decisions.[65] The unfortunate result is the continued loss of materials; minor clerks very often imagine that paper once written upon has completed the purpose of its existence and can be discarded.[66] This problem plagues the preparation of the current law reports as well

---

[62] The collection was selected from the more than 100,000 pages selectively salvaged from the district headquarters. The work from 1961 to 1964 is described in Thompson, op. cit. supra note 58, at 158, 179. During 1965-1966, Mr. A. T. Hunt of the faculty of law of the University of Khartoum completed a comprehensive and uniquely detailed document index that transformed an unwieldy collection into an efficient research tool.

[63] THOMPSON, THE LAND LAW OF THE SUDAN, CASES AND MATERIALS (3 vols. 1965). The next immediate use of the Project's documents will be a research-writing program for students of law at the University of Khartoum.

[64] The majority of the cases distributed to various persons for editing in 1964 had not been returned by mid-1966, and the danger was that another salvaging campaign would be necessary.

[65] Although the Sudan Law Project Trek Team searched all judicial headquarters for the 1900-1956 law reports, the only comprehensive collection of other legal documentation was in the southern Sudan. The documentation treks were reinstituted in April 1966. Following a training program carried out by the faculty of law of the University of Khartoum in cooperation with the African Law Center at Columbia University, Ustaz Mohamed El Fatih Hamad left with a team of students for work in western Sudan.

[66] Another explanation for the consistent destruction of materials is that where the name of God appears in a document, as it does frequently, a devout but unsophisticated Muslim clerk might prefer to destroy the document rather than to leave it in what he considered disrespectful circumstances. But the general mistreatment of documents suggests the problem is secular. The method and success of minor clerks sent to find a document is not exaggerated by a sequence in Kafka's The Castle in which
> Mizzi and the assistants, left so long unnoticed, had clearly not found the paper they were looking for, and had then tried to shut everything up again in the cabinet, but on account of the confusion and superabundance of paper had not succeeded. Then the assistants had hit upon the idea which they were carrying out now. They had laid the cabinet on its back on the floor, crammed all the documents in, then along with Mizzi had knelt on the cabinet door and were trying now in this way to get it shut.
KAFKA, THE CASTLE 71-72 (Penguin Books 1957). The active files, however, are normally well ordered.

as the collection of materials from noncurrent files.[67] The key to overcoming these difficulties is the recurrent theme that the number of trained persons must rise to the number of necessary tasks.

But whatever the number of personnel, the willingness of people to initiate work beyond their obvious duties continues to be a crucial factor in the success of the program. A remarkable feature of most of the efforts to increase the availability of legal materials to an acceptable minimum is that members of the faculty of law of the University of Khartoum were involved. Work initiated primarily to support scholarly commentary on Sudanese law has attracted the support of the government. Although oversight by the legal profession has permitted some problems to arise since independence, the predominant pattern has been an increasingly successful effort to establish the preconditions necessary for the operation of the legal system. The continued necessity for such an effort demonstrates just how formative this era of their law is.

IV. SIGNIFICANT GAPS AND UNCERTAINTIES

Each of the three major sources of law as presently constituted has two major characteristics: (1) a remarkable degree of permissiveness for officials administering the source, and (2) substantial gaps or uncertainties, caused in part by the undetermined consequences of the permissiveness.

A. Islamic Law

The Grand Kadi's power to issue judicial circulars has been used to reform the personal law of Muslims.[68] The juristic basis of the reforms has included *talfiq* ("patching" between different schools of jurists) and, more significantly, *ijtihad* (contemporary interpretation of original sources of the Shari'a law).[69] These judicial circulars are often phrased in the most general terms when indicating which juristic school should guide the Shari'a courts. Moreover, within any one juristic school rules may be at variance with each other. Thus there is doubt as to the actual law being applied by the Shari'a courts and the extent of any differences between courts.[70]

---

[67] Despite numerous circulars from the Chief Justice beginning in 1961 requesting that judgments from the province courts be sent to Khartoum (see 1960 SUDAN L.J. REP. 279), it is still necessary for the general editor of the *Sudan Law Journal and Reports* to go personally to the courts to insure full coverage of reportable cases.

[68] See text at pp. 135-36 *supra*.

[69] Anderson, *The Modernisation of Islamic Law in the Sudan*, 1960 SUDAN L.J. REP. 292, 302. Professor Anderson's study is an admirable one containing details of the changes. *Id.* at 302-05.

[70] A study of this problem was a major point of a projected research program planned by the faculty of law of the University of Khartoum in 1965.

A further complication arises because Muslims who appear before local courts are often governed by a combination of Islamic
law and customary law. In theory and practice, customary laws
may supplement Islamic law.[71] Also in theory and practice, Shari'a
and customary law conflict.[72] In the first textbook about Sudanese
laws,[73] Dr. C. D'Olivier Farran made a thorough study of the types
of conflicts that may arise from the statutory, the customary, and
the Islamic matrimonial laws. But published information is otherwise limited to scattered examples, and there has been no systematic study of the fusion of any particular system of customary laws
with Shari'a rules.

If the conflict between the Shari'a law and the customary law
arose in a civil division court, the customary law would prevail
according to statute.[74] No case has tested the issue, and it remains
a lively source of debate because the theory of the Shari'a (translated literally as the "prescribed path") is that it is immutable.
When civil division courts have applied Islamic law, they have not
always understood the correct procedural steps[75] or, more disturb-
ingly, they have simply ignored the general rule that questions of
Islamic law in civil division cases must be referred to Shari'a
courts.[76] This is probably not so much due to the willful increase
of power by the civil division courts as to the fact that nearly all of
the civil division judges are Muslims, and they feel qualified to
rule independently upon Islamic law questions.

B. Customary Law

Regrettably, customary law is the nearly forgotten source of

---

[71] Abu Rannat, *The Relationship Between Islamic and Customary Law
in the Sudan*, 1960 J. AFRICAN L. 9, 10.

[72] These conflicts are illustrated by the question of the legal status of
the estate of a married woman of the Massariya, who inhabit western
Kordofan Province, and by certain questions of divorce among the Humr,
a Muslim tribe of the Baggara people. *Id.* at 11-12.

[73] FARRAN, MATRIMONIAL LAWS OF THE SUDAN (1963).

[74] Civil Justice Ordinance, 1929, § 5, 10 LAWS OF THE SUDAN 12 (1955).

[75] See, *e.g.*, Fatma Abdel Rahman v. Heirs of Mahamed El Azrak, HC-
REV-1956, 1960 SUDAN L.J. REP. 1 (Article 80 of the Judiciary Act dealing
with conflicts of jurisdiction between Shari'a and civil courts wrongly invoked by the civil district court, but the Chief Justice's action under Article 80 subsequently bound the civil high court).

[76] See, *e.g.*, Ali El Hiwaires v. Mohamed Ramadan, AC-REV-240-1958,
1961 SUDAN L.J. REP. 136 (civil Court of Appeal judge corrects Shari'a
court's opinion by unauthorized procedure: "The Grand Kadi, to whom
I showed this case, confirms [the correction]," conflicting with proper procedure in Civil Justice Ordinance, 1929, §§ 38, 39, 10 LAWS OF THE SUDAN
17-18 (1955). *But see* Heirs of El Niema Ahmed Wagealla v. El Hag
Ahmed Mohamed, AC-APP-5-1960, 1961 SUDAN L.J. REP. 221, where a civil
division court referred a question to a Shari'a court in order to avoid what
it perceived as the necessity of rendering an undesirable decision according
to the general territorial statute. See also Perrott, *A Note on the Case of
Heirs of El Niema Ahmed Wagealla v. El Hag Ahmed Mohamed*, 1961
SUDAN L.J. REP. 280.

Sudanese law. With the exception of Dr. P. P. Howell's *A Manual of Nuer Law*, based on the pioneering work of Professor Evans-Pritchard, there has been no extended study of any of the systems of customary law in the Sudan, and none is planned or underway. The isolation of the Three Towns from the remainder of the country partially explains the lack of official interest in customary law. That the Sudan is not entirely south of the Sahara also contributes, for some Sudanese see customary law as the rival of the personal law of Islam and therefore reject it. Finally, the shortage of information about customary law created a vicious circle in which it was difficult to stimulate the interest that would lead to further investigation.

Paradoxically, the disturbances in the southern Sudan that presently prevent research there also may have created greater awareness of the need to know about the customary law of that region. The materials collected by the Sudan Law Project from the south before the disturbances and from other parts of the Sudan are another crucial step in encouraging intensified research into customary law.[77]

Customary law in its original form was neither written nor influenced by Western legal traditions.[78] Because it reflects the life of a people, customary law changes with the internal social and economic evolution of a tribal group. Some of the most significant changes are due to the impact of external influences,[79] primarily those brought by the Anglo-Egyptian condominium and by the government since independence. As stated by a Sudanese administrator of the Dinka, "a lot of development has taken place in their customs according to the spread of Education and Civilization and this simultaneously developed their laws."[80] Very little is known about the method or extent of the adaptations.

To what extent and with what success have courts used the tests of "justice, morality or order"[81] or of "justice, equity and good

[77] The first published results are two important sets of documents edited by Mr. R. A. Cook, research associate of the Sudan Law Project: Stubbs' "Customary Law of the Aweil District Dinkas," 1962 SUDAN L.J. REP. 450 and *Blood Money and the Law of Homicide in the Sudan, A Documentary Survey*, 1962 SUDAN L.J. REP. 470.

[78] See generally Schiller, *Law*, in THE AFRICAN WORLD: A SURVEY OF SOCIAL RESEARCH 167-72 (Lystad ed. 1965).

[79] *Id.* at 169.

[80] Ghorashi, Dinka Customs and Laws, undated (1961?) (unpublished manuscript in the Sudan Law Project collection at the University of Khartoum).

[81] Chiefs' Courts Ordinance, 1931, § 7, 10 LAWS OF THE SUDAN 166-67 (1955); Native Courts Ordinance, 1932, § 9, 10 LAWS OF THE SUDAN 172-73 (1955). In Sudan Government v. Rainando Legge, Central Bari Regional Court-210-1962, 1963 SUDAN L.J. REP. 54, the Bari custom prescribing punishment for a man who has premarital intercourse with a virgin he is unwilling to marry was held in accord with the standard. See generally Schiller, *op. cit. supra* note 78, at 172.

conscience"[82] to strike down or modify customs? What value judgments have been involved in pursuance of this policy, and are they in any way uniform? What precisely is the role of the state's judicial procedures as an agent of change in the development of customary law? For example, the introduction of state courts can modify the original functioning of the customary law system. A district commissioner reported in 1934 that the Beja, with no sense of state, merely viewed a wrong as it touched the individual or tribe. Thus, crime was regarded more as a civil injury. However, "the spread of Native Courts and their responsibility for public security and justice are rapidly changing this outlook . . . . [P]icturesque compromise[s] are being ousted by more prosaic but deterrent sentences of gaol and fine."[83] Knowledge of such transformations is essential for scholarship, for effective administration, and for assessing possible innovations.

The conflicts between different systems of customary law require investigation because these conflicts are increasing as people flow from the tribal areas to urban centers and mix.[84] But the continuing disparity in social and economic development between people in the cities and in the rural areas also requires attention. The civil division courts are inclined to permit different legal consequences for the same act when done by different people, the consequence varying according to where the act occurred.[85] For example, the criminal defense of "grave and sudden provocation" is judged by the standard of the "reasonable man," but each particular

---

[82] Civil Justice Ordinance, 1929, § 9, 10 Laws of the Sudan 13 (1955). No apparent significance attaches to the use of "or" rather than "and" in the standard in Civil Justice Ordinance, 1929, § 5(a), 10 Laws of the Sudan 12 (1955). In Administrator-General v. Thoraya Ibrahim Salama, AC-APP-41-1955 (unreported) (cited by Abu Rannat, supra note 71, at 10), the Court of Appeal held a Coptic law of succession in conflict with the standard even though the law was identical to a Shari'a rule. There is no reported case in which a custom is voided by the standard. But see Farran, op. cit. supra note 73, at 14-15. Compare Mustafa Mohamed Gasmalla v. Alfred Tawfik Ibrahim, KHT-HC-CS-68-1954 (unreported) (unsafe to depart from established English law applied under the standard unless application is unjust in the Sudan), with Joseph Tabet v. Osman Saleh, KHT-HC-CS-986-1942 (unreported) (local custom dealing with liability for commission to an auctioneer held in accord with the standard although English law considered more reasonable).

[83] Letter From District Commissioner, Beja District, to Kassala Province Governor, November 12, 1934 (Sudan Government File DCB/42.A.1 in Sudan Law Project collection at the University of Khartoum). See also Howell, A Manual of Nuer Law (1954). The introduction of the state's mechanisms for enforcement caused the customary formulas for composition to be applied more frequently and with greater rigidity. Id. at 22-38, 225-37.

[84] One aspect of this, intertribal marriages for "detribalized" southern Sudanese, is considered in Farran, op. cit. supra note 73, at 183-85.

[85] See, e.g., Sudan Gov't v. Musa Gibril Musa, DPC-Major Court-2-1959, AC-CP-2-1959, 1959 Sudan L.J. Rep. 12 (pursuing and killing a thief of water justified as no offense by reference to local standards); Sudan Gov't

locality has its own reasonable man.[86] Questions that need answering, therefore, include whether the differential application of sanctions in urban and tribal areas is necessary or desirable for the maintenance of the legal order, or whether it merely inhibits the development of homogeneous national law.[87]

What little is known about customary law from the judgments of the state courts is potentially suspect because the judges who are expert in dealing with custom are outnumbered by those who, through no fault of their own, have neither experience nor training in either the nature or substance of customary law. The potentiality of error is increased by the surprising fact that there are no official guidelines for determining customary rules. Where relevant anthropological research is available, a court may use it,[88] but otherwise the methods of determination vary considerably, particularly in the lower courts. Within a single province there may be one district judge who relies on the evidence of tribal elders, another who depends on the advice of his clerk because he happens to be a member of the tribal group concerned, and yet another who strictly applies his predecessor's memorandum on the local customs.[89] Because some of these judicial techniques are of doubtful merit, there is an urgent need for a study leading to the drafting of minimum standards for the methods by which courts determine the substance of customary law.

C. General Territorial Law

The method of reception of foreign law into Africa differed from country to country.[90] A common British formula imported into a territory all of the common law, the doctrines of equity, and the statutes of general application that were in force in England on a

---

v. Abdullah Makhatar Nur, Major Court-3-1957, AC-CP-9-1957, 1959 SUDAN L.J. REP. 1 (belief in ghost allowed as a mistake of fact). See Brewster, *Punishment of Homicide Offenders—Exceptions to Penal Code*, § 251, 1963 SUDAN L.J. REP. 229, 234.

[86] Sudan Gov't v. El Baleila Balla Baleila, AC-CP-218-1958, 1958 SUDAN L.J. REP. 12.

[87] Comparative materials covering these issues are contained in Milner, Criminal Responsibility in African Law (preliminary collection of materials, University of Pennsylvania Law School, 1966).

[88] *E.g.*, "It is not necessary to go at length into Nuer customs and customary payments of cattle for marriage, birth, divorce, adultery, blood money, etc. Most of it is in Evans-Pritchard, which you should read very carefully; in general, he is most accurate, though not so accurate when he goes from the general to the particular." Handing Over Notes of the District Commissioner, Fangak District, Upper Nile Province, January 23, 1936 (Sudan Government File UNP/57.D.6 in the Sudan Law Project collection at the University of Khartoum) ("Handing Over Notes" constitute a manual of cumulative knowledge passed to a successor).

[89] These varieties of methods were all observed within the compass of the district headquarters of the west bank of Equatoria Province from May to June 1962 by the Sudan Law Project Trek Team.

[90] See generally Schiller, *op. cit. supra* note 78, at 172-74.

specified date.[91]   In contrast, the authorization of section 9 of the
Civil Justice Ordinance to "act according to justice, equity and good
conscience"[92] in cases not covered by local legislation is strikingly
permissive.   This formula provides great flexibility but also creates great uncertainty, for it is obviously not self-defining.

The tendency of Sudanese courts to be guided by English law
when acting under the authority of section 9 has contributed to the
existence of a cumulative heritage of lawyers' law derived from the
common law.[93]   But adherence to this heritage is not mandatory.
Where there is a gap in Sudanese law, an English statute or English judge-made law may be on point.   The basic uncertainty is
whether a court will adopt, adapt, or reject the English rule.   Uncertainty also arises because a court in certain situations may have
power to apply an English rule although there is relevant Sudanese legislation.

If a court must decide a point of law covered by an English
statute but not covered by local legislation, it will usually apply
the English statute as if it were enacted in the Sudan.[94]   But occasionally it will not.[95]   This uncertainty is an acute problem since
the Sudan lacks legislative equivalents for English statutes dealing with subjects such as installment buying or the sale of goods.

Further uncertainty results from some of the methods the courts
use to fill a gap when they do not apply the English legislation.
For example, the Court of Appeal has filled a gap "by analogy" to a
Sudanese statute after rejecting *ab initio* a relevant rule from the
English Sale of Goods Act, which it had applied in previous cases.
But the analogy was so attenuated that the causal link was all but
invisible.   That part of the Sudanese statute relied upon referred
to the physical recovery of property, but the rule created "by analogy" granted the cash value of property that had disappeared.[96]

---

[91]   For extended discussion of the problem raised by this type of formula,
see generally HARVEY, LAW AND SOCIAL CHANGE IN GHANA 239-71 (1966).

[92]   10 LAWS OF THE SUDAN 13 (1955).

[93]   See text at p. 139 *supra*.

[94]   See, *e.g.*, Apostolou Enterprises Co., Ltd. v. Mohamed Saleh Gireis,
AC-REV-172-1958, 1958 SUDAN L.J. REP. 69, where the Court of Appeal decided the case "on the authority of" § 29(2) of the 1893 English Sale of
Goods Act.   Interestingly, the editorial headnote does not indicate that it
is an English statute being applied.   For a pre-independence application of
the same statute by a Sudan court, see, *e.g.*, Abu Fatma Sharif v. Mansour
El Shouehi, AC-APP-3-1920 (unreported).

[95]   See, *e.g.*, Hassan Abdel Rahman v. Satti Mohamed Satti, AC-REV-
135-1958, 1958 SUDAN L.J. REP. 66, where the district court's application of
the English statute was sustained by the province court.   The Court of
Appeal, however, did not apply the English statute.

[96]   *Ibid.*   It is interesting that distinguished High Court Justice Babiker
Awadalla, who is thoroughly knowledgeable in the common law, also
ignored established tortious and quasi-contractual actions of the common
law that deal with the point raised. See Perrott, *Appendix to "Some Notes
on Possession and Title in the Sudanese Law of Personal Property, Part II,"*
1963 SUDAN L.J. REP. 221, 222-24.

Whether this is a bold judicial stroke or simply usurpation of the legislative function, it contributes to the uncertain condition of Sudanese legal sources.

A problem arises where Sudanese legislation is modeled upon an English statute, and subsequently the English statute is substantially amended but the Sudanese legislation is not. For example, some of the changes in the English legislation that was the model for the Sudanese Companies Ordinance[97] are thought desirable by members of the Sudanese legal and business communities. But the legislative draftsmen, dulled by six years of submission to an inactive military government and for a variety of other reasons,[98] have never considered these changes. A similar problem arises in regard to a portion of the Wills and Administration Ordinance of 1928, adapted from the Indian Succession Act of 1865, which in turn was based upon an English common-law rule statutorily abolished in England in 1934.[99]

Nothing in section 9 of the Civil Justice Ordinance, 1929, requires Sudanese courts to follow the English change.[100] The significant question is whether the courts could adopt the English amendment if they felt it was necessary or desirable. Arguably such action is jurisprudentially permissible. The court could declare the relevant portion of the Sudanese statute no longer "for the time being in force" under section 9, which does not specifically forbid such a declaration. As additional justification, the saving clause of the Civil Justice Ordinance states that nothing in the ordinance "shall be deemed to limit or otherwise effect the inherent power of the Court to make such orders as may be necessary for the ends of justice . . . ."[101] The court could then apply the English rule as being in accord with "justice, equity and good conscience." Although acceptance of this argument would create great uncertainty in the law, courts may be greatly tempted to accept it when the alternative is the inability to apply a modern amendment considered necessary for a just decision.

Despite the extreme expansion of judicial discretion suggested by this argument, the courts have already moved towards accepting it. They have applied English legislation that has not been enacted in the Sudan in order to supplement the provisions of existing Sudan-

97 Companies Ordinance, 1925, 4 LAWS OF THE SUDAN 125 (1962).

98 The pressure of routine business on a small staff is an important reason. The effect of the uncertain fate of the common-law heritage on the legislative draftsman is analyzed in part VI *infra*, pp. 167-71.

99 See Perrott, *supra* note 76, at 287.

100 Civil Justice Ordinance, 1929, § 9, 10 LAWS OF THE SUDAN 13 (1955) reads: "In cases not provided for by this enactment or any other enactment for the time being in force, the courts shall act according to justice, equity and good conscience."

101 Civil Justice Ordinance, 1929, § 226, 10 LAWS OF THE SUDAN 60 (1955).

ese legislation.[102]   The jurisprudential justification for this is less difficult.   Because the English amendment is one that supplements rather than alters the Sudanese statute, it is a rule that covers one of the "cases not provided for by this enactment or any other enactment."   The courts, therefore, are free to apply the English legislation as being in accord with "justice, equity and good conscience."[103]

Where there is a gap in Sudanese law that is covered by English judge-made law rather than by English legislation, the courts apparently feel easier about referring to the English rule.   There is no legally compelling reason for this since each is guiding and not binding on Sudanese courts.   But a reading of the reported cases indicates that, when there is no applicable rule in the Sudan for a subject covered by English case law, the courts have never rejected this law *ab initio*.   They have consistently considered English rules found in English law reports or, more likely, in English common-law treatises.[104]

The reception of foreign law with too little alteration is one of the problems in the development of the sources of law.   All too often a court in the Sudan feels that its job is done by citing a foreign authority in support of the rule it applies.[105]   For example, the district court of Gedaref decided a case of cattle trespass by reference to dictum in an English case instead of creatively producing an appropriate rule.   Opposed to the government's desire to settle farming areas was the interest of the nomadic cattle owners in their traditional grazing methods.   Whether there should be strict liability for cattle trespass or liability only for negligence could have been decided after a full examination of the relevant facts and customs and in light of conscious policy judgments about the best resolution of the competing interests.[106]

---

[102] See, *e.g.*, Heirs of Imam Ibrahim v. El Amin Abdel Rahman, AC-REV-53-1963, 1962 SUDAN L.J. REP. 228.

[103] See *id.* at 234, where Mr. Justice Babiker Awadalla states: "What we apply in the Sudan is not the English statutory provision itself but the general principles of justice which prompted the legislature in England to cater for the situation."

[104] One reason for this is the shortage of English and other law reports, particularly outside of Khartoum.   See note 41 *supra*.   English cases cited in a judgment of the Sudan courts often follow the development of cases in a major English text on the relevant subject, whether the text is cited or not.

[105] That this is common practice may be seen by perusing any volume of the *Sudan Law Journal and Reports*.   See, *e.g.*, Heirs of Hussein Abdalla v. Mohamed Mohamed El Amin, AC-REV-96-1958, 1961 SUDAN L.J. REP. 113, where, in a judgment of less than a page, a strong Court of Appeal applied two rules of English contract law without discussion.

[106] This case, which was not reported and not appealed, was discussed at length in Gedaref in January 1963 by members of the Sudan Law Project Trek Team and the judicial staff there.   The relevance of the importance of methodology as distinguished from mere knowledge of rules in legal education is obvious.

In some cases the courts have adapted English law so that the rule conforms to Sudanese conditions,[107] and in others they have used indirect techniques to create a rule different from the English rule.[108] The extent of such adaptation is one of the most important areas for further research if the development of Sudanese judge-made law is to be fully appreciated.

The rational development of judge-made law is also hindered by the too frequent occurrence of conflicting rules on the same legal question.[109] This result is doubly unsatisfactory when each judge, assuming the correctness of his interpretation, does not give reasons for his decision.[110] Although the lag between the time when a judgment is written and when it is reported creates a situation ripe for conflicting decisions, better judicial coordination might prevent conflicts between members of the Court of Appeal.

The binding rules of the judge-made source of law are uncertain because a doctrine of judicial precedents in the Sudan is far from established. The general pattern is for lower courts to pay deference to the decisions of higher courts, a natural result of the judicial pyramid with the Court of Appeal at the top.[111] Developed in the English tradition of strongly coercive precedents,[112] the Sudan's Court of Appeal generally states that it is bound by its own deci-

---

[107] See, *e.g.*, Heirs of El Tayeb El Melik v. Ahmadiya Zawya, AC-REV-262-1962, 1962 Sudan L.J. Rep. 135 (relief granted by lower court based on concept of constructive trust not allowed on appeal because the concept was applied to a wakf, which was held to be entirely different from the English conception of trust); Khartoum Municipal Council v. Cotran, AC-APP-31-1958, 1958 Sudan L.J. Rep. 85 (question of damages to be fixed by local considerations and not by strict adherence to English or other laws). See generally Twining, *Khartoum Municipal Council v. Cotran; A Study in Judicial Techniques*, 1959 Sudan L.J. Rep. 112.

[108] See, *e.g.*, Heirs of Hussein Farah v. Abdel Rahman Gasmil Seed, PC-REV-56-1958, 1962 Sudan L.J. Rep. 47, where Mr. Justice Tayeb refused to apply the English statutory rule requiring a sale of land to be evidenced in writing, but he did so solely on the ground that English statutory rules are not applicable in the Sudan. But since the area of law has not been preempted by a local statute, there would have been no theoretical difficulty in applying the English rule if the judge had so wished. See note 94 *supra* and accompanying text; the same conclusion follows a fortiori from notes 101 and 102 *supra* and accompanying text. Possibly the judge used a presumed rule of reception to avoid the application of a rule that he felt inappropriate to the situation, *i.e.*, a sale in a rural district in 1944 (a situation in which it would be likely for most sales to be unwritten?).

[109] See, *e.g.*, Thompson, *The Sudan Law of Landlord and Tenant and the Judicial Interpretation of the Rent Restriction Ordinance, 1953*, 1962 Sudan L.J. Rep. 411, 432-36.

[110] *Id.* at 422-24, 432-38.

[111] See Guttman, *A Survey of the Sudan Legal System*, 1956 Sudan L.J. Rep. 7.

[112] See Cross, Precedent in English Law 4, 103-17 (1961). *But see* the announcement that the House of Lords will no longer necessarily be bound by its own decisions, N.Y. Times, July 27, 1966, § 1, p. 1, col. 6.

sions.[113] In contrast to the general pattern, however, lower courts have consciously defied a rule set down by a higher court, and the Court of Appeal has overruled itself.[114]

The unsettled status of the decisions in the Court of Appeal poses acutely the traditional arguments concerning stare decisis. This self-imposed restriction in the formative era of law could prevent the loss of confidence in the judicial system that might follow if the Court of Appeal frequently overruled itself, and it would contribute to greater certainty in the law. The opposing argument is that the court's prudent use of the power to overrule itself could provide an essential flexibility to conform to rapidly changing conditions. It is important that the choice of a doctrine of judicial precedents be well considered and not merely an automatic adoption of the English practice. A responsible resolution of this problem is intimately connected to the ability and willingness of the legislative power to act quickly to remedy weaknesses in the law, for this would mitigate the potential danger of the Court of Appeal being bound by unwanted rules.

The authority of judicial precedents from 1900 to 1956 is a special problem primarily because the pre-1956 cases are not yet generally available to the courts. The current practice is that cases decided before independence are as binding as cases decided after independence. The Court of Appeal has even said that dictum in a pre-independence case, "though not authoritative, will be accorded the greatest respect by the court and will not be disregarded unless it runs counter to previous and binding decisions governing the

---

[113] See, *e.g.*, Ahmed Mohamed Ahmed v. Wali Hammad, AC-REV-60-1958, 1960 SUDAN L.J. REP. 45, 46.

[114] The history of the courts' interpretation of the relationship of § 11 (a) and § 20 of the Rent Restriction Ordinance, 1953, 7 LAWS OF THE SUDAN 95 (1955), is illuminating. The critical question was whether an estoppel issue could be pleaded. Ibrahim Mohammed Wagealla v. Ahmed Shawgi Mustafa, HC-REV-55-1957, 1957 SUDAN L.J. REP. 24, allowed the pleading of estoppel. This decision was affirmed. Ibrahim Mohammed Wagealla v. Ahmed Shawgi Mustafa, AC-REV-85-1957. Abdullah Mohamed El Fadil v. Batoul Beshir El Dabi, HC-REV-264-1958 (unreported), did not allow the estoppel issue to be pleaded. There was no appeal. The possibility of an estoppel was assumed by the court in Ibrahim Osman El Arabi v. Hassan Ahmed El Hakim, AC-REV-137-1958, 1961 SUDAN L.J. REP. 124. In Fatma Habib v. El Sarra Bint Fideil, HC-REV-24-1959, the judge of the high court was faced with two decisions by the Court of Appeal that upheld the pleading of estoppel, Ibrahim Mohammed Wagealla v. Ahmed Shawgi Mustafa, *supra*, and Ibrahim Osman El Arabi v. Hassan Ahmed El Hakim, *supra*. The judge, refusing to be bound by them, ruled against estoppel and gave reasons for doing so. The Court of Appeal sustained him, thus reversing its prior decisions. Fatma Habib v. El Sarra Bint Fideil, AC-REV-137-1959, 1962 SUDAN L.J. REP. 64. The Court of Appeal returned to its original position and permitted the estoppel issue to be raised in Aslan Seroussi v. Derbedrossian Bros., AC-REV-185-1959, 1961 SUDAN L.J. REP. 174. For the first time, the Court of Appeal gave reasons for this interpretation, and, for the second time, it overruled itself.

point in controversy."[115]   Just as independence did not guillotine
the prior development of the judicial structure,[116] neither did it
guillotine the sources of judge-made law.

The publication of the 1900-1956 cases will require reconsideration
of the current policy. The absence of systematic law reporting for
the 1900-1956 period resulted in conflicting decisions on particular
points of law. Some of the cases now being published will conflict
because they were selected for the merit of the opinions, not for
their compatibility. The dramatic increase in the number of available precedents will also probably include judgments that the
courts will feel are inappropriate to present conditions. Finally,
the possible influence of nationalistic sentiments cannot be ignored
nor accurately predicted if Sudanese judges are faced with an un-
popular decision by a British-staffed Court of Appeal sitting in
1915. But whatever modifications occur to the theory that all pre-
independence cases are binding, these cases will at least be valuable, persuasive authorities because they deal with actual Sudanese
legal problems and often contain cogent analyses.

The jurisprudential uncertainties in the law of the Sudan have
unfortunate practical consequences. For example, the legal foundation upon which an expanding economy can be built remains unsettled. Sometimes the commercial community must take extra-
judicial steps to calm apprehensions born of uncertainty. The Sudan Bills of Exchange Ordinance of 1914 was modeled after an
English act of 1882. The English act has undergone a number of
minor changes and a major amendment in 1957, but none of the
changes have been enacted in the Sudan. The 1957 amendment
has important consequences for bankers' liabilities, and it was
uncertain whether Sudanese courts would apply it. To solve the
uncertainty, bankers agreed among themselves not to regard the
change as applicable.[117]

A recurrent feature of this analysis has been the legislative authority's failure to take the initiative in filling the gaps in Sudanese
law. Fortunately, but not inevitably, the judiciary has taken an
increasingly active role in developing the general territorial law.
Despite numerous difficulties, the judiciary has created a series of
rules in a number of areas (for example, landlord-tenant) that are
binding and that are truly Sudanese common law.[118]

---

[115] Mr. Justice B. Awadalla, with Chief Justice Abu Rannat and Mr.
Justice K. El Amin concurring, in Kattan v. Kattan, AC-REV-47-1957, 1957
SUDAN L.J. REP. 35, 51.

[116] See FARRAN, op. cit. supra note 73, at viii.

[117] The author is indebted to Mr. J. S. R. Cole, Q. C., and Mr. D. Perrott
for this information.

[118] See Thompson, supra note 109, at 429-31.

V. KEY ISSUES FOR THE FUTURE

A. Merger of Shari'a and Civil Court Systems

The dichotomy between the civil and the customary courts that exists in many African nations has not plagued the Sudan.[119] But the proper relation between the civil division and the Shari'a courts in applying Islamic law is an issue likely to attract increased attention. Some Shari'a judges have demanded greater insulation from civil division courts partly because of incursions into their jurisdiction, but mostly because of dissatisfaction with the civil division's control over Shari'a courts' administrative matters.[120] In contrast, there is support, particularly in the academic community, for merging the Shari'a and civil division courts into one system, possibly along lines followed in the United Arab Republic.[121] The key factor in a merger is legal education, for such a change would require judges competent to adjudicate both civil and Shari'a law questions. Elimination of the present dualism in the courts would, therefore, compel an alteration in the educational program that currently provides separate lines of studies for prospective Shari'a and civil division judges.[122]

B. Development of Customary Law

The silence that characterizes the interest in customary laws in the Sudan is a sharp contrast to the lively discussions in nations like Tanzania, where President Nyerere has made unification of customary law a part of his country's program for progress.[123] The Sudanese Government's only official statement about customary law indicated that customary rules would be sustained on appeal unless found to conflict with existing state law or with the repugnancy clause. It also indicated that judicial circulars would note developments of general interest.[124] In theory, this is a cau-

---

[119] At the African Conference on Local Courts and Customary Law (Dar es Salaam, September 9-19, 1963), the Sudan took a lead in urging the elimination of this dichotomy.

[120] The administrative powers that were most attacked related to terms of service and the supply of court equipment. Dissatisfaction became especially articulate in January-February of 1965 and has not yet been fully resolved.

[121] In the summer of 1963, Ustaz Mohamed Saleh Omar of the faculty of law (Shari'a department) made a study of the Egyptian system. His writings on the subject were interrupted when he became a minister of the new government following the 1964 Revolution.

[122] Professor Anderson states that when Islamic laws are "reduced to the form of a code, it at once becomes much more feasible for a judge who has had his legal training in a modern law school to administer it." Anderson, *The Modernisation of Islamic Law in the Sudan*, 1960 SUDAN L.J. REP. 292, 312.

[123] See Cotran, *Some Recent Developments in the Tanganyika Judicial System*, 1962, J. AFRICAN L. 19, 26.

[124] Statement by Chief Justice Mohamed Abu Rannat at the African Conference on Local Courts and Customary Law (Dar es Salaam, September 9-19, 1963).

tious policy that recognizes the enormous differences in the country and that allows professional judges to adapt traditional rules to modern circumstances.

The most serious accusation against this policy is that it masked the military regime's actual policy in southern Sudan, that of "attempting by every possible means . . . to stamp out all traditional divergencies from their Arab-Mohammedan norm, however deeply rooted."[125] Reliable evidence on this issue is meager.[126] Part of it points in the opposite direction: there were northern officials in the south during the military rule who were concerned with applying customary law justly and accurately.[127] The causes of the intensified southern insurgency are so complex that it is unconvincing to argue back from armed rebellion and conclude that even one cause of it was the army's attempt to stamp out customary laws. It is similarly unconvincing to link causally the overthrow of the military regime with a desire by northerners to preserve and develop southern customary law.[128] The firm evidence is that the announced policy produced no significant judicial circulars and did not touch the outstanding problems of customary law. Inaction became a policy that amounted to a dignified complacency[129] matched by the intellectual nonfeasance of most of the legal pro-

---

[125] FARRAN, MATRIMONIAL LAWS OF THE SUDAN 141 (1963).

[126] See, e.g., ibid, where the only support for the accusation is a single example, an allegation from an unspecified source. However, at the time Dr. Farran was writing it was necessary to protect informants whose examples could have been multiplied. There was no systematic examination of whether these allegations were accurate and, if accurate, whether they constituted a conscious policy or isolated incidents. This is mentioned not to contradict Dr. Farran's contention but to indicate the difficulties of proof. His subsequent example of the closing of a southern secondary school followed by the placement of the students in northern schools is, of course, not proof of a policy in regard to customary laws. Nor is the prediction of a trend concerning the probable future treatment of customary laws the same as establishing proof of an ongoing suppression of customs.

[127] The Sudan Law Project Trek Team in 1962 found this to be the general rule, although the officials displayed varying degrees of proficiency in the handling of customary law. See note 89 supra and accompanying text. The Team's conclusion was based on observations of limited duration in each district but was bolstered by unlimited access to the government's files. The Team also observed an excessive readiness by most southern chiefs not to displease the northern officials, but any generalization arising from this would have to account for many facets of a complex relationship, including the norm of behavior during the British administration. See also Ghorashi, supra note 80, for evidence of a northern official in the south who specifically proposed that there be a customary law code for the Dinka. This is in sharp contrast with the government's official complacency and, a fortiori, opposite to any presumed policy of suppression.

[128] Criticism of the army's handling of the south was the origin of the incidents that led to the 1964 Revolution, but this criticism was soon submerged in a general attack on the government's competence.

[129] The causes are suggested at pp. 151-52 supra.

fession.[130]

The overthrow of the military regime and the civilian government's continuing efforts to stabilize conditions in the southern Sudan offer the opportunity to develop a new policy for customary law. Two alternatives are the enactment of customary law codes or a program of restating customary law along lines similar to the work of the Restatement of African Law Project.[131] Each would require systematic research that might well begin with the materials collected by the Sudan Law Project. The crucial need for research, planning, and a careful assessment of alternatives may be illustrated by three key challenges that seem unavoidable. The first follows from the likelihood, buttressed by an occasional government endorsement,[132] that the thousand or so local court judges will be replaced by professional magistrates who have received university training. Although demands for the immediate scuttling of the traditional authorities have failed,[133] the general tenor of opinion in the legal profession favors their gradual disappearance. Even in the southern Sudan, where the process of change would normally have been regarded as most difficult, the return of peaceful conditions may reveal in some areas that the authority of the traditional ruler-judges has been so shaken that replacement by professional magistrates may be plausible or even necessary.[134] An increase in the professional magistrates dealing directly with customary law questions in local courts must be matched by methods for increasing their professional capacity to handle those questions, or the consequences to the legal system will be unfortunate.

The second challenge is posed by economic development planning, which has at its core an increase in agricultural productiv-

---

[130] If it were ever established that the military government's real policy included the suppression of customary laws, then it would be necessary to conclude that the malfeasance was supported by the profession's nonfeasance.

[131] For a statement of the Restatement's purpose, see THE FUTURE OF LAW IN AFRICA 14-17 (Allott ed. 1960). Professor Allott is also editor of the *Journal of African Law,* which may be consulted generally in regard to the Restatement's work. See generally TWINING, THE PLACE OF CUSTOMARY LAW IN THE NATIONAL LEGAL SYSTEMS OF EAST AFRICA 37-51 (1964).

[132] See Statement by Chief Justice Mohamed Abu Rannat at the African Conference on Local Courts and Customary Law (Dar es Salaam, September 9-19, 1963). Informal statements by members of the high court reflected a similar view as recently as April 1966.

[133] Following the 1964 Revolution, the abolition of the "native administration" was urged by the Communists and supported by others as a precondition for the holding of national elections, which, nevertheless, were eventually held in late April 1965.

[134] The consensus of opinion among northerners and southerners who were on official tours to the troubled areas between December 1964 and April 1966 is that the chiefs are caught between the rebels and the government officials. They can only please one side by displeasing the other, and they often succeed only in attracting the wrath of both sides.

ity.[135] This will include increasing and altering landholding in subsistence areas now governed by customary laws. Experts will be necessary, not to guarantee success, for that is the impossible dream of social engineers, but to avoid foolish failure. At least two tasks suggest why the lawyer must become sufficiently knowledgeable in customary law so that he may join the work of experts such as anthropologists and economists. The lawyer should be able to phrase the customary rules so as to relate them to the concepts of modern lawyers' law, a step toward incorporating the traditional into the modern system.[136] The lawyer must also construct the development scheme in terms that are legally sound and consistent with the existing law because the legal framework fundamentally reflects the implementation process.[137]

The general use of legislation to accelerate the modernization of the nation constitutes the third challenge. Many of the changes will touch traditional relationships covered by customary laws. The danger is that such legislation can result in "fantasy law"[138] that will be neutralized by insufficient attention to local conditions. That this is possible in the Sudan may be illustrated by the ineffective 1951 Standing Orders of Zande District in Equatoria Province. These regulations prescribed five minimum requirements for a valid local marriage and, to the administrator, seemed sensible. But they proved to be unenforceable and, more significantly, had the undesirable side effect of repelling people from the regular court system.[139] Such incidents could have disastrous consequences for the legal system if multiplied across the nation.

---

[135] See generally Meagher, Public International Development Financing in Sudan 20-26, 1965 (Report No. 11, Public International Development Financing, a Research Project of the Columbia University Law School).

[136] For a comparison of the phraseology used by a lawyer and an anthropologist, see TWINING, op. cit. supra note 131, at 43. For a pessimistic assessment of the possibilities of converting traditional relationships into the methods of a modern economy, see McLoughlin, Economic Development and the Heritage of Slavery in the Sudan Republic, 32 AFRICA 355 (1962).

[137] See generally Allott, Legal Development and Economic Growth in Africa, in CHANGING LAW IN DEVELOPING COUNTRIES 194 (Anderson ed. 1963); NYHART, LAW, LAWYERS,AND PRIVATE SECTOR INSTITUTIONS IN AFRICA (Hausman ed. 1963); Schiller, The Changes and Adjustments Which Should Be Brought to the Present Legal Systems of the Countries of Africa to Permit Them to Respond More Effectively to the New Requirements of the Development of the Countries, in LEGAL ASPECTS OF ECONOMIC DEVELOPMENT 193 (Tunc ed. 1966); Nyhart, The Role of Law in Economic Development, 1962 SUDAN L.J. REP. 394.

[138] The phrase used by van Vollenhoven to describe the attempted introduction of a model civil code into the Dutch East Indies in 1920. Quoted by Schiller, op. cit. supra note 137, at 200.

[139] Reining, A Social Study of the Azande of the Nile-Congo Divide, pp. 68-83, 1959 (unpublished manuscript on file with the Institute of Social Anthropology, Oxford University).

C. Development of the General Territorial Law

Three ideas prevalent among members of the legal profession will influence efforts to deal with the gaps and uncertainties in the general territorial law. Briefly characterized, they are (1) Arabicization, (2) greater eclecticism, and (3) codification of common-law subjects. Each postulates key changes without rejecting the present core of the lawyers' laws.

1. ARABICIZATION

The idea that Arabic should more widely supersede English as the primary legal language has been labeled Arabicization, although this term also carries wider substantive connotations in other contexts. The decision of leading government lawyers to spend more time on a revision of the Arabic version of criminal legislation than on any other special project since independence exemplifies the high priority attached to Arabicization.[140] But this frequently heralded goal does not accurately reflect the decline in the use of English, the other official legal language. For example, Court of Appeal judges continue to write their decisions in English, and law teachers predominantly use English for instruction.

The advocacy of Arabic is tied intimately to elements of national pride. There are also convincing practical considerations, such as the need for the law to be comprehensible to the average citizen (who has no knowledge of English) or to the nonprofessional local court judges who are expected to apply specified national legislation as well as customary laws.[141] But practical considerations also work for the retention of English. It has proved valuable as a two-way bridge for information and experience to pass between the Sudan and the rest of the common-law world, and its comprehensive technical vocabulary, developed to deal with the problems of modern lawyers' law, has been usefully applied in the Sudan.

The potential Arabicization of legal sources is one aspect of a complex national issue that may be illustrated by the specific question of what language should be used for teaching the general territorial law. The increased use of Arabic in the secondary schools has contributed to a drop in the English proficiency of university

---

[140] The work was carefully done, but slowly—primarily because a large committee was working on a relatively imperfect first-draft translation. Work was accelerated after it was calculated that, at the past rate of progress, the final version would take 216 years.

[141] There is no general training program for local court judges. The efforts initiated by Mr. Justice H. A. Rahim in 1962 to remedy this problem in Kassala Province are noteworthy. For an example of the difficulty experienced by local courts in understanding general territorial law, see Perrott, *Some Notes on Possession and Title in The Sudanese Law of Personal Property* (pt. 1), 1962 SUDAN L.J. REP. 323, 367-68.

entrants[142] and is, therefore, a pressure for accelerated Arabicization of legal training. The University of Khartoum is not now prepared to venture such a transition, partly because of the unresolved problems of accommodating classical Arabic to the technical terms of the common law and of providing research and teaching materials in Arabic. An unfortunate consequence of the situation is that the faculty of law has had to become involved in attempting to improve the English capabilities of its students.[143]

The one experiment by the faculty of law in Arabic instruction for lawyers' law inadvertently could not be concluded,[144] but it did identify yet another aspect of the national character of the language issue. The southern Sudanese students requested that special classes be conducted in English because their preparation in classical Arabic was inadequate.

Concentrated Arabic training and increased exclusion of English and local languages in the southern Sudan could eliminate this problem and help unify the country, but this would be a distant achievement and one with which many southerners do not presently agree. The language issue thus forms part of the current national debate about the proper constitutional status for the southern Sudan.

Because of the enormous complexities surrounding Arabicization of the legal sources, neither the pace nor the extent of the trend is forseeable. It would be valuable for the instances of the increased use of Arabic to be examined now. For example, there is evidence that, while some lower court judges have written their opinions in Arabic to better inform the litigants, others have used Arabic in their decisions as an excuse to avoid discussing any legal issues.[145] The danger is that insufficient investigation of the contingencies of a language shift could result in hasty and hazardous moves in the future.

2. GREATER ECLECTICISM

There is growing support for an eclectic marketing among the legal products of many countries as a basis for new legislation or

---

[142] This conclusion was independently determined by studies of the faculty of law of the University of Khartoum during 1964. See generally ENGLISH IN THE SUDAN CONFERENCE, PROCEEDINGS (Dep't of Extra Mural Studies, University of Khartoum 1966).

[143] For example, a substantial portion of the time of the entering law class during the 1964-1965 academic year was spent with a member of the British Council, who taught what amounted to a remedial reading course.

[144] It was initiated in 1964 by Dr. Hassan Tirabi, who reported satisfaction with the progress of the course. Unfortunately, Dr. Tirabi left the university in early 1965 to become national leader of the Islamic Charter Front.

[145] The general editor of the *Sudan Law Journal and Reports*, Mr. Justice El Amien, reports that, even using Professor Goodhart's theory of the *ratio decidendi* of a case, it is difficult to justify reporting most of the cases because they merely summarize the facts and state a holding.

for judicial action under the formula of "justice, equity and good conscience." Like Arabicization, this idea is also a withdrawal from heavy reliance on the colonial heritage, and it is frequently expressed as "benefitting from the mistakes of others."

Since the Sudan is one of the branches of the English common-law tree, the most exacting test of the eclectic method will be the attempt to transfer rules from a country with a continental law system growing from the Latin soil of Roman law. Although the common-law and continental systems demonstrate great similarities in developed practice,[146] there may be differences that could cause a legal transplant from one system to die in the other. This question is raised, for example, by the efforts of the legal officers who approached the problem of drafting an act for installment purchases by writing to the foreign embassies in Khartoum for their relevant legislation.[147] Would a continental system statute, however brilliant, blend harmoniously with the common-law concepts that form at least ninety percent of the Sudan's commercial law? The need for caution in mixing laws from the two systems is suggested by the Sudan's Recovery of Lost and Stolen Property Ordinance of 1924. Primarily derived from the continental system and arriving in the Sudan by way of Egypt, where it was introduced from France, this law is based ultimately on the Roman law concepts of ownership and restitution. They are alien to the concepts of possession and damages found in the common law of personal property that otherwise prevails in the Sudan, with the result that there are confusing conceptual conflicts.[148]

3. CODIFICATION OF COMMON-LAW SUBJECTS

Codification of common-law subjects, like contracts and torts, along the lines of the codification of the common law of crime in the Sudan is often advocated but has never been implemented. The principal supporting argument is that it would end a major cause of uncertainty in the sources of lawyers' law while also permitting Sudanese adaptation, both during the original enactment and through the process of judicial interpretation. While Arabicization and eclecticism have attained sufficient momentum to be called trends, codification remains suspended in a world of conflicting ideas. To better understand this world requires a closer examination of the legal profession, the origin of the ideas.

---

[146] See AMOS & WALTON, INTRODUCTION TO FRENCH LAW 9-14 (2d ed. 1963); THE CODE NAPOLEON AND THE COMMON LAW WORLD 55-80, 267-98 (Schwartz ed. 1956); Scott, *The Recovery of Lost and Stolen Property*, 1958 SUDAN L.J. REP. 239, 240-53.

[147] The experiment died in the excitement of the 1964 Revolution and its aftermath.

[148] See Atiyah, *S. G. v. Bakheit Adam Mohammed and the Recovery of Lost and Stolen Property Ordinance, 1924,* 1956 SUDAN L.J. REP. 47; Perrott, *Some Notes on Possession and Title in the Sudanese Law of Personal Property* (pts. 1-2), 1962 SUDAN L.J. REP. 323, 1963 SUDAN L.J. REP. 221.

D. The Legal Profession and the Need for a Law
Revision Committee

Most of the nearly 200 advocates were trained at the University of Cairo or its Khartoum branch, which opened in 1955 as a non-residential institution offering evening classes.[149] Not surprisingly, they tend to favor the substance and form of the continental system with which they are familiar. But the power to shape the sources of law has been in the judiciary and Attorney General's Chambers, which are composed of some 175 persons who, with few exceptions, were trained in the common-law tradition at the University of Khartoum and who often take an advanced degree in England. Many of these persons favor increased legal eclecticism, but their inclination has been to look to English common law. Those who are judges have expected the advocates to do the same.

Quite separately from the issue of the quality of the two different kinds of university education,[150] the difference in legal backgrounds itself makes the exchange of ideas within the legal profession difficult. Widening the common ground for the members of the profession would be an important step in improving the chances of accelerated legal progress. The Sudan bar examination, after many vicissitudes,[151] may become one leveling factor, but compromise from both sides will be necessary.

The shortage of trained lawyers in the Sudan is not so grave as in the rest of Eastern and Central Africa,[152] but the glut of advo-

---

[149] The two institutions have contributed approximately the same number of graduates. They form the overwhelming majority of the bar association, whose president, Sayed A. T. Shibli, served as a senior official of the Sudan Law Project from 1961 to 1963. This constitutes the most active cooperation that has taken place between the civil law and the common-law elements in the Sudan.

[150] The results of the 1963 bar examination that tested all recent law graduates (the University of Khartoum was originally exempt) gave support to the feelings of superiority openly expressed by staff and students at the University of Khartoum, which takes the cream of the Sudan's secondary school graduates and operates as a residential institution. But there are distinguished lawyers who are graduates of the University of Cairo—one of them received the highest score in the 1963 examination. The question of the quality of legal education at the University of Khartoum is itself under constant review. See generally Khalil, *A Plea for a Shorter LL.B. Course in Khartoum*, 1963 J. AFRICAN L. 125; W. Twining, *Legal Studies at the University of Khartoum*, 1962 J. AFRICAN L. 145.

[151] The bar examination initially applied only to graduates of the University of Cairo. After independence in 1956, members of Parliament, many of whom were educated at the University of Cairo, abolished the exam rather than extending it to all graduates, despite the opposition of the heads of the two major political parties. In the summer of 1963, an examination was introduced for all graduates but was subject to controversy and change until mid-1966, when it appeared that it would be retained. See Khalil, *supra* note 150.

[152] "The colonial period can be symbolised by a single fact: that on the

cates in Khartoum should not obscure the seriousness of the fact that the necessary tasks exceed the qualified people.[153] For example, just when it was thought that the faculty of law at the University of Khartoum was substantially Sudanized, three of the five senior Sudanese on the faculty left as the result of the 1964 Revolution. Two became ministers of the government and one accepted the leadership of a major political party.[154] Yet these same persons were among the only persons available to do such small jobs as compiling legal bibliographies on Sudan law or such large jobs as writing legal treatises.

The successful development of the general territorial law depends more upon insuring the quantity and quality of the output of those presently employed than upon increasing the number of personnel. Both the Chief Justice and the Attorney General are attempting to inspire activity beyond a "business as usual" routine and to enforce considerably more than the three hour workday practiced by those who disregard the standard set by the more industrious members of the profession.[155]

As urgent as the need for greater productivity is the need for the members of the profession to reach a consensus on a number of policy points that are necessary for the development of the general territorial law. Bringing the leading members of the legal profession into a law revision committee is the most important step that can be taken for the progressive improvement of the laws. During the past fifteen years there have been repeated exhortations for such a committee.[156] The systematic evolution of the

attainment of Independence in December 1961, Tanganyika had but two African lawyers. The position in other East African territories was only slightly better." Twining, *Legal Education Within East Africa*, in EAST AFRICAN LAW TODAY 115, 116 (1965).

[153] The major foreign contribution has been by the Project for the Staffing of African Institutions of Legal Education and Research (SAILER), which is directed by Mr. John S. Bainbridge and financed by a Ford Foundation grant. As of July 1966, SAILER had sent nine lawyers in response to university and government requests.

[154] This does not reflect the full seriousness of the situation, since three other Sudanese, though remaining as members of the faculty, became engaged in virtually full-time work on government investigatory committees.

[155] In a circular to all judges preceding the Judicial Conference of December 12, 1964, the first such meeting following the revolution, Chief Justice Babiker Awadalla warned that promotions would depend on the quantity and quality of output and not, as in the past, merely upon seniority and academic qualifications. The Morning News (Khartoum), Dec. 3, 1965, p. 1. In mid-1966, the major problem was the Chief Justice's difficulty in finding effective sanctions to increase the number of cases being decided in the district courts.

[156] See NATIONAL CHARTER, in Republic of Sudan Gazette ii (Special Supp. 1964); Gow, *Law and the Sudan*, 1952 SUDAN NOTES AND RECORDS 299, 307; Guttman, *Editorial*, 1956 SUDAN L.J. REP. 3, 4; Thompson, *Research into the Law of the Sudan*, in THE PHILOSOPHICAL SOCIETY OF THE SUDAN: RESEARCH IN THE SUDAN 152, 169 (12th Annual Conference 1964). The Attor-

sources of law requires the services of a standing committee that
meets at regular intervals and is competent to decide what legislation should be enacted and with what priority. The need for
such deliberations has been a salient theme in the earlier discussion
of the gaps and uncertainties in the law.[157] A working body of
lawyers could also play a significant role in the planning and
conduct of programs of economic development.[158] Two important
tasks face such a committee. It should prepare the next revised
edition of Sudan legislation in order to eliminate the archaic condition of the existing *Laws* and supplements[159] and should improve
the unfortunate state of the Sudan's commercial laws.[160] The committee must also thoroughly consider Arabicization, legal eclecticism, and codification.[161] Weaving these ideas into a viable policy
will be immensely difficult, and the following analysis will demonstrate why there are even more difficulties than those previously
suggested.

VI. PRESSURES FOR FUNDAMENTAL CHANGE

The analysis of the gaps and uncertainties in Sudanese general
territorial laws has been based on the present orientation of the
legal system, which projects a pattern characterized by the retention of the common law as the core of the lawyers' laws. But the
greatest uncertainty in the Sudan is whether the pattern will remain the same. Some members of the legal profession would go
far beyond reforming or modifying the general territorial laws, far
beyond merely increasing the use of legal eclecticism or extending the use of Arabic. These persons would fundamentally alter
the existing sources of the general territorial laws.

The success of the 1964 civilian revolution provided to the proponents of radical change a freedom of discussion and an atmosphere of renewed national pride that insured them a sympathetic,
if uncommitted, audience. The National Charter made the first
official call for a law revision committee "for the purpose of pro-
posing new laws consistent with our traditions."[162] But there is
tremendous doubt as to the extent and nature of change implied
by "new laws." Even the drafters of the National Charter were

---

ney General announced the formation of such a committee, but nothing
came of the announcement. The Morning News (Khartoum), May 5, 1965,
p. 2.

[157] See pp. 147-57 *supra.*

[158] See generally the references cited in note 137 *supra.*

[159] See pp. 140-41 *supra.*

[160] See particularly the text accompanying note 117 *supra.* A draft of
a commercial law that attempts to take account of conditions in the Sudan
is in Atiyah, *A New Sale of Goods Bill* , 1957 SUDAN L.J. REP. 107.

[161] See pp. 162-64 *supra.*

[162] NATIONAL CHARTER, Republic of Sudan Gazette ii (Special Supp.
1964).

delayed by dispute.[163] That the law revision committee has yet
to be formed can be attributed, at least in part, to these doubts and
disagreements.[164]

The only clear consensus among the members of the legal profession is the vague but powerfully felt opinion that there must be
"Sudanese law." The intensity with which this revived nationalist
sentiment is expressed may forestall hard thinking about the methods of achievement. The unimpeachable goal of "Sudanese law"
requires precise definition if it is to be meaningful.

In some quarters of the legal profession, "Sudanese law" is primarily a negative sentiment, a desire to reject what is felt to be
alien. After the 1964 Revolution, some of the advocates circulated
a petition asking for the "execution" of English law, and students
in the Khartoum branch of Cairo University condemned the "im-
perialists' law" taught at the University of Khartoum.[165] These
reactions are better appreciated when one recalls that four states
forbade the citation of English cases following the American Revolutionary War[166] and that an effort to impeach the justices of the
Pennsylvania Supreme Court relied upon charges that the justices
were guilty of contact with "the hated and exploded English common law."[167] Despite all this, within "seventy-five years at most,
the English seventeenth-century legal materials were made over
into a common law for America . . . ."[168] Thus, the critical question is whether the Sudan will also make over the common law
into its image or whether it will embark on a wholly new course.

Those who believe in a radical departure from the common-law
heritage fall into four different groupings of indeterminate
strength. The first is composed mostly of advocates trained in the
continental system who would carry legal eclecticism to its limit.

---

[163] The proposal for the committee came on the morning of October 30,
1964, during the final editing of the Transitional Constitution and followed
more than 15 hours of continuous deliberation between the representatives
of the military and the civilian negotiating group. As initially conceived,
the committee was to propose "new Arab codes," but after lively debate
the more ambiguous wording was accepted. In the Arabic version of the
National Charter, "laws" is perhaps more correctly read as "codes." Conversations With Members of Both Negotiating Groups in November 1964
and March-April 1966.

[164] There are also other, more fundamental tasks yet incomplete, such
as the drafting of a constitution to replace the transitional document.

[165] The extra mural studies department of the University of Khartoum
took notice of these attacks in The University Forum, No. 28, Jan. 1965.

[166] Pennsylvania, New Jersey, and Kentucky so legislated, and the
courts of New Hampshire created a rule to the same effect. See POUND,
THE LAWYER FROM ANTIQUITY TO MODERN TIMES 180-81 (1953).

[167] Wister, *The Supreme Court of Pennsylvania*, 3 THE GREEN BAG 58,
68 (1891), as cited in POUND, *op. cit. supra* note 166, at 180.

[168] POUND, *op. cit. supra* note 166, at 185. See also Pound, *The Development of American Law and Its Deviation from English Law*, 67 L.Q. REV.
49, 56 (1951).

They would reopen existing laws to the winds of change from all foreign sources but especially from continental system countries. The second group[169] is a spearhead of pan-Arab solidarity in the Sudan and would prefer importing codes from the Arab countries in the Mediterranean crescent, particularly the United Arab Republic. The result sought by this group is Arabicization in the widest sense of the term, since the language shift would be accompanied by a change in the substance of the laws.

The third group, chiefly represented by the Muslim Brotherhood,[170] would require close adherence to Islamic principles by all the lawyers' laws. The consequences of this policy are difficult to foresee because Shari'a rules deal primarily with personal laws despite the more inclusive general theory of Islamic law.[171] One view is that the rigid requirements of Islam regarding lawyers' laws are few, reflecting an origin in an era prior to modern industrial complexities. The main control is that a rule of lawyers' law "must not fly in the face of accepted Islamic principles."[172] But some proponents of Islamic legal principles argue that they would profoundly alter the existing general territorial laws. The first test of the theory of Islamization is likely to occur in the deliberations of the constitutional study commission, where details of an Islamic constitution will be required.[173]

The final grouping is dominated by members of the Communist Party, now officially banned,[174] and its sympathizers. They have a sweeping though undetailed reform program, but their chief sig-

---

[169] A leading figure is Chief Justice Babiker Awadalla, who has, nevertheless, performed his judicial role expertly and predominantly in accord with the common-law tradition.

[170] The Brotherhood is basically an intellectual Islamic renaissance movement. In the Sudan it is politically amalgamated into the Islamic Charter Front. For an account of the role of the Muslim Brotherhood in the United Arab Republic, see HARRIS, NATIONALISM AND REVOLUTION IN EGYPT (1964).

[171] See ANDERSON, ISLAMIC LAW IN THE MODERN WORLD (1959).

[172] This statement represents the consensus of a number of leading Sudanese lawyers who are sympathetic to the views of the third group but who are not within its hard core. See generally Mahmasani, *Transactions in the Shari'a*, in LAW IN THE MIDDLE EAST 179 (Khadduri & Liebesny ed. 1955); Onar, *The Majalla*, in LAW IN THE MIDDLE EAST 218 (Khadduri & Liebesny ed. 1955). See also COULSON, A HISTORY OF ISLAMIC LAW, 120-34, 218-25 (1964). FYZEE, OUTLINE OF MOHAMMEDAN LAW (3d ed. 1964) deals with no lawyers' laws, with the exception of preemption of land sales. The major purpose of such sales, however, is the exclusion of strangers from the family groups of co-owners.

[173] Shortly after independence, the Grand Kadi of the Sudan prepared a twenty-one page discussion of relevant principles. MUDDATHIR, A MEMORANDUM FOR THE ENACTMENT OF A SUDAN CONSTITUTION DEVISED FROM THE PRINCIPLES OF ISLAM (1956).

[174] N.Y. Times, Dec. 19, 1965, § 1, p. 24, col. 1. The party thus had about a year of legitimate existence following the 1964 Revolution. In mid-1966, party officials had not been driven into hiding to the extent that they had found necessary under the military government.

nificance is their influential opposition to the existing legal structure, opposition that they often develop by supporting the criticisms of other groups.

The identification of four groupings, though useful in delineating the contrasting ideas favoring change, does not imply a formalized opposition by organized groups. The opposition is in an extremely nascent condition and is normally expressed by individuals in private conversations about particular legal questions. Moreover, the groupings are not necessarily mutually exclusive. Some individuals may support the viewpoints of different groups, depending on the issue in point. For example, a particularly strong affinity exists between the pan-Arabic groupings and those favoring extensive borrowing from continental systems, because a continental system derived from France prevails in the United Arab Republic. Finally, proponents of increased codification are part of each grouping as well as being among those who support the common-law heritage.

The opposition to the common-law heritage has three characteristics that add confusion to the unsettled debate. First, the opposition remains oral although the complexity of the issues requires written exposition as a basis for discussion. Second, the quality of the debate is weakened by an excess of unexamined notions. For example, it is frequently asserted that there are sufficient secondary materials in Arabic to supplement the study of Egyptian codes, which are based on French law. If there are sufficient materials, proponents of Egyptian codes score an important point; if there are not, there is a formidable obstacle to adopting Egyptian codes in the Sudan, where the second national language is English, not French. To preclude premature opinions, an authoritative assessment of this, and other issues, is necessary. Third, "red herrings" complicate discussions. For instance, some persons who favor greater codification, but who oppose the common-law heritage, often equate codes exclusively with the continental legal systems. Consequently, they overlook compilations of the common law, such as the Liberian Code of Laws, or legislation such as the Uniform Commercial Code. Also, many opponents of the common-law heritage obscure the difference between lawyers' laws and personal laws, a difference that distinguishes the general territorial law from the Shari'a and the customary law. They therefore make it appear that "Sudanese law" requires dismissal of the common-law heritage of lawyers' laws in order to preserve the traditional customs and Shari'a rules. But the undisputed need to adapt the common law to Sudanese conditions and philosophies is different from replacing or altering the specific personal laws that form the bulk of Islamic and customary law.

The dispute about the fate of the sources of the general territorial law is generally characterized by the need to clarify the real issues. The situation is so nebulous that some persons' opinions about the proper source of lawyers' law are not consciously formulated, remain hidden, and are revealed only by the shadow they cast in discussions. As a result, arguments about needed legal reforms may be useless because of the failure to focus on the actual basis of dispute. Disagreement about the reform of the Sudan Companies Ordinance, for example, may rest less upon the merits of specific changes than upon the protagonists' unstated idealizations of what they think the sources of law should be. One argument for reform may be urged with the unarticulated goal of strengthening the existing common-law structure through statutory reforms. An opponent's objection may rest on the unstated assumption that the common-law heritage should be replaced by continental codes, while yet another person's position may be based on the unspoken belief that the ordinance will best be molded to local conditions by Sudanese judicial interpretation. Of course, it is possible to make the unstated premises articulate, but the basic difficulty is not always obvious nor is the clarification always easy. When the clarification is made, the parties must move back from the specific law being discussed and reengage at a more general level regarding the merits of different systems of laws. This is likely to be frustrating because the parties will have even less power to influence a decision about the basic direction of the legal system than they will have to influence a needed reform in a specific corner of the law.

VII. CONCLUSIONS

If the Sudan's policy of national unity and the history of legal growth in other nations are reliable guides, the three major sources of Sudanese law will inevitably form a common legal fabric. But inevitability does not imply speed. The crucial question is how far it will be possible to smooth the way instead of allowing the weight of passive events to take a passage of more than six centuries, as they did in England. The Sudan is thus beginning the tasks that can profoundly influence the character of its laws.

Perhaps the most important factor is the role of the trained lawyer in forging the fundamental laws of a new nation. In his book, *Facing Mount Kenya*, Jomo Kenyatta provides a lyrical picture of the young African who learns the law of the tribe from revered elders. Such pictures have not disappeared from the Sudan, but the men who are responsible for the legal future are those who are educated at a modern university.[175] They are the ones who will assist the creation of a stable legal order that can support the progressive improvement of the society and who will construct the legal infrastructure that is needed for economic modernization.[176]

---

[175] See p. 165 *supra*.
[176] See p. 161 *supra* and references cited in note 137 *supra*.

A legal profession trained in a Western tradition is one aspect of the continuing influence of foreign legal concepts and institutions. The National Charter and the Transitional Constitution of 1964 confirm the use of Western legal institutions,[177] and the daily practice of the courts affirms the usefulness of foreign legal concepts. Not even the severest critics of imported law have suggested that the Sudan be sealed away from the experience of others. The importance of imported legal traditions is settled. But equally important is that we not underestimate the intense determination of the Sudanese to mold their future in accord with their own heritage. The policy to have new laws "consistent with our traditions"[178] is vague, but it will not be ineffectual. A more institutionalized effort to refine the process of defining and applying these "traditions" is one of the promises of a law revision committee. At a minimum, the adaptation of imported laws to local conditions can be expected to continue.[179]

Thus, the policy of the Sudan is to use Western legal developments to assist modernization but to keep the changes consistent with its traditions. Occasionally, either side of this policy may become oddly isolated and distorted. This may be illustrated by two contrary attitudes prevalent among some members of the legal profession. On one side, some have myopia about the importance of Khartoum and fail to see the difference between the legal concerns of the Sudan's most modern center and the remainder of the country.[180] On the other side, some have a self-depreciating clarity about presumed national limitations and thus regard certain Western legislation as too sophisticated for the Sudan. This view may be accurate, or it may conceal an unwillingness to undertake the difficulties of adaptation.[181] When the two sides of the policy are combined, the mixing of traditional rules with new legal forms may require the resolution of conflict[182] and may risk the neutralization of what is new.[183] There is an inherent tension that must be overcome in the fulfillment of a policy to meld harmoniously an ancestral order with a new society. The attempt to do

---

[177] See note 7 *supra* and accompanying text.

[178] NATIONAL CHARTER, Republic of Sudan Gazette ii (Special Supp. 1964).

[179] See, *e.g.*, Heirs of El Tayeb El Melik v. Ahmadiya Zwawya, AC-REV-262-1962, 1962 SUDAN L.J. REP. 135 (relief granted by lower court based on concept of constructive trust not allowed on appeal because the concept was applied to a wakf, which was held to be entirely different from the English conception of trust); Khartoum Municipal Council v. Cotran, AC-APP-31-1958, 1958 SUDAN L.J. REP. 85 (question of damages to be fixed by local considerations and not by strict adherence to English or other laws).

[180] See, *e. g.*, pp. 148-49 *supra*.

[181] See, *e.g.*, text following note 117 *supra*. This attitude is also reflected in the failure to consider the draft commerical legislation in Atiyah, *supra* note 160.

[182] See particularly McLoughlin, *supra* note 136.

[183] See text accompanying note 139 *supra*.

this will be the Sudan's most difficult responsibility in the coming decades.

Progress requires continued efforts to make available the essential legal materials[184] and to deal with gaps and uncertainties in the law.[185] Progress also requires a resolution of the dispute about the future of the common-law tradition.[186] The confused condition of this debate will delay its conclusion. Until a resolution is reached, the most unfortunate consequence will be the postponement of needed reforms. Whether the common-law tradition is retained or rejected, commercial law reform, for example, is necessary. But the uncertainty about the future source of lawyers' laws either consciously or subconsciously creates feelings of fear and futility that frustrate action.

Ideally, a law revision committee would make decisions about the basic sources of the general territorial law as a prelude to making specific decisions to eliminate the gaps and uncertainties in the law. The potential flaw is that the disagreements between those who would retain the common-law heritage and their opponents, and the divisions among the opposition groups, may be of sufficient strength to foredoom any effort to organize a law revision committee. Substantive disputes may thus defeat any procedural efforts to provide a forum for reaching agreements. Although the clusters of opinion about the sources of law are often closely related to political affiliations,[187] there is no consistent pattern of opinion related to the major parties that suggests that a particular resolution would follow from a government by one of them or by a coalition.[188] But if present attempts to secure a firm national leadership are successful, the improvement in the government's decisionmaking process will facilitate the solution of political problems that can delay progress, such as those that exist in regard to the southern Sudan. A stable political base will also facilitate action in the legal arena and will make available leading members of the profession presently preoccupied by politics.[189] Because no

---

[184] See part III *supra*, pp. 139–47.

[185] See part IV *supra*, pp. 147–58.

[186] See part VI *supra*, pp. 167–71.

[187] See *supra* note 170 and accompanying text.

[188] The two major parties are the Umma and the National Unionists Party (NUP). Both count among their members persons in each of the four groupings discussed in the text at pp. 168-71 *supra,* including some of the Communists.

[189] The general but unsteady pattern since the 1964 Revolution has been for the major political parties to join in a coalition to share the political power. On July 27, 1966, Sayed Sadik El Mahdi, thirty year old president of the Umma, became Prime Minister. N.Y. Times, July 28, 1966, § 1, p. 4, col. 3. An Oxford graduate and descendent of the Mahdi who defeated General Gordon in 1885, he is the youngest premier in the Sudan's history. Although he is untested, many observers believe him to have the best chance of forming a stable civilian government.

concerted effort has yet been made to form a law revision committee, pessimism about its creation would be premature.

But if it is not possible to construct a mechanism for reaching a
consensus in the legal profession as a whole, there is one major
alternative to a continued policy of drifting development.   The
separate institutions that presently have power to influence the
sources of law must increase the informal exchange of ideas and
must take more initiative within their spheres to deal with existing
problems.   In particular, the faculty of law at the University of
Khartoum could play a vital role.   It is the major training ground
for future judges and legal draftsmen, and it has already demonstrated that it can stimulate cooperative projects in the legal community.[190] The faculty is in a favorable position for conducting the
studies that are needed for important policy decisions on issues such
as the increased use of Arabic for lawyers' laws.   Increased activity
by other institutions, such as the judiciary, could result in increased conflicts if, for example, the superior courts were to fill
gaps in the law with sections of Egyptian codes while the University of Khartoum continued to educate future judges in the common law.   But even these conflicts might well have the beneficial
effect of necessitating important decisions.

The desirable prospect is the achievement of a general consensus
about the sources of the law so that legal development in the
Sudan will move forward at a quickened pace. Drawing upon the
experience of others and by conscientious research, review, and
reform, the Sudanese can bring a large measure of accelerated and
rational development to their law during its formative era.

---

[190] See pp. 142, 145-47 *supra*.

INDEX

INDEX

Administrative law, 40, 67, 68
Adu, A. L., 39
African Conference on Local Courts and Customary Law (1963), 158
African Courts Act (Kenya), 100
African Courts (Amendment) Ordinance No. 50 of 1962 (Kenya), 80, 100
African Courts Ordinance No. 65 of 1951 (Kenya), 77, 78, 100
Agreement of 1900 (Buganda), 54
Agriculture Act (Kenya), 102
Akufo-Addo, Edward, 114
Alienability of land, 51, 52, 53, 56
Allodial ownership, 9, 51
Allott, Anthony N., 16, 28, 53, 160
Ankrah, J. A., 114
Apaloo, M.K., 112
Apartheid, 19
Apter, David, 121
Arabicization, 162–63, 164, 167
Asante, S. K. B., 55

Bankruptcy law, 33
Bantusans policy, 19
Bills of Exchange Ordinance of 1914 (Sudan), 157
Bohannan, Paul, 31
Brewster, C. W., 143
Buganda, 16, 54

Chiefs' Courts Ordinance of 1931 (Sudan), 136, 137
Civil Justice Ordinance of 1929 (Sudan), 138, 152, 153
Civil Service, 38, 39, 40, 42, 67, 93, 106, 123
Clarity of title, 50, 53, 64
Codification, 33, 34, 72, 162, 164, 167, 170
Collectivism-individualism, 128–32
Colonial Development and Welfare Acts, 58
Colonialist enclave, 7, 8, 13, 14, 18
Colonial Model Income Tax Ordinance (1922), 62
Commercial Law, 34, 36, 90, 164, 167, 173
Commission of Enquiry into Trade Malpractices (Ghana), 35, 37, 70
Common law: administrative, 67, 69; Arabicization of, 162, 163; codification of, 34, 162, 164; English, 10, 11, 90, 139, 151, 152, 153, 164, 165, 168; in Ghana, 34, 47; property, 24, 32; and public law, 36; in Sudan, 139, 141, 152, 153, 157, 164, 165, 167, 168, 170, 171, 173; torts, 60; transition to national, 92

Communist Party, 169–70
Companies Ordinance of 1925 (Sudan), 153
Company Code in Ghana, 35
Contract: between Africans and non-Africans, 16, 17; breach of, 17; in English law, 12, 16, 17, 22; freedom to, 17, 18; between government and private enterprise, 44, 70–71; as jural postulate, 21, 25, 45, 60, 65; and planning, 22, 23, 55, 56; and private enterprise, 36; and property rights, 12, 21, 32, 56
Contract law, 17, 35, 43–44, 59
Convention Peoples' Party (Ghana), 105, 111–15 *passim*, 126–27
Corruption: extent of, 27, 69; in Ghana, 70, 104, 112, 115, 117, 126; in government, 69–71; in Nigeria, 70; and party financing, 70; and price rises, 35
Cotran, Eugene, 103
Courts Act (Kenya), 100
Court structure: in Kenya, 76–78, 80, 85, 100; in Sudan, 136–37, 155
C.P.P. *See* Convention Peoples' Party
Credit, 33, 61
Criminal Code (Amendment) Bill of 1961 (Ghana), 27
Criminal law: customary, 14, 15, 19; English, 14, 15, 16, 19; Islamic, 16; in Kenya, 103; and policing of managerial performance, 44–45
Crown lands, 54, 81–82, 101, 102
Crown Lands Act (Kenya), 101
Crown Lands Ordinance of 1915 (Kenya), 81, 101
Customary law: adaptability of, 29, 53; and alienability of land, 51, 52; applicability of, 11, 12–14, 18, 46, 47, 77, 91; in Buganda, 16; and commercial transactions, 48; criminal, 14–15, 19; determination of, 30; and economic development, 13, 48; and English law, 10, 30, 31, 48, 91, 92; in Ghana, 31, 47, 110, 118; Islamic law as, 31; jural postulates of, 20; and "justice, equity and good conscience," 29, 137, 142, 149–50; in Kenya, 83, 88, 89, 90, 102, 103; land, 9, 49, 55, 65, 80, 83, 85, 90; and land tenure, 47, 48, 50, 51, 53, 54, 55, 77, 87; as people's choice, 28, 31; property, 11, 20; in Sudan, 134, 135, 137, 144, 148, 149, 150, 151, 158–62 *passim*, 170; sufficiency of, 28, 31, 32, 45, 49, 50, 91; in Tanzania, 47, 158; and tax policy, 64